Shakespeare's Acts of Will

Shakespeare's Acts of Will: Law, Testament and Properties of Performance

Gary Watt

Bloomsbury Arden Shakespeare
An imprint of Bloomsbury Publishing Plc
B L O O M S B U R Y
LONDON • OXFORD • NEW YORK • NEW DELHI • SYDNEY

Bloomsbury Arden Shakespeare
An imprint of Bloomsbury Publishing Plc

Imprint previously known as Arden Shakespeare

50 Bedford Square
London
WC1B 3DP
UK

1385 Broadway
New York
NY 10018
USA

www.bloomsbury.com

BLOOMSBURY, THE ARDEN SHAKESPEARE and the Diana logo are trademarks of Bloomsbury Publishing Plc

First published 2016
Paperback edition first published 2018

British Library Cataloguing-in-Publication Data
A catalogue record for this book is available from the British Library.

ISBN: HB: 978-1-4742-1785-9
PB: 978-1-3500-5957-3
ePDF: 978-1-4742-1787-3
ePub: 978-1-4742-1786-6

Cover design: Dani Leigh

Cover image: David Tennant as Richard II. Photo: Kwame Lestrade © RSC

Library of Congress Cataloging-in-Publication Data
A catalog record for this book is available from the Library of Congress.

Typeset by Fakenham Prepress Solutions, Fakenham, Norfolk NR21 8NN

To Jamie

'There are more things in heaven and earth …
Than are dreamt of in your philosophy'

CONTENTS

ACKNOWLEDGEMENTS

To write a book about Shakespeare is a beautiful burden. Most thanks of all go to my wife Emma and to my sons Jamie and Michael for sharing the beauty and bearing the burden with me. I am grateful to Emma and Jamie for listening, reading and checking line references – and for making invaluable suggestions for improvement. For comments on draft chapters, I am immensely grateful to the kind and perceptive critique of colleagues and friends. Thomasin Bailey, Kimberley Brownlee, Richard Dawson, Andrew King, Roger Leng, Keith Osborn, Paul Prescott and James Boyd White have all improved this book with their insights. I am also grateful to Daniela Carpi and Jeanne Gaakeer who convened a seminar at the *Shakespeare 450* conference, Paris, where I presented some work in progress, and to Sidia Fiorato for guiding it to publication in the journal *Pólemos*. Daniela has always been a kind encourager of my efforts to know Shakespeare better. My gratitude also to Elaine Ho and Marco Wan for giving me the opportunity to share some thoughts in a public lecture at the University of Hong Kong, and to Frederick Blumberg and others for their responses on that occasion. I am grateful to Stephanie Tillotson and Thomasin Bailey for giving me the opportunity to deliver a seminar in the *Sidelights on Shakespeare* series at the University of Warwick, and to Mairi Macdonald for convivial conversations on Shakespeare's will and wise guidance on how to read between the lines and when not to. Paul Raffield, my co-editor of the journal *Law and Humanities*, deserves standing thanks for encouraging and exemplifying imaginative engagement with Shakespeare and the law. A great deal of this book has grown out of thoughts hatched in preparing and delivering workshops on rhetoric for the Royal Shakespeare Company over many years. For giving me that opportunity and with it the chance to learn from theatre professionals, I am grateful to the members of the voice department and to Jane Hazell in particular. The editorial team of Margaret Bartley and Emily Hockley at Bloomsbury Arden Shakespeare deserve special thanks for their support and sound supervision, and not least for arranging immensely helpful reviews at every stage of the process. I am indebted to the guidance of those anonymous reviewers and thank them for it. Finally, on the four-hundredth anniversary of his testament, I am grateful to Shakespeare for making me a beneficiary.

Kenilworth, 2016

1

'Performance is a kind of will or testament'

This book is about the way words work. It is about words written and words spoken and how they relate to the speaker's silence, gesture and movement through space. We are concerned with the metre and rhythm of spoken and written lines, which is a sort of movement through time. It is about the relation of words to their physical context, which in the playhouse includes the materials of stage structures, fixtures, costume and moveable props. Above all it is about the capacity of words to affect those who speak them and those who hear them. The words of Shakespeare's dramatic works exemplify this capacity and it will be our happy task to unfold them and to get a feel for them and to find some of their hidden ways of working.

To be concerned with the ways that words touch people, move people and change people is to be concerned with the art of rhetoric. The Greek adjective *rhetorikos* denoted the profession of the *rhetor* or orator.[1] These were the public speakers and legal advocates of ancient Greece. The word ultimately derives from Proto-Indo-European for the spoken word (**wretor*). The related Greek word *rhetra*, which over time denoted a ceremonial or authoritative utterance, an agreement, a contract or a legal resolution, reminds us that rhetoric is especially concerned with the power of words to express will to bring about changes of social state. This brings us to the word 'will' appearing in the title of this book. The pun on Shakespeare's name is fortunate (or unfortunate),[2] but the word figures in this study for the more substantial reason that we are concerned with the way words express will and move wills. We shall see that the related idea of 'testament' denotes the expression of will before witnesses and, for this reason, can reveal a great deal about the nature of dramatic performance in law, theatre and the rest of social life. Testament performs the work of will in the world and in the world we leave behind.

This is not, primarily, a book about the technical minutiae of testamentary law, although we will occasionally find it helpful to consider the details of statutes, case reports and legal treatises. This book is more concerned with the cultural practices – and specifically the creative practices – that connect theatre to law and connect both theatre and law to the wider world of the witnessing public. It might seem strange to an outsider to think of the law as a creative practice. If so, this might be due in part to the fact that insiders seem dead set in their denial of law's imaginative dimension. Since the enlightenment, lawyers have looked to the new professional paradigms of empirical and medical science to dignify the common law with a doctrinal sense of schematic structure and a reputation for laboratory predictability from case to case. Anybody with intimate familiarity with the progress of the common law at its cutting edge in the highest courts will see that this 'scientist' account is a myth.[3] Law is a creative construct, and an example of the most ancient rhetorical profession playing with language in the creative way that it has always done best. Part of the lawyers' rhetorical pretence is to deny that rhetoric or creative fiction is at work in their professional practices. Even legal scholars routinely contrast rhetoric with reality, with no acknowledgement that rhetoric is what lawyers really do.[4] In one recent case heard in the highest court in the land, one of the Justices of the United Kingdom Supreme Court went out of his way to say that there is no place for 'fairy tales' in the law.[5] My own opinion is that the law is deeply committed to the fairy-tale business of moving property and people from one state to another by means of magic words. The irony is that the same senior judge in the very same case had opened his speech with a line of exemplary rhetoric in which he likened the tension between the legal and equitable aspects of the common law to a garment being pulled apart at the seams.[6] The ubiquitous and necessary presence of metaphoric language ensures that the law continues to spin a good yarn.[7]

The major part of this book is focused upon a group of Shakespeare's Elizabethan plays that can be dated (with all the usual caveats) to the period 1595–1603. In fact, three of them fall in 1599 (*As You Like It*, *Julius Caesar* and *Henry V*), and *Hamlet* was probably substantially complete a year or two thereafter. This is not to suggest that the testamentary theme is irrelevant to the Jacobean plays. On the contrary, I hope to show that all theatrical drama is in a deep sense testamentary. Nevertheless, the themes and language of testament, inheritance and succession are more prevalent in Shakespeare's Elizabethan works. Some of the Jacobean plays engage with the broadly testamentary concern that an aging father would naturally have for his daughter (think Lear, Prospero and Shakespeare himself), but in the Elizabethan plays a legal last will and testament appears as a plotting device and even as a physical prop, and it is only in the Elizabethan plays that the word 'testament' is ever repeated and (with the exception of that very late, and seemingly valedictory, work *The Tempest*) it is only in the Elizabethan plays that the testamentary word 'executor' ever appears. If Shakespeare was particularly engaged with testamentary concerns in the Elizabethan period, this might have been down to public concern over matters of royal succession (we consider this below, but suffice to say here that such tensions might be more tactfully touched upon through talk of testaments than by direct handling). It might, by the same token, have been down to Shakespeare's literary 'sources' or 'precedents' (many of which, we will see, were concerned with issues of testament and succession). Shakespeare's interest in issues of testament in the Elizabethan period might also be attributable to more personal factors. His only son died on 9 August 1596 and his father died on 7 September 1601.

The title of this chapter quotes the painter in *Timon of Athens*.[8] Given that the main focus of this book is upon Shakespeare's Elizabethan dramas, the Jacobean play *Timon of Athens* might seem an unlikely starting point. We start with it because Timon's painter spoke more wisely than he knew. In that one line (with a little licence of interpretation) he has conveniently indicated a number of premises for the present study. Before we consider the merits of the quote, we should briefly attend to its context. On the way to seeking a commission from Timon, the painter asserts that it is 'most courtly and fashionable' to promise to act without actually doing the deed spoken of ('the deed of saying'), and that people who actually perform are 'the plainer and simpler kind of people' (*Tim*, 5.1.24–5). These are amusingly self-deprecating lines for an actor to utter in the very act of performing a play. The painter implies that anyone who performs today what they might put off until tomorrow must lack a future, or lack imagination to foresee a future. They might as well be on their deathbed, for 'performance is a kind of will or testament which argues a great sickness in his judgment that makes it' (*Tim*, 5.1.27–8). In early modern England it was rare to make a will unless illness or violent threat gave cause to fear impending death (see *Per*, 1.1.42).[9] Shakespeare himself wrote his will shortly before he died. It was drafted in January, amended and executed in March, and he died on 23 April 1616.[10]

The first thing we learn from the statement 'performance is a kind of will or testament' is that Shakespeare appreciated the drama inherent in the performance of a last will and the drama of legal testamentary language. Words uttered at thresholds between states of being have a quality that is called in various contexts 'ceremonial', 'ritual', and even 'magical'. All liminal language is potent, but none more so than words spoken at the threshold between life and death. Shakespeare acknowledges elsewhere that 'the tongues of dying men / Enforce attention like deep harmony' (*R2*, 2.1.5–6).[11] In theatre, the language of the play performs a sort of magic as it passes from the world of the stage to the world of the playgoers. In law, so-called 'operative words' (such as 'I agree', 'I declare' and 'I swear') have a comparable capacity to move people from one state of social being to another. When Shakespeare was writing, legal forms of words had power to marry, adopt, bastardize and kill. The words of a last will and testament have a distinctive liminal power to cross the threshold of death itself. Through words of will and the performance of the testamentary document, one acts now to expresses one's will over the properties of a future world. (It has been said that all 'law is the attempt to build future worlds'.)[12] The performance of will is not complete in the form of the words alone, but requires the complicity of witnesses, the agency of executors and the confirmation of probate.[13] Legal and theatrical modes of performance are in many respects vastly different, of course, but theatre is 'testamentary' in the way it engages actors to execute the dramatist's will and playgoers to witness it, test it and hopefully approve it. The judgment that a play calls for is not passive, but participatory: '[t]he art of the drama makes a primary demand on us: to leave our armchair throne of judgment and descend into the mellay of contradictory passions – which the action of a play is'.[14]

The second thing we learn from Timon's painter is that performance was a concern of early modern culture that pervaded and connected such seemingly disparate practices as law, theatre and painting. Lorna Hutson advises that we should be cautious in resorting to the performance trope in literary studies, including studies in law and literature. She does not deny the metaphor's 'explanatory power', but suggests that its dominance might obscure the merits of other analyses, including one based on 'narrative'.[15] It is an excellent point, but 'performance' still seems the best metaphor to describe the central concerns of the present study. This book aims to appreciate the practices by which will is expressed in the form of words, and specifically to appreciate how words produce physical forms in the mind and how the materiality of the playhouse contributes to this process. Of course, it is necessary to take narrative seriously, even within the wider trope of performance. The sense that narrative produces material forms in the mind is so strong that Shakespeare frequently writes of narratives that 'break' off (e.g. *CE*, 1.4.96; *R2*, 5.2.2; *KJ*, 4.2.235; *Ham*, 1.1.40). In Chapters 2 and 6 we will examine how Shakespeare sometimes employs on-stage witnesses to narrate accounts of events involving the handling of material stuff. We will see that this device is especially effective in conveying a felt experience of the drama.

A third thing we learn from Timon's painter is that Shakespeare employed legal notions of performance playfully and without undue respect for thresholds between technical categories. The painter blithely borrows the language of testamentary law to make a point about contractual performance.[16] Shakespeare enjoyed the protean possibilities of legal language and was adept at moving lawyers' terminology from one technical category to another, thereby diverting the power of legal language to his own dramatic use while simultaneously subverting law's authority to restrict legal subjects to its own terms. In the special context of testaments, the law itself was capable of imaginative indulgence and looked to the intent rather than the form of words, on the presumption that the testator 'has not time to settle every thing according to the rules of law, and wills are most commonly made on a sudden, and in the testator's last moments'.[17] Without neglecting technical boundaries between legal categories, my main focus will be upon the interplay of words between legal categories and upon the interplay of linguistic cultures and practices between drama and the law. This requires us to attend to cultural appreciation of 'word play', and above all to the arts of rhetoric that informed legal practice and theatrical practice in Elizabethan England.[18]

A fourth thing we learn from the painter is that performance in all its forms has the capacity to perfect what is otherwise imperfect and incomplete. (A legal testament, for example, is not fully performed until the testator's death and due execution of the terms of his will.) It is in this sense that 'the text of a play' can be considered to be, in Granville-Barker's phrase, 'a score waiting performance'.[19] Fifth, and related to the previous point, we learn that the 'deed of saying' (assuming that it goes beyond the deed of *merely* saying) can perfect the performance of words by enacting them through appropriate deeds. There is something of this sense in Hamlet's suggestion that theatrical performance should 'suit the action to the word' (*Ham*, 3.2.17). In *King John,* Constance talks of actions as signs that confirm words. Her rhetorical questions (addressed to Salisbury, whom she fears has come to confirm bad news concerning her son's prospects of attaining the English throne) have the effect of inviting the playgoers to witness with her, and to join her in forming a judgment:

> What dost thou mean by shaking of thy head?
> Why dost thou look so sadly on my son?
> What means that hand upon that breast of thine?
> Why holds thine eye that lamentable rheum,
> ...
> Be these sad signs confirmers of thy words? (2.2.19–24)[20]

The performative process of word confirmed by act is even observable at the governmental level when an 'Act' of Parliament confirms the speech ('*parlement*') of the legislative body. In this example, the speech is to a great extent the very essence of the authoritative Act (see the discussion of 'speech acts' below). While we are discussing 'acts', it should be noted that *actio* originally described the gestural action of orators and that 'action' described legal proceedings long before 'acting' became a byword for playing in the public playhouses.[21] If we extend our retrospective to prehistory, we will conclude that forms of words were originally the perfection of gesture, as gesture was the perfection of word. Thus Dietrich Stout and Thierry Chaminade see similar 'cognitive control processes' in the 'hierarchically complex, multi-stage action sequences' of prehistoric handaxe production to 'those involved in modern human discourse-level language processing'.[22] Or, as Elias Canetti wrote more than half a century earlier: 'Words and *objects* are ... emanations and products of a single unified experience: *representation by means of the hands*.'[23] To handle language well, one must develop one's embodied sensitivity to the feel of words. Accordingly, one of the rehearsal strategies recommended by Cicely Berry, the founding Voice Director of the Royal Shakespeare Company (hereafter 'RSC'), is to encourage the actors to speak their lines while simultaneously finding physical objects, handling them and building them into structures.[24]

A sixth – and, for present purposes, final – thing we learn from Timon's painter is that the expression of 'will' is a prime objective of performance. According to the *Oxford English Dictionary*, among the earliest records of the Anglo-Norman word 'performance' are those in the twelfth century, in which it was 'frequently in legal use' in connection with the object 'will'. Shakespeare himself refers to the performance of 'will' (*AW*, 2.1.204) or 'desire' (*2H4*, 2.4. 262–3; *Mac*, 2.3.29–30) or 'purpose' (*H8*, 4.2.41–2) more often than the performance of plays (*H5*, 3.prologue.35). Frequently, as in *Timon*, he writes of the performance of a 'promise'. 'Performance' did not acquire its distinctive theatrical sense until during Shakespeare's lifetime. For the purpose of this book, I take it that 'performance' is the expression of will in and through artificial forms, or through artistic engagement with natural forms, and that performance is perfected not only by the people who are the principal actors in the performance but by the community of people who interact with the performance and approve it.

As intimated earlier, it is not a primary aim of this book to establish that Shakespeare had knowledge of particular laws or that legal matters directly influenced his work. Causal inquiries of this kind are fascinating, but their results are always highly contestable. That said, we will occasionally identify similarities between Shakespeare's texts and contemporary legal treatises. On the subject of testaments, Henry Swinburne's *Treatise of Testaments and Last Willes*[25] and William West's *Symbolæography*,[26] both appearing as first editions in 1590, are especially noteworthy. It is likely that Shakespeare knew these works, but whether, and in what ways, they might have contributed to the content of his plays is hard to say. There is also significant correspondence between Shakespeare's plays and the English law reports of Edmund Plowden that were published in French during Shakespeare's lifetime, but we can only speculate as to how Shakespeare encountered them.[27] There is equally compelling correspondence between some of Shakespeare's lines and the content of the English language rhetoric manuals, including Thomas Wilson's *The Arte of Rhetorique*.[28] Shakespeare was almost certainly familiar with Wilson, and with other contemporary rhetoric manuals in English (such as George Puttenham's *The Arte of English Poesie*), but surface similarities between English expressions used in the manuals and the plays might obscure the possibility that Shakespeare was more deeply 'influenced' by the Latin originals that he had used during his grammar school days.[29] What does 'influence' mean anyway? More interesting, and more provocative to thinking about how we might be 'influenced' by Shakespeare today, is to see Shakespeare as a lively mind writing and working in a highly productive creative culture that was both collaborative and acquisitive. To quote Holger Schott Syme, connections between 'early modern theatrical, legal, historiographical, and political modes of authorization ... speak less to a rich network of mutual influences and interconnections ... than to a pervasive cultural preoccupation that found expression in various areas of life'.[30]

Early modern culture was a culture of performance of every sort – including performance of law, dress, architecture, music and plays – and in tension with all these was the overriding sense that this was a culture in which a life was performed not merely in the expression of self in an (emerging) modern sense, but performed also in furtherance of the forms of social order. This called for service to one's social superiors and, lest we forget it, service to Church and to God. There is no more extensive and direct textual influence on Shakespeare than the words of the Geneva Bible. At the heart of early modern Christianity was belief in the Divine performance, wherein 'Word was made flesh' in the figure of Christ.[31] The central ceremonial performance of the age, the Christian Eucharist, was at the heart of the Protestant schism concerning the capacity of sacramental words to transform bread into Christ's flesh. This was an age in which the spoken performance of words was deeply material. It has been said that theatrical performance is in several senses 'material', and that the most important is the sense in which 'theatrical performance has real social and physical consequences'.[32] The same was true of performance in religion and law during Shakespeare's lifetime. Like the theologians, the common lawyers appreciated materiality in the microscopic minutiae of forms of words. Sir Edward Coke, Shakespeare's contemporary and the preeminent common lawyer of his age, once contemplated a single short statement of law (the maxim '*possessio fratris de feodo simplici facit sororem esse haeredem*'),[33] and concluded that almost 'everie word' should be considered 'operative and materiall'.[34] Appreciating the performative and rhetorical culture that law shares with theatre will help us to appreciate in Shakespeare's lines what Coke appreciated in legal lines, which is nothing less than the power of words to wield matter and to do the work of performing will in the world. It will also help us to appreciate the pliability and playfulness of words. Most important of all, an understanding of the capacity of real rhetoric to touch and move us through words and action will yield appreciation for a type of performance that has the capacity to transform lives and reform society. This is the sort of performance we can hope for in the law and it is the sort of performance that continues to be the promise of Shakespeare's plays.

An initial spur for this book was the observation that many of Shakespeare's plays recognize the dramatic power inherent in testamentary wills. We can observe by way of overview (with representative examples in parenthesis) that in some plays the opening scene presents a point of legal testamentary contention (*AYL*, *H5*, *3H6*, *KJ*), that another deploys the physical form of a testamentary will at the dramatic climax of the play (*JC*), and that another employs a testamentary provision as a significant sub-plot (*MV*). Even where the performance of an individual's will does not take a form that the law would consider to be testamentary, it might nevertheless exhibit a testamentary power to disrupt default schemes of succession and inheritance (*R2*, *KJ*, *Ham*, *KL*); or an individual's will might be enforced in life with such stubborn finality that it feels as inflexible as the testamentary wishes of the dead. Where the performance of stubborn will is aligned with such sources of authority as the regal or ducal (*AW*, *CE*, *KL*, *MM*), the contractual (*MV*) or the marital (*TS*, *WT*), its dramatic power is all the more pronounced. Most common of all is alignment with parental authority. A father's will ruling over a daughter's will appears frequently in ways that are not technically 'testamentary' in the legal sense of the word (*KL*, *MND*, *MA*, *RJ*, *TGV*). Then there are plays in which an individual's will and performance, which should be conjoined, are instead alienated from each other. This can be effective in comedy (*AYL*, *LLL*), but in cases of radical alienation the effect is tragic (*Ham*, *R2*). Not only does Shakespeare make extensive use of will as a plot or premise for his plays, but his use of testamentary language is impressive in its diversity and extent – so much so that a barrister working in Victorian Liverpool devoted a short book exclusively to the topic.[35]

It is notable that John Austin's theory of the 'speech act' or 'performative utterance' – the theory that certain forms of words enact changes in the world – was premised on the example of legal language, and specifically upon testamentary language. He appreciated that testamentary terminology is deeply imbued with the sense that spoken and written words have the capacity to perform powerfully upon the world of 'real' things:

> Lawyers when talking about legal instruments will distinguish between the preamble, which recites the circumstances in which a transaction is effected, and on the other hand the operative part – the part of it which actually performs the legal act which it is the purpose of the instrument to perform ... 'I give and bequeath my watch to my brother' would be an operative clause and is a performative utterance.[36]

The word 'bequeath' is perfectly suited to Austin's argument. According to the Oxford English Dictionary it was originally 'a strong verb' in the Anglo-Saxon. It is not merely the 'quote' or 'quoth' of saying, but an emphatic sense of saying with binding power. The difference between the spoken 'quoth' and the binding 'bequeath' might be compared to the difference between the regular Anglo-Saxon sense of speech as 'spiel' and the sense that some speech has a potency and power to bind that makes it 'gospel' or magical 'spell'. To bequeath connotes the sense of attempted authority over the material world that we still use when we say that something is 'spoken for'.

The etymology of 'testament' is a clue to the fact that since ancient, even prehistoric, times testaments have acquired their legitimacy as performances played out before witnesses. The English word derives from the Latin *testamentum*, which connotes a witness (*testa-*) to the mind (*-mentum*). A great deal of the language of Roman law was derived from very ancient roots,[37] and the 'testa-' of testament is a case in point. The sense of 'witness' originates in the idea of a third person standing by, which in the reconstructed Proto-Indo-European lexicon approximates to **tri-st-* ('third'-'standing'). As a result of a 'sound change', this became ters(t) and tes(t).[38] In Roman law, witnesses gave the testament its 'testamentary' quality. They were the spectators and audience to a ceremonial performance that had a director, a script, props, and actors with allocated parts to play. As 'performance is a kind of will or testament', so in Roman law testament is a kind of performance. Leaving aside the testament made before the army in anticipation of war (*testamentum in procinctu*), Roman law originally recognized two main methods for making wills. By the most ancient method, the will was made or confirmed in a committee (the *comitia calata*) which was called together twice yearly for the purpose,[39] but '[t]he comitial will was obsolete before real history begins'.[40] It was succeeded by, and in due course superseded by, the mancipatory testament 'performed by bronze and balance' (*per aes et libram agitur*), which was 'the will of the classical age'.[41] The mancipatory testament was an ancient ceremonial mode of sale (*mancipatio*) performed before witnesses, which had been adopted for use in testamentary transfer. The word *mancipatio* indicates that the subject matter of the transfer was physically handed over (literally 'captured in the hand'). The *aes* ('bronze') was ancient currency in the form of crudely cast pieces of the metal, later superseded by coinage of the same name. According to Gaius, the heir was represented by a person playing the part of the 'purchaser' and 'the testator directed him with reference to what he desired to be given to anyone after his death'.[42] The heir in this ceremony was more closely akin to the executor of an English testament (that is, the one who carries out or 'executes' the will according to its terms) than to the beneficiary of an English testament (the one who benefits from the assets passed on by the will). The 'purchaser' (playing the part of the heir) had this scripted line to speak: 'Let your family and money pass into my charge and custody, and, in order that you may make your will properly in accordance with the public law, let them be purchased by me with this bronze.'[43] Having said these words, the 'purchaser' struck the balance with the bronze, and delivered it to the testator as symbolic purchase money.[44] Then the testator spoke his part while holding the will in his hands: 'As is written in these tablets of wax, so I give, so I bequeath, so I declare my will, and so do you, citizens, bear witness.'[45] In course of time the ceremony of mancipatory testament continued as a matter of form, but the person performing the ceremonial role of purchaser no longer played the part of heir. Instead, a different person was 'appointed heir under the will' and 'charged with the distribution of legacies'. This later form of will was not published until after the testator's death.[46] Even later, the Romans introduced a third form of will called the 'Praetorian testament', by which the praetor accepted the seals of seven witnesses instead of mancipatory performance, and other forms of will followed that, but this sketch will suffice to show that the idea of testament was intensely performative in its origins and that the performance was 'testamentary' because it required the participation of witnesses.

In the early modern playhouses, witnesses to the performance included 'the understanding men in the yard'[47] and those sitting in the higher-priced 'stands' or 'galleries', including those sitting in the 'lords' rooms'.[48] Had Prince Hamlet visited the playhouses of late Elizabethan England, 'Th'observed of all observers' (*Ham*, 3.1.153) would certainly have had a seat in the lords' room, or even (depending upon how one interprets the debatable evidence) a seat on the edge of the stage itself.[49] In the Elizabethan playhouse, the playgoer in the gallery seats 'not only sees everything well, but can also be seen'.[50] The popular metaphor of *theatrum mundi* ('all the world's a stage') implied 'a showing and seeing place or a showing off and being seen place'.[51] Today, as then, playgoers have a 'creative role as imaginers of the drama',[52] and the playing of this role can be assisted by material efforts to incorporate playgoers into the action. The most obvious assistance provided by the physical structure of the Elizabethan playhouse was to use a thrust stage to place the downstage action in the very midst of the throng of playgoers.

Playgoing witnesses play their part, but actors of a more active sort take centre-stage. In the case of an Elizabethan testament, it was the executors who performed the testator's wishes 'by arranging probate and the distribution of the estate'.[53] In a simple case, the executors produced the testament to the clerical judge in the ecclesiastical court (this official was known as the 'Ordinary', for reasons we will consider in Chapter 6) and swore an oath to affirm or 'prove' that the document represented the testator's last will and testament and undertook to administer the estate according to its terms.[54] All that was required was that the will be made in writing, but in the event of any doubt regarding the testament, witnesses might be called to prove the testament *per testes* in solemn form of law.[55] It therefore became standard practice to have witnesses attest the will when the testator made it. Henry Swinburne recommended at least two witnesses.[56] Swinburne distinguishes testamentary wills from non-testamentary wills on the technical basis that the former name executors, but is content to use 'testament' in the general sense to cover wills with or without executors.[57] William West calls the testator and executor the 'principall persons', distinguishing them from the witnesses and 'legatories' (persons taking benefits under the will), whom he calls 'lesse principall'. For West, only the testator is involved in the 'active makynge of a Testament', whereas the executor, witnesses and beneficiaries are involved in the 'passive makynge of a Testament'.[58]

What is critical for present purposes is that West acknowledges all parties to be participants with some part to play in constituting the efficacy of the will. He also acknowledges the constitutive effect of the testamentary speech act. We saw earlier that John Austin was impressed by the performative power of bequeathing, which is a sort of speaking or 'quothing' into being. William West seems to have been similarly impressed. He calls a testament a 'just sentence, or declaration of our minde, concerning that which wee would have done after our deathes, with the ordayning of an executor thereof'.[59] If the testator's words in the will supply the script of the testamentary play, then the executor must be considered its principal actor. The executor's role is metaphysically sublime. The executor is a mediator between the living and the dead, and it has long been the rule that when the testator dies, and even before probate, 'the property of the goods which was in the testator, is cast upon and vested in the executors'.[60] In Elizabethan England the testator's debts would also be passed on to the executors.[61] In fact, the real 'actor', or active instrument that connects the work of the executor to the work of the stage actor, is the 'hand'. An early modern treatise on palm reading states that 'our Hands are the most Noble Members in perfecting of al manner of Actions; they are the executors of our Primary Conceptions'.[62] A treatise on the art of gesture states in similar vein that 'the hand ... by gesture makes the inward motions of the minde most evident'.[63] The idea goes back to Aristotle, for whom the hand was 'the instrument of instruments'.[64]

Shakespeare flourished in a particular historical period in which significant legal reforms were transforming the social power of individual will. The Statute of Wills (32 Hen. 8 c.1), which came into force on 20 July 1540, had empowered feudal tenants to devise two-thirds of their land by will, but, most significantly, it went even further in the case of tenants holding under the most common form of feudal tenure ('socage' tenure). On them it conferred freedom to dispose of their entire interest in the land by will. In the words of the statute, it conferred a new

> full and free liberty, power and authority to give, dispose, will and devise, as well by his last will and testament in writing, or otherwise by any act or acts lawfully executed in his life, all his said manors, lands, tenements or hereditaments, or any of them, at his free will and pleasure.[65]

The pronoun 'his' was intended to be discriminatory. The 1540 statute was supplemented in 1542 by *An Act for the Explanation of the Statute of Wills*, which confirmed that a married woman ('woman covert') had no power to leave land by will.[66] Neither was the Statute of Wills concerned with the non-freeholding masses, including those many outside London and at the labouring level of society, who held their land by customary copyhold tenure (a form of 'tenancy at will' held from the lord of their local manor).[67] The Statute of Wills conferred testamentary freedom, but it was not free for all. (It should be noted in passing that many landholders in the City of London did not need the assistance of the statute, for in matters of testament, as in matters of trade, the City of London had always been something of a law unto itself.)[68] The main beneficiaries of the statute were the landed nobility and gentry. It liberated their land-holdings from the feudal scheme of inheritance and represented, for them, a triumph of individual will over the prerogative will of the monarch. The statute can therefore be seen as an incident, and an instigator, of what Stephen Greenblatt identified as the tension in the early modern period between 'a new stress on the executive power of the will' and 'the most sustained and relentless assault upon the will'.[69] By legitimating land owners' testamentary control over their estates, the Statute of Wills incidentally promoted progress from the social scheme of the Middle Ages, which in its feudal aspect was committed to a hierarchy of 'fixed and traditional' social status,[70] to a society in which wealth and opportunity had some genuine potential to pass horizontally between people regardless of their social rank. S. B. Liljegren observed that:

> from the reign of Henry VIII down to the last days of James I, by far the better part of English landed estate changed owners, and in most cases went from the old nobility by birth and the clergy into the hands of those who possessed money in the period of the Tudors, i.e. principally the merchants and industrialists or the newly created nobility and gentry.[71]

The Statute of Wills was literally crucial. It marked, in the most important field of property rights, a crossing point between medieval and modern views of the world. The traditional default scheme (which preferred lineal descendants to collateral descendants, males to females, and first-born males to all others) was still in the background, and still applied to estates not disposed of by will, but individual testamentary will now had the power to oust the traditional feudal order. It is no exaggeration to say that 'since the Statute of Wills in 1540 the personal will as a legal instrument had become associated with the subject's rights in the face of the monarch's privilege'.[72] It cannot be denied that the early modern world view was still heavily influenced by the medieval concept of the 'chain of being', by which all Creation was understood to descend by fixed degrees downwards from the Godhead,[73] but the early modern mind was increasingly looking outwards along the horizontal plane to new horizons of place, politics and individual personhood. Richard Wilson provides a pithy summary when he observes that the 1540 Act 'installed the capitalist notion of the sovereign individual'.[74] By allowing individuals to substitute a testamentary scheme for the feudal scheme, the 1540 statute effectively established the individual landholder as monarch over his own private domain. He could leave land (or more accurately 'devise' land – which is etymologically to 'divide' it up) as he willed and the terms of his will were respected almost like a royal decree. By 1590, around the time that Shakespeare was embarking upon his career as a playwright, Henry Swinburne cited it as a maxim 'that the will or meaning of the testator is the Queene or Empresse of the testament'.[75]

Elizabeth I was a sort of Queene or Empresse of a testament. She had succeeded to the throne in accordance with the terms of the last will and testament executed by her father Henry VIII in 1547. The Third Act of Succession (1544) had authorized Henry, in the absence of a lawful successor by blood, to determine his successor by 'letters patents under the great seal, or by his last will in writing signed with his most gracious hand'.[76] Whether Elizabeth's accession was attributable to the operative power of Henry's testamentary will or to the power of parliamentary will expressed in the Act of Succession remains moot. Edmund Plowden and other leading common lawyers agreed with the orthodox opinion that '[t]he king as king had no power to determine the succession by testament'.[77] The provision in the Third Act of Succession that had empowered Henry to determine the succession by his testament followed a similar provision in the Second Act of Succession.[78] The close proximity of the Second Act of Succession (June 1536) to the Statute of Uses[79] (April 1536) is curious, for the Statute of Uses had purported to close down a conveyancing procedure (the 'enfeoffment to use' or simply the 'use')[80] which had successfully conferred a large degree of testamentary freedom on private landholders, whereas the Second Act of Succession conferred testamentary freedom on the king in relation to no less a thing than title to the Crown itself. The aims and principles of the statutes were inconsistent to the point of hypocrisy. As things turned out, clever conveyancers discovered a loophole in the Statute of Uses and found ways to create uses that could operate despite the statute. Just a few years after the Statute of Uses, the king relented in the face of demands for testamentary freedom and Parliament passed the Statute of Wills. Thus the 1540 Statute of Wills did not so much cause as re-confirm, and formally approve, an epochal shift from feudalism to 'free will and pleasure' (to quote the first section of the statute) in relation to the supremely important issue of transfers and testaments of land. What had previously been achieved indirectly by means of the equitable 'use' could now be achieved directly in law. The Statute of Wills was a development for which Henry (who by his various parliamentary 'acts of will' had authorized a statutory trend in favour of testament over tradition) had only himself to blame. It has been said that aristocracies are in principle 'opposed to wills as the means of conveying estates' because of their 'scope for whims and passions of all sorts' and in particular because they allow 'large scope for paternal affection',[81] but the traditional order of succession cannot stand when the monarch at the head of the aristocracy is the very embodiment of whim and passion.

Shakespeare's parents were born in the pre-1540 world of feudalism. Shakespeare was born into the post-1540 world of 'free will and pleasure'. There is always a danger of attributing a special unique historical context to the unique genius of Shakespeare, but there is an opposite danger of underestimating the scale of the social transformation that occurred during his lifetime. Shakespeare lived between the moment of the English monarchy's supreme sovereignty and the moment of its most profound subjection. Thirty-three years before Shakespeare's birth, Henry VIII had been newly installed as supreme head of the Church in England following the break from Rome.[82] Thirty-three years after the poet's death a commonwealth of citizens had been newly installed at the country's head in place of the recently decapitated Charles I.[83] The dramatic rise and fall of the monarchy in such a short span is attributable to innumerable historical factors, but significant among them is the factor of individual will and, in broad terms, a shift from monarchical to popular will. The short span in which royal sovereignty fell from its greatest height to its greatest depth contained within it the golden age of early modern English theatre. That golden age ended when Cromwell's Parliament closed the theatres in 1642, having begun (as is often supposed) with the appearance in 1561 of *Gorboduc*, the first English play in blank verse. *Gorboduc* was written by two common lawyers (Thomas Norton and Thomas Sackville) and first performed by lawyers before an audience of lawyers at Inner Temple. The play was on themes of royal succession and the wilful (albeit lifetime) disposition of a realm by its king.[84] *Gorboduc* was written early in the reign of Elizabeth I (1558–1603) and she is known to have attended a performance on 18 January 1562 (1561 Old Style). The young queen could hardly have failed to hear a lesson on succession in the lines of the final speech: 'No ruler rests within the regal seat; / The heir, to whom the sceptre 'longs, unknown.'[85] The question of succession to the English throne continued to be a vexed and vital one throughout the early years of Shakespeare's theatrical career, and his Elizabethan plays frequently connect testamentary concerns to concerns of traditional, especially royal, succession. For example, *Richard*

II and *King John*, which are the focus of Chapter 2, exploit the dramatic conflict between royal and testamentary succession. (William West divides succession neatly into 'royal' and 'civil', and civil into two sorts: the 'immediate or lawfull', which we call inheritance or intestacy, and the 'mediate or testamentarie', which is inheritance by will.)[86]

One way to express the distinctive quality of Shakespeare's historical moment is to talk in terms of transition from the medieval world of feudal tradition to the modern world of free trade. The transition can be conceived as a move from a social scheme arranged along the vertical axis according to hierarchies of status to a social scheme in which people deal with each other on the level, in the lateral plane. The testamentary freedom established by the 1540 Statute of Wills is a feature of this trend, because testament can be understood as a form of trade in the way that it enables individuals to depart at their own 'free will' from the default rules of inheritance and succession (we return to the idea of testament as trade in Chapter 2). None of this is to suggest that the distinction between feudal tradition and free trade was a clear one at any historical point, or to suppose that the move to free trade represents unambiguously positive progress,[87] still less to say that Shakespeare plotted his plays along two rigid axes. It is to claim, rather, that in the tension between feudal tradition and free trade Shakespeare found scope for infinite playfulness.

In modern usage the word 'trade' is resonant of hand-to-hand dealing and it has carried that sense for centuries. Bracton wrote in the thirteenth century that '*traditione*', or handing-over, of an asset was one of the 'five garments' 'necessary for the cloathing of contracts',[88] and even in Shakespeare's lifetime it was noted that the hand-to-hand business of free trade had produced a world in which a few people found themselves holding the lot.[89] In fact, the word 'trade' is etymologically more akin to the tread of feet than to dealing between hands (the word comes from the Old English verb *tredan*). What both senses – the 'hand-to-hand' and the treading foot – seem to agree upon is that trade operates on the level; in the lateral plane. Tradition, in contrast, is generally associated with handing down from generation to generation. Tradition need not imply hierarchy, but in many traditions, including the 'feudal', the hierarchy of handing down from social superior to social inferior is a defining feature of the scheme.

This dramatic tension between tradition along the vertical or hierarchical axis and trade in the lateral or horizontal plane was built into the physical fabric of the Elizabethan playhouse. The thrust stage was physically elevated above the yard by some four or five feet, but as the actors trod the boards downstage they were very much walking in the midst of the playgoers. Socially speaking, the downstage area was especially representative of street level and as such it was conceptually of one level with the groundlings treading in the playhouse yard. Sometimes, the stage was even used as a sort of village green or public highway for displaying thieves 'taken pilfring' at a play.[90] Robert Weimann's argument that the yard and the main downstage plane of the stage were united by a sense of communally shared space is important here. Weimann borrows the terminology of medieval theatre to suggest that the players on the foremost thrust part of the stage share with the groundlings the area of the 'platea'. Downstage is, as it were, 'down with the people'. The vertical structures of the stage (pillars, balcony, heavens and so forth) in the upstage area form the distinct area of the 'locus'.[91] In terms of social hierarchy, descent is from locus to platea and not from the downstage area to the yard. The exchange or trade that takes place in the platea (the word means 'street')[92] between the players and the playgoers is a trade of treading or walking together. It symbolizes shared economic enterprise and social mobility even as the vertical structures in the background stand for the unmoving hierarchies of feudal tradition.

As the dramatic tension between the vertical order of feudal tradition and the horizontal freedom of trade was played out in the physical structure of the playhouse, so it played out in the careers of the players themselves. It is only a slight oversimplification to observe that the course of Shakespeare's professional life mirrored the economic evolution of England from feudal tradition to free trade, for it was broadly one of progress from being a servant and dependent subject within a hierarchy of noble patronage to being (while still in official form a servant) a much more free agent operating within a horizontally ordered community of venturers.

It is unfashionable nowadays to talk in terms of such simple binaries as tradition and trade, heaven and hell, interior and exterior, male and female, true and false, but the early moderns used such simple pairings as a 'binary code' through which a mesh of great complexity could be fabricated and contemplated and played out. The moderns forgot the complexity. The postmoderns are in danger of forgetting the play. We will see in the chapters that follow that it is through their spirit of playfulness that Shakespeare's dramatic works continue to open more questions than can ever be closed. It is also through their playful spirit that they bear testament, even today, to the ongoing human struggle to perform individual will against the backdrop of status-entrenching social frames.

2

Handling tradition: Testament as trade in *Richard II* and *King John*

Richard II and *King John* exemplify Shakespeare's method of engaging the materiality of the playhouse to assist playgoers to handle the questions and dramatic conflicts of a play.[1] The vertical and lateral planes of the architecture, the movement and gesture of the actors, the performance of costume and hand props are all artfully suited to the logical and embodied sense that is produced by silences and words. Voice, movement and stage stuff combine to produce a totality of dramatic tension, and in these plays the tension is palpably that which arises from interactions between the vertical, hierarchical order of tradition and the lateral, horizontal potential of trade. In Chapter 1, where I outlined the etymological and stage significance of 'tradition' and 'trade', I stressed that Shakespeare does not assert a strict distinction between these ideas, but seeks to explore their playful and dramatic interaction. In *Richard II* and *King John*, Shakespeare presents worlds of traditional order in decline or under threat and invites playgoers to witness will expressed in these worlds in the language and actions of testament and trade. The participation of the playgoers as third party witnesses gives the performance a testamentary quality, but their participation is not passive. They are encouraged to subject the performance, and the will expressed in it, to a process of trial or testing. In legal testamentary terms, they are invited to subject the will to 'probate' or 'probation',[2] which means that they are asked to approve what they have seen. I should stress again that as we think in testamentary terms, our focus should not be upon legal technicalities for their own sake but upon the ways in which the rhetorical, material and communal practices and effects of law are broadly akin to those of theatre. It has been said that modern playgoers approaching *Richard II* (and the same is true of *King John*), 'are a bit like anthropologists dropped into a village just as a ritual begins; our task is to make sense of what we see'.[3] The sense we are looking for 'lies in the gesture, the object, the act, the person' and 'not in any secondary explanations, or reasons, or justifications'.[4] To assist us in this task of sensing the full make-up of the play, Shakespeare presents on-stage witnesses, including manipulators and manual workers. They help the playgoers to handle great questions of crown and country ('crown' is conveniently uncapitalized in this chapter). In *King John*, the chief witness is Philip the Bastard; in *Richard II* it is the gardener.

When the gardener observes that the crown has been 'quite thrown down' by Richard's 'waste of idle hours' (3.4.66), he plants a question in the minds of the playgoers.[5] The question is whether Richard's 'waste' is of the active or the passive sort. The word 'thrown' suggests the former. The word 'idle' suggests the latter. This question presents choices for the scene in which the physical crown changes hands from Richard to Bolingbroke. Should Richard cast it aside, or willingly hand it over, or willingly let it fall, or should he involuntarily lose his grip? If the latter, is it because of his own weakness or because of Bolingbroke's force? There is talk of Richard's 'willing soul' adopting Bolingbroke as his heir (4.1.109–10), but at the crux of the dramatic action Richard equivocates: 'What you will have, I'll give, and willing too; / For do we must what force will have us do' (3.3.206–7). To the great advantage of the play, the text does not close the question of free will and possession of the crown, but leaves it to the playgoers to test the issues and reach conclusions. They might conclude that Richard's neglect of the crown justified Bolingbroke's possession of it, but however that question is settled on the surface it will merely disturb this deeper question: 'can the destination of the crown be determined by individual will?' That question had been revived by Henry VIII's attempt to devolve the crown by his last will and testament and 'was never settled'.[6] Shakespeare declines to resolve the debate and instead exploits its dramatic tension. The debate is a deep one. It calls for nothing less than to ask whether the right to govern can pass by human handling or must be allocated by the lottery of birth and blood. Deeper still is the challenge to divine on which side of these possibilities the will of God is at work. For early modern playgoers, informed by such schools of thought as Richard Hooker's 'latitudinarian' Anglicanism (which regarded individual piety as more important to God than traditional ecclesiastical structures), such issues translated into nascent political questions of democracy and personal election.[7] Adam the gardener, representative of the biblical Adam,[8] was inviting the playgoers to question the power of individual agency to control events and to speculate with him that the high affairs of state might be better handled by common folk.

Let us suppose, as Andrew Gurr supposes, that Bolingbroke 'sees the crown as the title to a property which can be bequeathed by will like the property of an ordinary titleholder';[9] still we never learn if Bolingbroke is right. The openness of such questions maintains the ongoing life of the drama on the stage, and even in the study. We know that Bolingbroke took the crown into his own hands, but we are never sure if he stole it, or bargained for it, or merely picked up what had been dropped or thrown down. In *Richard II*, Richard calls Bolingbroke a thief (3.2.47), but it is not clear that Bolingbroke accepts the charge. Later in the tetralogy he admits that he 'stole all courtesy from heaven' (*1H4*, 3.2.50) and he confesses on his deathbed that he 'purchas'd' (*2H4*,

4.5.199) the crown. At worst the word 'purchase' indicates theft, for Shakespeare sometimes uses it as a synonym for 'steal' (*1H4*, 2.1.91; *H5*, 3.2.42) as he does 'convey' (*R2*, 4.1.317), and at best it makes Bolingbroke an enterprising businessman. His language is financially loaded even when he talks of friendship (*R2,* 2.3.60–2). 'Enterprise' means 'to take in hand', and from Bolingbroke's own mouth we learn, when he is king, that his 'hands are full of business' (*1H4,* 3.2.179). According to the gardener, even Richard himself 'is in the mighty hold / Of Bolingbroke' (*R2,* 3.4.83–4). In *1 Henry IV*, Worcester regards Henry as an opportunist and alleges to his face: 'You took occasion ... / To grip the general sway into your hand' (*1H4,* 5.1.56–7). Whether this was enterprise or theft remains unclear. The dying Henry acknowledges that the crown 'seem'd in me / But as an honour snatch'd with boist'rous hand' (*2H4*, 4.5.190–1), but to say it 'seem'd' so is not to say it was. The question remains open.

The passing of the crown is not just a question of having or taking laterally within the horizons of opportunity. It is also necessarily a question of traditional descent. The question of descent is central to the play's grand theme of Richard's fall and Bolingbroke's rise and it is amplified through the physical structures of the Elizabethan playhouse and stage. We consider two key episodes later in this chapter: Richard's descent from the castle walls (3.3.178–82), followed by the narrated account of the citizens' ascent to the 'windows' tops' of London (5.2.1–6). Considered as a connected pair of scenes, these episodes have the effect of staging a democratic displacement of the king from his elevated position. Spatial inversion on stage mirrors upheaval in the state. The vertical vectors of the play and the antithetical association of high to low is rendered dynamic by movement, props and such gestural points as the courteous bending of knees and the throwing down and picking up of gages.[10] In the very first scene, in the quarrel between Bolingbroke and the Duke of Norfolk (Thomas Mowbray), we have in quick succession John of Gaunt's 'Throw down, my son, the Duke of Norfolk's gage' (1.1.161) and King Richard's 'Norfolk, throw down his. / ... / Norfolk, throw down, we bid' (1.1.162, 164). A kinaesthetic effect induced by the continuous ups and downs of the stage action amplifies the conceptual contrast between the highs and lows of the characters' fortunes and status.[11] The gardener's reference to the high crown 'thrown down' is one of many dynamic instances of the vertical vector of the play. Indeed the word 'thrown', by punning on 'throne', concentrates the antithesis in itself. The fact that the throne (more properly 'the state')[12] is a major stage property, but one that the actors cannot wield physically, means that it must be handled in the mind – as much by the playgoers as by the players. In contrast, the gages (gauntlets) are the hand prop par excellence. We will pick them up again before the end of this chapter. For now it is important to stress that they move across the stage horizontally as well as moving up and down through the vertical axis. Gages are exchanged hand to hand by a kind of trade bargain that implies documentary performance made 'under hand', that is, with the signature or handwriting of the parties, hence Aumerle refers to his gage as a 'manual seal' (4.1.26).[13] The legal and trade sense of the gage is clear in Mowbray's declaration: 'I ... /... interchangeably hurl down my gage' (1.1.145–6). In Shakespearean usage, the word 'interchangeably' is inseparable from the legal performance of trade bonds and other deeds. It is used later in the play to describe the setting down of 'hands' in sealing a document (5.2.98), as it is elsewhere (*1H4*, 3.1.77; *TC*, 3.2.56–7).

There is, of course, another puzzle posed by the gardener's reference to the crown 'thrown down', beyond the immediate question of royal succession, and that is to know whose will is at work in the world and whose hand performs it. Intriguing here is the gardener's observation that Richard has insufficient weight on his side of the balance: 'In your lord's scale is nothing but himself / And some few vanities that make him light' (3.4.85–6). This may be an allusion to the supernatural, disembodied hand that wrote on the wall to warn King Belshazzar of his imminent downfall in the biblical book of Daniel. The writing recorded the judgment that the king had been 'weighed in the scale and found wanting' (Dan. 5.27).[14] However that may be, it is clear that the gardener, the manual worker, is inviting the playgoers to join with him in holding matters in the hands of the mind: grasping, wrestling, reshaping them, and weighing them in judgment. Shakespeare sometimes makes this invitation express, as when the chorus to *Henry V* concludes the first prologue by urging the playgoers 'Gently to hear, kindly to judge our play' (1.prologue.34). The chorus animates the playgoers to imaginative engagement of a hands-on sort: 'deck our kings' (1.prologue.28); 'Grapple your minds to sternage of this navy' (3.prologue.18); and, finally, he invites them to be conveyers of the king – to 'Heave him away upon your winged thoughts' and 'fetch' him in (5.prologue.8, 28). The invitation is expressly to 'behold / In the quick forge and working-house of thought' (5.prologue.22–3). Shakespeare would have his playgoers grapple like sailors, work like smiths and graft like gardeners. They are constituted hands-on participants in the play.

As the gardener is a biblical type of everyman, so he is a political everyman who works at the level of the ground and of the groundlings. We might be tempted to call him a 'levelling' type, but although his policy of humbling the haughty (he cuts the heads off 'too fast-growing sprays' [3.4.34]) might sound to modern ears like a policy of social equality ('All must be even in our government.' [3.4.36]), we should not ascribe twentieth-century individualistic notions of equality to the Elizabethans. They would have been quite as likely to hear the cutting-off of heads as a caution against social climbing and excessive ambition. The notion of 'even' government promoted by Shakespeare's gardener was unlikely to have been our modern idea of uniformity across all strata of social status, but something more akin to a just and unbiased ordering of the social scheme: 'Concord, not equality.'[15] The sense of even ground is enhanced when the queen, just prior to her encounter with the gardener, employs the metaphor of the sport of bowls (3.4.3–5). (Compare *King John*, discussed below, where the corrupting effect of 'commodity' on the 'world' is represented as a biased bowling ball.) The gardener's policy is one of balancing the constituents of society as a conscientious cultivator balances the elements of his garden. His desire for harmonious balance between justice of a horizontal sort and order of a hierarchical sort is confirmed by his image of the scales, and that image is supported in the stage action through the balanced choreography of two parties: the queen and her two attendants on one side, the gardener and his two workers on the other. There is no modern sense of social equality here, at least not in the crude form 'equality is uniformity', but there is a sense of common human dignity regardless of social status. This is confirmed by the fact that the gardener speaks verse, as do the citizens of Angiers in *King John* (see below). It is true that *Richard II* contains no prose lines, which is true also of *King John*, *1 Henry VI* and *3 Henry VI*, but if Shakespeare had wanted to denigrate the gardener he could have given him prose despite the predominance of verse, as he did with Jack Cade and the rebels in *2 Henry VI*.

Shakespeare's history plays can be regarded as extended rhetorical arguments designed to persuade the playgoing witness not to a particular verdict or point of view, but to an appreciation of what it feels like to handle the evidence and to participate in political discourse. The weight and 'feel' of the dramatic dispute is handled as matter in the mind, and occasionally a conceptual question is enlivened by a sensory conundrum. For instance, what weight should we associate with a king who is lighter than Bolingbroke in the gardener's image of the scales but heavier than Bolingbroke in Richard's own image of the buckets in the well (4.1.184–9)?[16] We are not compelled to resolve this apparent contradiction, but if the gardener's scales are indeed the biblical scales of the divine assessor, we can perhaps understand Richard to be thrown down in the affairs of men, even to death, and at the same time to be taken up in the hands of God. This approximates to Richard's own understanding. Addressing his wife en route to the Tower he tells her: 'Our holy lives must win a new world's crown, / Which our profane hours here have thrown down' (5.1.24–5). At a (perhaps unwise) distance from the stage we might see Richard's complete trajectory as down and then up, forming as it were the 'V' that makes the top half of a saltire. Bolingbroke's corresponding trajectory of rise and demise throughout the tetralogy would supply the lower half, with each half touching at the crossover point. Certainly there is a substantial crossing over of the characters' fortunes within *Richard II* and this is frequently emphasized through the rhetorical figure of *chiasmus*, which is a 'criss-cross' figure.[17] A sub-species of *chiasmus* ('*antimetabole*', in which words are exactly repeated and reversed in the form A-B-B-A) is pithily employed at the moment of formal transfer of the crown when Richard equivocates his consent: 'Ay, no. No, ay' (4.1.201). At the moment of his death, Richard confirms a crossroad even in his own divided being: 'Mount, mount, my soul! Thy seat is up on high, / Whilst my gross flesh sinks downward here to die' (5.5.111–12). The same sentiment is expressed in Shakespeare's *The Rape of Lucrece* (1594) which was written closely contemporary with *Richard II*: 'This brief abridgment of my will I make: / My soul and body to the skies and ground' (1198–9).[18] This antithetical treatment of soul and body is specifically the standard wording of an Elizabethan testament.[19]

Part of the appeal of Shakespeare's *Richard II* resides in references to the performative rituals of everyday life and death in early modern England, many of which required the hands-on participation of ordinary folk. For example, when King Richard laments that imprisonment divorces him from his wife 'hand from hand' (5.1.82), Shakespeare's playgoers would have recognized a reference to, and reversal of, the joining of hands in marriage and, more specifically, a reference to the ritual handfasting that sealed a betrothal.[20] Shakespeare himself might have been bound to Anne Hathaway by handfasting prior to marriage,[21] and it is likely that he acted as witness to this rite in 1604 when he 'made sure' the betrothal of Stephen Bellott to Mary Mountjoy at the moment of their '*giving each other's hand to the hand*'.[22] An effect of Richard's performative reversal of handfasting is to remind the playgoers of the preceding act of the play in which they had seen the seriatim reversal of the elements of Richard's coronation rite. As the un-fasting of the matrimonial hands implies Richard's separation from his wife, it also implies his imminent separation from life, since marriage lasts only until death.

The testamentary sense is even stronger in those communal performances alluded to, or incorporated, in Shakespeare's *Richard II* that specifically relate to death and burial. Among these we must include the documentary performance of the last will and testament, which we will consider in more depth when we consider Richard's 'talk of wills' (3.2.148). At this point we will concentrate on a material correspondence between the documentary performance of a will and the physical performance of funeral rites. In Elizabethan times, both performances involved an express passing of the soul into the hands of God, and of the body to the earth.[23] (We shall shortly see that there is significance in the fact that earth itself was passed from human hands as part of the Elizabethan burial rite.) The preamble to Shakespeare's last will and testament was in a form standard for the time:[24]

> In the name of god Amen I William Shackspeare of Stratford vpon Avon in the countie of warr[*wick*] gent[*leman*] in p[*er*]fect health & memorie god be praysed doe make & Ordayne this my last will and testam[*en*]t in mann[*er*] and forme followeing That ys to saye ffirst I Comend my Soule into the hand[*es*] of god my Creator hoping & assuredlie beleeving through thonelie merit[*es*] of Iesus Christe my Saviour to be made p[*ar*]taker of lyfe everlastinge And my bodye to the Earth whereof yt ys made[25]

This documentary form had a post-mortem counterpart in the dramatic performance of the funeral rite. The words spoken at

Shakespeare's funeral (and at the funeral of his son, Hamnet, which was roughly contemporary with *Richard II* and *King John*) would have been the words ordained to be spoken by the priest 'At the Burial of the Dead' according to the 1552 Book of Common Prayer. That ritual form of words, which was adopted without amendment by Queen Elizabeth in her edition of 1559, was as follows:

> FORASMUCHE as it hathe pleased almightie God of his great mercy to take unto himselfe the soule of our dere brother here departed: we therefore commit his body to the ground, earth to earth, asshes to asshes, dust to dust, in sure and certayne hope of resurreccion to eternal lyfe, through our Lord Jesus Christ, who shal chaunge our vyle bodye, that it maye bee lyke to his glorious bodye, according to the mightie working wherby he is hable to subdue all thinges to himselfe.[26]

This text had been significantly reformed from that of the 1549 first edition. The original wording had left the priest in his traditional position as mediator between God above and people below. The priest had uttered in the first person '*I* commende thy soule to God the father almighty, and thy body to the grounde' (emphasis added). The second edition talks instead of '*our* dere brother here departed' and uses the communal '*we* therefore commit his body to the ground' (emphases added).

Ritual power was taken not only from the mouth of the priest but also from his hands. The words of committal in the first edition are preceded by the direction: 'Then the priest castyng earth upon the Corps, shall saye.' In the reformed (second) edition of 1552, that direction is altered in a small but important detail, for it is now the bystanders, not the priest, who perform the ritual act of casting dust upon the corpse: 'Then whyle the earth shal be cast upon the body by some standing by, / the priest shall saye.' This exemplifies that genre of participatory public performance that I call 'testamentary', for the third party bystander (the 'tri-st' or 'testa') is not a passive observer but a participant without whom the performance would be incomplete.[27]

The ritual of the Roman Catholic priest casting dust down from a position somewhere between man and God, with the hierarchy that implies, was replaced by the horizontal ritual of brothers, members of a common priesthood of believers, casting dust upon one of their own.[28] The dust becomes a prop in a protestant drama with protestant script and protestant stage directions. The performative power of ordinary people taking matters into their own hands is an enduring one. Ben Whishaw, who played Richard II in *The Hollow Crown* (BBC, 2012) and who based his portrayal partly upon the dictator Colonel Gaddafi, notes that in footage of Gaddafi's capture 'people are throwing things at him'.[29] The footage shows shoes being wielded by his captors, and presumably the deposed dictator was struck by these in accordance with the Arab notion that the shoe is ceremonially unclean and to be struck by it is symbolically to be trodden down in the dust. In a famous incident at a news conference in 2008, the same insult was quite literally hurled at President George Bush Jnr by an Arab journalist. Bush managed to dodge the flying shoe, but his father had been forced to take a similar insult lying down. In 1991, President George Bush Snr had suffered the discomfiture of having a huge mosaic portrait of his face set into the floor at the entrance to one of Baghdad's major hotels. This cultural understanding of the shoe might be a reason why the celebrated Arab theatre designer Farrah (Abd'Elkader Farrah) employed a portrait of King Richard as a backdrop and lowered it to form a sloped stage for Bolingbroke to tread upon in Terry Hands' *Richard II* (RSC, 1980).[30]

The character of Northumberland, whom Richard labels 'thou ladder wherewithal / The mounting Bolingbroke ascends' (5.1.55–6), is a self-willing agent and an early modern protestant before his time. This is apparent from such lines as 'My guilt be on my head, and there an end' (5.1.69). He excises the priest from the proceedings. Likewise, when

Richard is deposed, there is no bishop to preside over the reversal of the coronation rites. Richard asks, 'Am I both priest and clerk?' (4.1.174). He answers his own question when he washes away the balm of his anointing with his own tears and gives away his crown with his own hands, thereby reversing the sacramental actions of the priest in the coronation ceremony. Richard is reduced to acting as his own agent, but the play's exemplar of the modern, self-determining agent is Bolingbroke. The Victorian critic Frederick Boas conceived him in typically Victorian terms, to be an 'iron-willed man of affairs'.[31] That may be overstating the efficacy of Bolingbroke's will, for there is truth in John Dover Wilson's suggestion that Bolingbroke is to some extent 'borne upward by a power beyond his volition',[32] but even if fate placed the ladder of opportunity at Bolingbroke's feet it is clear that he scaled it voluntarily: 'In God's name I'll ascend the regal throne' (4.1.114). From the opening scene of the play, he declares his will to enact what he speaks: 'what I speak / My body shall make good upon this earth' (1.1.36–7). This is the very manifesto of modernity, even post-modernity. He is a self-willing actor setting out to perform his individual identity on the political and theatrical stage. The historical Richard II has been described as 'the last king ruling by hereditary right, direct and undisputed, from the Conqueror',[33] and therefore as 'the last king of the old medieval order'.[34] The medieval nature of Shakespeare's Richard and his faction can be emphasized through costume, for example by adopting Tillyard's suggestion that Bushy, Green and Bagot were 'very plainly Morality figures and were probably marked in some way by their dress as abstract vices'.[35] If Shakespeare's Richard is medieval, he is nevertheless confronted with emerging modernity and ultimately his world is 'superseded by the more familiar world of the present'.[36] Again, the mode of costume can be employed to represent tension between the old order and the new. For example, in Michael Bogdanov's *Richard II* (English Shakespeare Company, 1989), epochal change was demonstrated by contrasting Richard's 'languid

Regency dandy' with Bolingbroke's 'sombre Edwardian civil servant'.[37]

The bystanders in an Elizabethan burial service who threw dust upon the coffin had their counterparts in the commoners who cast dust on the head of Richard as he entered London trailing behind the triumphant Bolingbroke. The scene of Bolingbroke's entry is reported by the eyewitness account of the Duke of York speaking privately to his wife. The duke had broken off his tale, so the duchess urges him to continue from 'that sad stop, my lord, / Where rude misgoverned hands from windows' tops / Threw dust and rubbish on King Richard's head' (5.2.1–6). The duke continues:

> As in a theatre the eyes of men,
> After a well-graced actor leaves the stage,
> Are idly bent on him that enters next,
> Thinking his prattle to be tedious,
> Even so, or with much more contempt, men's eyes
> Did scowl on gentle Richard. No man cried God save him!
> No joyful tongue gave him his welcome home,
> But dust was thrown upon his sacred head.
> Which with such gentle sorrow he shook off. (5.2.23–30)

The episode has a counterpart in the Old Testament. Not long after King David lost his throne to the rebellion of his son Absalom, we read that a Hebrew by the name of Shimei 'threw stones against him, and cast dust' (2 Sam. 16.13).[38] When Shakespeare's Richard 'shook off' (5.2.31) the dust, he was returning a biblical curse upon the London citizens.[39] A stage director might choose to represent the casting of dust on Richard by means of a confetti shower, shadow show, video projection or some other such device, but it might be better to leave the falling dust to York's narrative account and to omit any peripheral physical representation of the actual matter. The power of the scene may be heightened if the playgoers are required to hold the dust in the hands of their minds, there to weigh it up and grasp its significance. Imagined stage properties can sometimes have a more powerful hold upon playgoers' minds than physical props presented on stage. (The pound of flesh in *The Merchant of Venice* is a case in point.)[40] Held in the hand of the mind, the significance of the dust is something like the significance of the 'gage' considered earlier. Both things are taken up and thrown down in the vertical plane but they also have strong connotations of movement in the horizontal plane. We saw that the dust of the burial rite was taken up and thrown down in the horizontal plane of protestant brotherhood. The dust thrown down on Richard covers him in the shifting matter of the common highway and the *platea* (Greek 'street') that connects the low stage to the playgoers in the yard. 'Dust' would have a number of material implications for the Elizabethan playgoer. One playgoer would have thought of ashes scraped from the hearth, another of food scraps, and another of the contents of a chamber pot or 'jordan' (*2H4*, 2.4.32–3).[41] Encouraged by the players' repeated contact (by means of hands, knees and words) with the imagined stage soil of England, some playgoers – perhaps the groundlings especially – would have thought of the dust of the ground. For some, the reference to dust might have brought to mind the dust of the burial rite or (less likely) the dust of the biblical encounter between Shimei and King David. Whatever idea of 'dust' it brought to mind, York's description of commoners wielding dust would have encouraged mental grappling with material such as the chorus urges in *Henry V*. Through mental engagement, the London playgoer was turned from witness to actor even as the actor playing the Duke of York played witness to the actions of commoners in the London streets. The dust of the burial rite, which moved from the priest to the people and endowed them with performative agency, here moves from the theatrical players to the playgoers and endows them with the power of participation in affairs of state.

The drama of commoners casting dust upon the captive King Richard seems to have had an uncommon hold on Shakespeare's imagination. He even refers back to it from *2 Henry IV*, where the Archbishop of York condemns the commoners who 'threw'st dust upon [King Richard's] goodly head' and with 'loud applause' blessed Bolingbroke (1.3.103; 91). The word 'applause' here echoes the Duke of York's use of theatrical metaphor to describe the same event in *Richard II*.[42] The hold that the scene had upon Shakespeare's imagination was specifically a theatrical hold.

On King Richard's return to England from Ireland, his first act had been to touch the ground. He blessed it, communed with it and pleaded with it to 'Throw death upon thy sovereign's enemies' (3.2.22). Yet in the event of Bolingbroke's triumphal entry into London, Richard's subjects become his enemies and they throw death upon him in the form of dust. In this expressly theatrical scene, the dramatic prop of the burial rite is thrown on Richard's head as if he were already dead. The kingship lives in Henry Bolingbroke and that which trails behind him in the form of Richard is the mere corpse of a king. It is perverse and paradoxical that the fleshy form of a king should outlive the sacred substance of his kingship, but here, as elsewhere (most profoundly in *King Lear*), Shakespeare exploits the drama inherent in the paradox. Richard presumes that 'The worst is death' (3.2.103), but worse than death is living death and worse for a king is to be treated in life and death as if he were no more exalted than any corpse laid low in the earth. When Bolingbroke's fellow subjects – the common bystanders who witnessed and participated in his triumph – cast dust upon Richard, they effectively buried their king in the road of the merchant metropolis of London. Shakespeare had earlier caused Richard to anticipate this fate:

> Or I'll be buried in the King's highway,
> Some way of common trade, where subjects' feet
> May hourly trample on their sovereign's head;
> For on my heart they tread now whilst I live,
> And, buried once, why not upon my head? (3.3.155–9)

This passage begins with the antithetical pairing of 'buried' and 'the king's highway', but the antithesis is more nuanced than a commonplace contrast between high and low, for the way of the king in Shakespeare's play is not as high as it should be; it is imagined as a low road of 'common trade'.[43] The substantial contrast being made here is not between high and low along the vertical axis, but between the vertical order of tradition and the horizontal plane of trade.

Richard confesses that his 'coffers ... / ... are grown somewhat light' and that he is 'enforced to farm our royal realm' (1.4.43–7) (compare *H5*, 5.2.124–7). This confirms that he has turned from tradition to trade. The word 'farm', which derives from the French *ferme* ('lease') and ultimately from the Latin *firma* ('fixed sum'), indicates that Richard is landlord of a lease.[44] Gaunt establishes this with his complaint that England had been 'leased out ... / Like to a tenement or pelting farm' and his indictment of Richard: 'Landlord of England art thou now, not king' (2.1.59–60; 113).[45] Shakespeare is here presenting landlord and king as incompatible offices. The well-known labels 'landlord' and 'tenant', which even today attach to the parties to a lease, might suggest that the arrangement was akin to the feudal relationship between lord and tenant. The basic scheme of the feudal system was that all land in the realm was owned by the crown and every land holder (tenant) held his estate from his superior (his lord) and so on all the way up the chain to the monarch as supreme overlord. In fact, the farm lease 'had ... nothing ... feudal in its nature, and was, consequently, exempt from the feudal rule of descent to the eldest son as heir at law'.[46] The lease was essentially contractual in its origins and the feudal terminology of tenant and lord was adopted out of familiarity or as a rhetorical pretence. England 'leased out' is for Gaunt an England in legal and commercial bondage (2.1.63–4, 114). Feudal land holding was understood in terms of 'tenure', which described the terms on which a tenant held the land from his superior lord. The species of 'tenure' denoted the sort of duties that accompanied the holding. For example, tenants holding under the tenure of 'Knight-service' had the very onerous obligation of supplying military service to the crown, or (as it evolved) a substantial cash equivalent. The relational nature of feudal land holding meant that it was a sort of 'hand-holding' between the tenant and his lord.[47] In *Richard II*, feudal tradition loses its grip and the realm itself is handled as an object of commercial trade. In Gregory Doran's production (RSC, 2012), the throne of state took the form of a movable platform that reached its elevated position above the stage by descending from the fly loft. The 'state' should be stable and static. (Shakespeare consciously juxtaposes 'state' and 'change' [3.4.29–30].)[48] Its descent in this production signals that the political state itself is unstable and set on a tragic downwards trajectory. Richard abandons tradition for the low road of trade in other actions too, the most significant being the seizure of the inheritance that should have been handed down to Bolingbroke from John of Gaunt. This act, discussed further below, was the one by which Bolingbroke was, in his own words, 'trod down' (2.3.126).

In the context of land transfer, legal inheritance by 'heirs' under traditional default rules of descent can be displaced by lifetime sales and other legal 'acts of trade' but also by the legal 'act of will' we call the testament. It follows that testament and trade both effect lateral hand-to-hand transfer in opposition to vertical hand-down by tradition. A lifetime purchaser of a fee simple was said to be an 'assign', and in early modern England the same label properly applied to the recipient of a fee simple under a testamentary will.[49] It is fitting, then, that David Tennant's Richard crawled along the ground – effectively representing the king as a downtrodden subject of trade, and one who treads or trades horizontally – as he spoke the play's most obviously testamentary line: 'Let's choose executors and talk of wills' (3.2.148) (Gregory Doran, RSC, 2013). When Lepidus contrasts 'hereditary' to 'purchased' (1.4.13–14) in *Antony and Cleopatra*, Shakespeare is accurately alluding to the legal distinction between acquisition as an heir and acquisition as an assign by testament or trade. A testament produces succession but it does not produce 'inheritance' properly so called. When a testator writes his will, he cannot name his heir, because nobody can know who will be their heir at the future date of their death (for one thing, the present 'heir apparent' might predecease the testator). Hence the doctrine, recited by Sir Edward Coke, that heirs 'in the legall understanding of the Common Law, implyeth ... he to whom lands, tenements, or hereditaments by the act of God, and right of blood doe descend of some estate of inheritance, for *Solus Deus haeredem facere potest non homo*' ('Only God has the power to make an heir, not man').[50]

King Richard's reference to 'common trade' comes immediately after the 'list of exchanges'[51] that Richard 'must' (a most unprincely word)[52] perform as a result of his having traded places with Bolingbroke. The lengthy, itemized list is rendered in the form of rhetorical anaphora and reads like a trader's ledger of bargains. It starts 'I'll give my jewels for a set of beads' and concludes 'And my large kingdom for a little grave' (3.3.147–53). Charles Forker notes that the word 'tread' in Richard's 'Some way of common trade ... / ... / ... on my heart they tread' (3.3.156, 158) is 'quibbling on *trade*'.[53] Both words share the same etymology and in some Elizabethan dialects were very likely pronounced the same.[54] Even modern ears can hear the sound of 'tread' amplified through the consonance of its elements in the adjacent words 'trade' and 'head', but why does Shakespeare emphasize the word 'tread' in connection with dust and a King's demise? It seems likely that Shakespeare is recalling the Psalms of King David, and in particular the lines: 'Then let the enemie persecute my soule and take it: yea, let him treade my life downe vpon the earth, and lay mine honour in the dust' (Ps. 7.5).

The words of King David begin with a personal prayer in the style of a rhetorical apostrophe to God in which he calls upon the Lord to be his defender against his enemies or else, *if* He judges David to be wicked, *then* to let his enemies triumph and tread him in the dust. According to the Book of Common Prayer's 'Order how the Psalter is appointed to be read', every Psalm was required to be recited every month in every parish in England. Shakespeare would have heard many of those readings and he would also have been familiar with Miles Coverdale's English translation of the Psalms from their appearance in the Geneva Bible.[55] On the evidence of *Richard II*, we can speculate that Shakespeare was impressed by the inherent drama of King David's high-stakes wager with God. Quite certain is the fact that the same biblical drama would make a significant impression a generation after Shakespeare's death on opposing sides in the debate surrounding the deposing of Charles I. King David's wager figured in polemics pleading the Royalist cause on the one side and the Parliamentary cause on the other. The Royalist polemic was the *Eikon basilike*, a tract attributed (somewhat dubiously) to Charles I during his time in prison awaiting trial. In the section entitled 'Upon His Majesties going to the House of Commons',[56] Charles calls God to be his Witness: 'But thou, O Lord, art my witnesse in heaven, and in my Heart: If I have purposed any violence or oppression against the Innocent: or if there were any such wickednesse in my thoughts', and, continuing, makes the wager that King David had made in Psalm 7.5: 'Then let the enemy persecute my soule, and tread my life to the ground, and lay mine Honour in the dust.' If the Psalm was at the front of Charles's mind, so Shakespeare's play might have been in the rear of it. Charles is known to have personally annotated his own copy of the 1632 second folio of Shakespeare's *Complete Works*.[57] (The evidence is even stronger to suggest that Shakespeare's play featured in high-stakes political drama in February 1601. Supporters of the Earl of Essex had paid for a performance at the Globe of a play by the Lord Chamberlain's Men called the 'kyllyng of Kyng Richard the Second',[58] which was presumably Shakespeare's play.[59] It was performed on 7 February and the very next day the Earl led the so-called 'Essex rebellion' for which he was later executed.) In response to the *Eikon basilike*, Parliament commissioned John Milton's *Eikonoklastes*, which was published following the trial and execution of Charles I. Milton cleverly quotes Charles's own words as evidence of God's judgment against the king: 'What need then more disputing? He appeal'd to Gods Tribunal, and behold God hath judg'd, and don to him in the sight of all men according to the verdict of his own mouth.'[60] Milton inevitably had the last word, but had Charles lived he might have cited another Psalm in which the downtrodden King David attributes his fallen state not to divine judgment, but to betrayal by the people. David is confident that in the eyes of God he 'shall stand fast for evermore as the moon, and as the faithful witness in heaven', but of the people he hears God complain: 'Thou hast broken the Covenant of thy servant, and profaned his crown, casting it on the ground ... Thou hast caused his dignity to decay, and cast his throne to the ground' (Ps. 89.39, 44). This Psalm perhaps inspired Shakespeare's 'crown ... quite thrown down' (3.4.66).

When Shakespeare's King Richard utters those plaintive lines, 'For God's sake let us sit upon the ground / And tell sad stories of the death of kings' (3.2.155–6), it will have called to playgoers' minds *The Mirror for Magistrates*, which was popular in various editions from 1559 to 1610. Thomas Sackville, one of the co-authors of *Gorboduc* (see Chapter 1), was a key contributor. Richard's lines might also have evoked John Lydgate's *Fall of Princes* (c. 1431–8) to which *The Mirror*, according to its Preface, was a sequel. Both works were collections of didactic tales, mostly metrical, on the *de casibus* theme of the fall of (or of that which befell) great historical figures. The earliest royal life reflected upon in *The Mirror* is that of Richard II and it is now trite to say that Richard's troubles as portrayed in Shakespeare's play were popularly considered to be a cautionary tale on the dangers of uncertain royal succession. It therefore held up a mirror to the aged and childless Elizabeth. There is even an oft-repeated legend that Elizabeth once remarked to the jurist William Lambarde: 'I am Richard II, know ye not that?'[61]

Scene 3.2, in which we find Richard on the ground talking of graves, is the first of the two central scenes of the play. Together the pair of central scenes form the fulcrum on which the fortunes of the characters turn. Referring to the play's dominant image of a set of scales, Andrew Gurr summarizes the structure of *Richard II* in the single word 'balance'.[62] Mark Rose suggests that the 'play pivots' in Scene 3.3.[63] The deposition scene that follows (4.1) is not so much a substantial shift in the status of Richard and Bolingbroke as a formal confirmation of the substantial changes that have already occurred in Act 3. The deposition scene was nevertheless symbolically potent enough to prompt its tactful (or perhaps tactical or compulsory) omission from all printed forms of the play during Elizabeth's reign.[64] The first of the two central scenes of the play, Scene 3.2, places the action on the coast of Wales where King Richard has just returned from Ireland. His first action is to salute the earth with his 'hand', and (presumably) to stoop down to do it 'favours' with his 'royal hands' (3.2.6; 10–11). In the BBC production *The Hollow Crown*, Ben Whishaw paws at the sand, hollows out a handful and scoops it up. This was an inspired choice. Richard will shortly 'talk of graves' and specifically of a 'little grave', and here he grabs burial dust in his hand and engraves a little grave in the earth.[65] Richard's stoop to the ground represents his declining status. The supreme overlord of all land is reduced to manual holding of the earth's base matter.[66] In feudal terms, he becomes the lowliest form of land-holder. A related image of decline appears near the end of the play where the queen likens Richard to the king of beasts and cautions him against passivity. She advises that 'The lion, dying, thrusteth forth his paw / And wounds the earth, if nothing else, with rage' (5.1.29–30).

On the coast, hand-on-ground, King Richard feels the threat of 'the treacherous feet / Which with usurping steps do trample' (3.2.16–17) on his land. This is the threat of those levelling subjects who would tread down tradition and the threat of Bolingbroke, in particular, who would trade places with his king. A sense of trade is present again when the Bishop of Carlisle counsels Richard to have respect for the divine power that made him king. Speaking in terms of Richard's 'will' to accept the divine 'offer' (3.2.29–31) is more appropriate to describe a contractual deal than a divine gift.

Richard attempts to reassert his traditional hierarchical status when he urges his followers to raise their sights: 'Look not to the ground, / Ye favourites of a king. Are we not high? / High be our thoughts' (3.2.87–9). His fortunes and his mood fluctuate with each fresh piece of news and are finally downcast by Sir Stephen Scroop's report of general rebellion among the king's subjects: men and women, young and old. Without the prop of popular support, the king's mind now plummets to thoughts of death: 'Revolt our subjects? That we cannot mend. / They break their faith to God as well as us. / Cry woe, destruction, ruin and decay. / The worst is death, and death will have his day' (3.2.100–3). Richard's reference to 'subjects' and 'God' invokes the settled hierarchy in which the king is situated above his subjects and below his Divine Lord, but the words 'revolt' and 'decay' acknowledge that the traditional social settlement is being overturned and is falling away. The play's grand motif of Bolingbroke's rise and Richard's fall is immediately reiterated by Sir Stephen Scroop's report that Richard's closest confidants, Bagot, Bushy and Green, have been executed by Bolingbroke and now 'lie full low, graved in the hollow ground' (3.2.140). It is these burial words that finally throw Richard down into the dust: 'For God's sake let us sit upon the ground' (3.2.155).[67] To emphasize their continuing hold on the king's mind, Shakespeare plots the words 'grave', 'hollow' and 'ground' throughout Richard's next speech. It is the famous speech in which the king, confronted with the immediacy of death and his own mortal state, turns testamentary:

> Of comfort no man speak!
> Let's talk of graves, of worms and epitaphs;
> Make dust our paper and with rainy eyes
> Write sorrow on the bosom of the earth.
> Let's choose executors and talk of wills.
> And yet not so, for what can we bequeath
> Save our deposed bodies to the ground?

> Our lands, our lives and all are Bolingbroke's,
> And nothing can we call our own but death
> ... For within the hollow crown
> That rounds the mortal temples of a king
> Keeps Death his court; and there the antic sits,
> Scoffing his state and grinning at his pomp,
> Allowing him a breath, a little scene,
> To monarchize, be feared and kill with looks. (3.2.144–52, 160–5)

The combination of performance and introspection in this scene is typical of many in which Richard appears to sit in witness to the execution of his own will. Palmer suggests that he may be 'the only appreciative witness of his tragedy',[68] echoing Chambers' suggestion that he 'becomes an interested spectator of his own ruin'.[69] (Richard is his own audience too.)[70] He witnesses events, but he has so lost his grip on them that he cannot even think to hold a writing instrument in his hand. Dust is his paper and his writing rains down in tears.[71] Richard's hand grows weak as Bolingbroke's hand is strengthened.

There is something shocking in King Richard's overt 'talk of wills' and executors. It has long been standard practice for monarchs of England to write wills, but in the matter of succession of the crown the individual monarch's will can only be a hollow performance. Richard's question 'for what can we bequeath / Save our deposed bodies to the ground?' was very much a live one for the monarchy when Shakespeare wrote the play, and the orthodoxy then, as now, is that the crown passes by traditional rules of succession which cannot be altered by the testamentary will of the particular king or queen. (See the discussion in Chapter 1.) The reason for this is that the incumbent ruler may die, but the monarch never will. The monarchy is a corporation perpetual.[72] The doctrine of the 'king's two bodies' provides that when a king dies his 'body natural' perishes but his 'body public' does not.[73] This means that when a monarch dies (the principle applies to a queen as well as to a king), the crown passes immediately to the new monarch and the deceased monarch's last will and testament, even if it purports to pass the crown, has no crown to give. It is a basic principle of logic and law that people cannot give what they do not have ('*nemo dat quod non habet*'). Richard perceives that he will not have to wait for death to take his crown, for it is already slipping from his grip. The concluding call of Richard's speech is inevitably a call to dispense with tradition. Shakespeare has just placed in Richard's mouth the theatrical image of his reign as a 'little scene' and now he has him speak a stage direction to his followers who, as etiquette demanded, are bareheaded in their sovereign's presence: 'Cover your heads, and mock not flesh and blood / With solemn reverence. Throw away respect, / Tradition, form and ceremonious duty' (3.2.171–3). With these words, the actor playing Richard might choose to throw away the crown prop.[74]

The second of the pair of pivotal scenes at the centre of *Richard II* is Scene 3.3. It is the one in which Richard encounters Bolingbroke face-to-face for the first time since Bolingbroke's illegal return to England. The scene is loaded with the antithetical motif of rise and fall and therefore presents an image of the play in microcosm. It begins when Northumberland reports the news that 'Richard', refuged in Flint Castle, has 'hid his head' (3.3.6). Northumberland's omission of the title 'King' lowers Richard as surely as if his head had been physically removed from his shoulders. Richard is a master of ceremonial courtly display, as will soon be apparent from his celestial appearance high on the castle walls, but Bolingbroke knows better how to stage-manage political theatre for common consumption. One of his favourite performative points is the courteous kneel, sometimes accompanied by the courteous kissing of an offered hand. The real Bolingbroke was required, as a vassal, to kneel and kiss the hand of his liege lord during the feudal ceremony of homage and would have done likewise out of courtesy on other courtly occasions, but Shakespeare has him turn the obligation into a performative opportunity. It has been observed that '[e]ach time after his exile that Bolingbrook kneels ... he rises with his powers enlarged', whereas each time 'Richard sinks to, kneels, or sits upon the ground after his return from Ireland, he rises weaker than before'.[75] Before the trial by combat that preceded his banishment, Bolingbroke had requested permission of the Lord Marshal to 'kiss my sovereign's hand / And bow my knee before his majesty' (1.3.46–7). King Richard's response, 'We will descend and fold him in our arms' (1.3.54), anticipates his future descent from king to subject.

Bolingbroke does not reserve his courtesies for the king. On at least one occasion he doffs his hat to an oyster-wench, and we are told that a 'brace of draymen ... / ... had the tribute of his supple knee / With "Thanks, my countrymen, my loving friends"' (1.4.32–4). Bolingbroke knows the trick of bending low to pick up the favour of the people, and the king is actor enough to know that he is being upstaged by him. Richard complains that Bolingbroke is acting 'As were our England in reversion his, / And he our subjects' next degree in hope' (1.4.35–6). In the scene of Bolingbroke's illegal return to English soil, Shakespeare employs Bolingbroke's uncle, the Duke of York, to alert the playgoers to the hypocrisy in Bolingbroke's genuflection (2.3.83–4), but Bolingbroke is undeterred. He performs his gestural trick even as late as Scene 3.3 in which he offers to kiss Richard's hand and bend *both* his knees in obsequience to the king (3.3.35–7; 48). In this scene, Shakespeare causes Bolingbroke to fall into a trap of metaphor and *paronomasia* (pun). Bolingbroke identifies himself with water and the king with fire: 'Be he the fire, I'll be the yielding water; / The rage be his, whilst on the earth I rain' (3.3.58–9). At first sight these metaphors seem a wise choice if Bolingbroke wishes to communicate his humility (flames rise up ambitiously and water tends humbly downwards to the lowest level), but Bolingbroke is betrayed by the metre of a line that leaves him hanging on the damning consonance of 'rain' and 'reign'. Hence the hasty enjambment: 'My waters – on the earth and not on him' (3.3.60). The actor has the choice to pause at the end of the verse line or continue to the end of the clause. The former will betray Bolingbroke's subliminal treachery; the latter will suggest loyalty.

When Richard appears resplendent on the castle walls, his first words indicate his readiness still to believe the physical formalities of deference: 'long have we stood / To watch the fearful bending of thy knee' (3.3.72–3). He berates Northumberland for his failure to perform: 'how dare thy joints forget / To pay their awful duty to our presence?' (3.3.75–6). The king from the upper stage makes an optimistic apostrophe to the divinely ordered hierarchy – the 'chain of being' – in which God is the lord over kings, kings the lords over men, and men mere 'vassal' subjects (3.3.85–90). Confirmation that the 'chain of being' is undone comes when Richard descends into the base court of the castle: 'Down, down I come, like glist'ring Phaëthon, / ... / In the base court? Base court where kings grow base / ... / In the base court? Come down? Down court, down king!' (3.3.178–82).[76] When Richard reaches the level ground of the stage, he finally sees the insincerity of Bolingbroke's genuflectory posturing: 'Fair cousin, you debase your princely knee / To make the base earth proud with kissing it. / ... / Up cousin, up. Your heart is up, I know, / Thus high at least, ... although your knee be low' (3.3.190–5). (The actor may choose to lower the register of their voice on the word 'low', which can serve to intensify both the king's gravity and the sense of his downwards trajectory.)[77] Shakespeare places a scene late in the play (5.3) in which Bolingbroke is made to arbitrate a contest of supplicatory kneeling that verges on the comic. Bolingbroke urges throughout that all parties – the Duke of York on the one side and York's wife and son on the other – should rise to their feet, but Shakespeare obliges him to witness a mockery of his own genuflectory excess. The points of his own performance are played against him, and the playgoers enjoy seeing him pricked by it. Played one way they will laugh with him; played another they will laugh at him.

Just before his descent from the castle walls, Richard remarks that Bolingbroke 'is come to open / The purple testament of bleeding war' (3.3.93–4). George Steevens made the common-sense observation that 'purple' indicates the effusion of blood and that 'testament' is used in its legal sense: 'Bolingbroke is come to open the testament of war so that he may peruse what is decreed there in his favour'.[78] Instead of submitting to succession by lineal descent, Bolingbroke is content that the crown should descend by bloody acts of will.[79] Does this necessarily imply that Bolingbroke's will is opposed to the will of God? Shakespeare, ever keen to keep open the question of the rights and wrongs of Bolingbroke's actions, has Bolingbroke dispute any such suggestion. When the Duke of York urges Bolingbroke to have regard to the heavens above his head, Bolingbroke claims to 'oppose not myself / Against their will' (3.3.18–19). Bolingbroke can be understood to regard war as a traditional mode of direct appeal to divine authority, which is how he regarded his personal trial by combat with Mowbray. On this view, Bolingbroke is prepared to act by rolling the dice and to leave it to God to decide the outcome, whereas his father had been content, in more passive mode, to leave the 'quarrel to the will of heaven' without taking up arms to test the point (1.2.6). For Bolingbroke, the outcome of a war witnesses to the divine will, so that war is a 'purple testament' in that sense too. To open a testament of this sort, by way of trade or bargain with God, supports our suspicion that Bolingbroke is ever the businessman. On his illegal return to England, Bolingbroke confirms with heart and hand his bond of friendship with his allies: 'My heart this covenant makes; my hand thus seals it' (2.3.50). The language here is the biblical language of the divine covenant written directly on the heart,[80] but it is also the language of commercial trade (it is preceded by references to 'count', 'fortune' and 'recompense').

Shakespeare emphasizes Bolingbroke's self-conscious agency when, wrongly put out of his rightful inheritance, Bolingbroke takes matters into his own hands: 'I am a subject, / And I challenge law. Attorneys are denied me, / And therefore personally I lay my claim / To my inheritance of free descent'

(2.3.133–6).[81] We know that Bolingbroke subsequently went further than this when he laid claim to Richard's royal inheritance. Bolingbroke was bound to claim that the usurpation was righteous and in accordance with God's will. On his deathbed he confides in Prince Hal that all his reign had 'been but as a scene / Acting that argument' (*2H4*, 4.5.197–8), adding that 'what in me was purchas'd / Falls upon thee in a more fairer sort; / So thou the garland wear'st successively' (4.5.199–201). Henry asserts that his death 'Changes the mood' (*2H4*, 4.5.199). Not the 'mood' only, but also the 'mode'. Bolingbroke acquired the crown by trade 'purchase' (*1H4*, 2.1.93), but his son will take it by traditional descent. Henry V's settled state of possession is what lawyers call 'quiescence of title', hence Henry IV's dying words to his son: 'To thee it shall descend with better quiet' (*2H4*, 4.5.187). At the last, Bolingbroke (King Henry) appeals to God to grant a gift by his divine grace, signalling that his days of bargaining with God are over. Addressing Prince Hal, he says: 'How I came by the crown, O God forgive, / And grant it may with thee in true peace live!' (4.5.218–19). His prayer is that God will fill up the crown that he had hollowed out.

In *Richard II*, Henry Bolingbroke's hollow performance was not restricted to his knee. It extended to his hand, as when he threw down his gage in the opening scene and in doing so purported to discard his high status: 'I throw my gage, / Disclaiming here the kindred of the King, / And lay aside my high blood's royalty' (1.1.69–71). Despite this disclaimer, he takes the chance at every turn to bring up his status again, as, for example, when he refers to 'the glorious worth of [his] descent' (1.1.107). When King Richard invites Bolingbroke to pick up his gage, Bolingbroke replies: 'Shall I seem crest-fallen in my father's sight? / Or with pale beggar-fear impeach my height' (1.1.188–9). His refusal to pick up his gage is a deliberate assertion of his status. He only bows when it suits his own performance. No wonder Richard gives Bolingbroke the mock title 'high Hereford' (1.4.2). In Shakespeare's lifetime, and as far back as the reign of Richard II, the throwing down of a gauntlet in gage of combat was employed ceremonially in the celebrations following the coronation of English monarchs.[82] Few people, if any, in Shakespeare's audience would have been aware of that obscure ceremony, but many would have witnessed the use of a glove or gauntlet in a ceremony known as 'livery of seisin' and many would have taken an active part in it. In the Middle Ages, the ceremony of livery of seisin was 'the most essential part' of the conveyance of inheritable estates and interests in land.[83] Even during Shakespeare's lifetime, this hands-on method remained the standard mode of acquiring land by purchase or gift.[84] The general rule requiring land transactions to be made in writing did not enter the law until the enactment of the Statute of Frauds in 1677 (29 Car 2 c 3). Holdsworth notes that, whereas the English relied on actual public performance of the ceremony of livery of seisin, on the European mainland 'under the influence of Roman law, there was a tendency to allow the delivery of a document, stating that seisin had been delivered, to operate as an actual livery of seisin'.[85] As part of the ceremony, an item of material stuff – normally a sod of earth, a twig or such like, but occasionally something more exotic like 'the door, the hasp, or the ring of the house'[86] – was held in hand to symbolize transfer of title to the land. Holdsworth records that 'a sod from the churchyard will do, or a knife without any sod, or a glove, or indeed any small thing that lies handy'.[87] (Compare the use of earth from the churchyard in the ritual 'passing' of the dead in the Elizabethan burial rite, discussed earlier.) One might assume that the use of a glove was simply intended to symbolize the 'handing over' of the land. Perhaps it was, but it might also have been a vestige of something more violent. The legal historians Pollock and Maitland record that it was frequently required that the donee should *wear* a war glove or gauntlet transferred to him by the donor and that this glove was the '*vestita manus* that will fight in defence of this land against all comers'.[88] The hand vested in a glove or gauntlet therefore connects the gage thrown down in offer of combat with the land offered in lifetime purchase or gift. In both combat and contract, the gage of a glove is a material token of the fact that traditional matters of honour and landholding are being grasped into human hands by human will.

Bolingbroke is not the only self-willing trader in town. When Richard appropriates Bolingbroke's Lancastrian inheritance (the estate which should have passed to Bolingbroke on the death of his father John of Gaunt), the wording of Richard's 'speech act' betrays him: 'Think what you will, we seize into our hands / His plate, his goods, his money and his lands' (2.1.209–10). Here we glimpse the historical Richard whom Holinshed records 'began to rule by will more than by reason' and by whose parliamentary authority 'diuerse rightfull heires were disherited of their lands and liuings'.[89] In *Troilus and Cressida*, Ulysses observes that 'when degree is shaked, / Which is the ladder to all high designs, / The enterprise is sick' (1.3.101–3). Ulysses is talking here of such subversive acts as Richard's enterprise in pulling the ladder of inheritance away from Bolingbroke and Bolingbroke's enterprise in pulling the ladder of royal status away from Richard. Ulysses' point is that commercial ventures are no bad thing in themselves, but that trade is detrimental when it subverts the traditional order of things, for it is only 'by degree' that 'Peaceful commerce ... / The primogeneity and due of birth, / Prerogative of age, crowns, sceptres, laurels, /... stand in authentic place' (*TC*, 105–8). Under feudal law a traitor's estate was automatically forfeited into the hands of his lord,[90] but until he broke his banishment Bolingbroke was no proven traitor (as York points out at 2.1.192–4) so Richard's seizure of Bolingbroke's estate is illegitimate. Rejecting tradition, he has treated Bolingbroke's noble inheritance as if it were common stuff of trade to be grabbed and handled and passed from person to person regardless of due descent. It is surely no coincidence that the sound of 'seisin' is concealed in Richard's 'seize into'. The very next line betrays him further, for his inventory of the Lancastrian estate is in the itemized form that one associates with a bill of trade or a testament made by private will. Richard should take heed. Kings who favour trade over tradition might one day have to hand over their crown.

The Duke of York is so incredulous that Richard intends to seize Bolingbroke's inheritance, he dares to challenge him directly: 'Seek you to seize and gripe into your hands / The royalties and rights of banished Hereford?' (2.1.189–90). This is surely the chief offence to which York was alluding, a few lines earlier, when he referred to 'England's private wrongs' (2.1.166). The word 'private' is apposite. By seizing into his own hands that which ought to have been handed down to Bolingbroke by inheritance, Richard effectively privatizes the public dignity of the nobility. Traditional inheritance becomes no better than the hollow subject matter of common trade, valued only as a commodity of bargain and exchange. York is in no doubt about the serious implications of Richard's offence: 'Take Hereford's rights away, and take from Time / His charters and his customary rights; / Let not tomorrow then ensue today; / Be not thyself, for how art thou a king / But by fair sequence and succession?' (2.1.195–9). York contrasts Richard's privateering to the dignity of Richard's royal predecessors, whose hands had won glory by battle and blood – a mode traditionally approved as being dependent upon the providential hand of God (2.1.171–2, 179–81). Richard's act of seizing Bolingbroke's Lancastrian inheritance pre-empted and denied the providence of God. His hand had seized where God's hand should have granted. Bolingbroke's response – we might say, his revenge – is to seize Richard's royal inheritance.

The play's final and climactic use of the word 'seize' comes in King Richard's line: 'Here, cousin, seize the crown / Here cousin: / On this side my hand, and on that side thine' (4.1.182–3). Director and actor have significant choices to make in the suiting of gesture to these words. Should Richard stretch towards Bolingbroke the hand that holds the crown? This would be to 'tender' the crown in the etymological sense of ex-tending it in offer. David Tennant's Richard did something subtly but effectively different to this when he extended his arm not towards Bolingbroke, but into neutral space, and without looking towards Bolingbroke, beckoned him as a dog to a bone with a small, high-pitched 'Here cousin' (Gregory Doran, RSC, 2013). Or should Richard merely hold the crown and require Bolingbroke to make all the moves? Fiona Shaw's Richard set the crown on the ground and, with a little gesture of her hands, goaded Bolingbroke to pounce on it (Deborah Warner, National Theatre, 1995). Ben Whishaw's Richard (BBC, 2012) remained rooted and Bolingbroke (Rory Kinnear) slowly walked towards him. When Bolingbroke took hold of the crown, Richard tightened his grip, and, contracting his arm, moved in to meet Bolingbroke at close quarters over the golden hollow. Eventually, Richard relinquished the crown by rolling it along the ground towards Bolingbroke, who wisely declined to stoop but stood in silence. Bolingbroke's agent, Northumberland, picked up the crown for him.

The physical passing of the crown is the moment of formal handover from Richard to Bolingbroke, from tradition to trade. Richard employs the language of commerce when he laments the trading of his name: 'I have no name, no title / ... / if my word be sterling yet in England, / Let it command a mirror hither straight, / That it may show me what a face I have, / Since it is bankrupt of his majesty' (4.1.255; 264–7). When he throws down the mirror, it symbolizes the casting down of that aspect of himself that was king. The moment Richard performs the stage direction '*Shatters glass*' (4.1.288), his regal image turns to dust. The gesture echoes the moment that Richard threw his warder (ceremonial staff) down to halt the trial by combat between Bolingbroke and Mowbray (1.3.118). Jorgensen notes that '[t]his simple motion, halting the empty ceremony of the combat, has solid repercussions for Richard'. Jorgensen cites the observation made by Mowbray in *2 Henry IV* that 'when the king did throw his warder down, /... / Then threw he down himself' (4.1.125, 127).[91] It has been said that King Richard 'mistook his warder for an enchanter's wand',[92] but in Shakespeare's hands the warder does have magical properties on stage (compare Richard's 'senseless conjuration' of the soil [3.2.12–23]). Sir James George Frazer divided the 'sympathetic magic' of material objects into two main branches: the 'imitative' (or 'homeopathic') and the 'contagious'.[93] The glove (or gauntlet or gage), which performed so powerfully in early modern ritual, is magically potent in both of Frazer's senses. Its physical form imitates the hand, and because it has been in contact with the hand it carries the 'contagious' magic of continuing contact. The mimetic and contagious qualities that we see in the throwing down of a glove as gage are also present in the casting down of Richard's warder. The contagious quality is present in the fact that the warder has been in contact with the king and the mimetic quality is present in the warder's capacity to represent the rectitude of regal rule. The phallic implications of the metonymic object and the symbolic implications of its removal from the king are self-evident. Richard seems to assert his royal power when he throws down the warder, but by interrupting divinely supervised combat it is arguable that the true effect is to curtail a traditional basis for determining royal right to rule. As such the throwing down of the warder can be seen as a symbolic and prophetic act of self-emasculation.[94]

Richard had said 'show us the hand of God / That hath dismissed us from our stewardship; / For well we know no hand of blood and bone / Can gripe the sacred handle of our sceptre, / Unless he do profane, steal or usurp' (3.3.77–81), but Richard's own anointed hand acts as the 'hand of God' to dismiss him from the throne. Richard's hand trades with Bolingbroke's in the shared business of deposing the true king. York reports to Bolingbroke that Richard is willing to yield his sceptre 'To the possession of thy royal hand' (4.1.111). He then proceeds immediately to the pretence that the trade has effected an orthodox succession when he invites Bolingbroke to 'Ascend his throne, descending now from him' (4.1.112). The truth is that the crown did not descend by the traditional mode. It became a hollow commodity of trade the moment Richard took it off. A few lines later, at the point of transfer of the physical crown, Richard's words emphasize the work of his own hand in the business of handover: 'I give this heavy weight from off my head, / And this unwieldy sceptre from my hand, /… / With mine own hands I give away my crown' (4.1.204–5, 208). The form of his words might seem to suggest that this is a unilateral and willing gift, but in substance it is a bilateral transaction. The reason we can never decide if Richard's hand gave or if Bolingbroke's hand took is because they were both complicit in transferring the crown. In the moment of their trade, in the joining of their hands either side of the physical crown, they shake hands upon a bargain.

And yet not so, for there can be no true bargain with a hollow crown, and no true bargain without consent, and Shakespeare embeds the sense (as must be common sense) that Richard is not a free and fully willing party to the deal. One of Shakespeare's most brilliant techniques for achieving this uncanny sense of unwilling volition is a method that I call 'fractional inference'. What I mean by this is that Shakespeare omits a key word but amplifies our sense of its absence by scattering fractions of the word throughout the text. In the following passage, for example, he omits the word 'will', but the sound elements of 'will' are included in such words as 'well' and 'fill' and 'whilst' and through the repeated sound of 'w'. This prompts a subconscious search for the word 'will' which makes us feel its absence all the more:

> Now is this golden crown like a deep well
> That owes two buckets, filling one another,
> The emptier ever dancing in the air,
> The other down, unseen and full of water.
> That bucket down and full of tears am I,
> Drinking my griefs, whilst you mount up on
> high. (4.1.184–9)

Bolingbroke's very next line – 'I thought you had been willing to resign' – by expressly using the word 'will', joins together the elements of 'will' that had been present in fractured parts in Richard's speech. We now sense more strongly than ever, if only subconsciously, that the word 'will' was absent from Richard's speech and we perhaps begin to feel deep down that Richard could not bring himself to say the word 'will' because his mind was fundamentally unwilling. Richard's response – 'My crown I am, but still my griefs are mine' (4.1.191) – purports to express his willingness to pass the crown, but through the assonance of 'still' it serves only to amplifiy again the absence of Richard's actual will. Like a stage silence, the absence of Richard's expressed 'will' demands our attention. Like a 'pregnant pause', it is a full absence. It fills up our attention. The placement of the static 'I am, but' between the 'w' of 'crown' and the 'ill' of 'still' adds another dimension. It produces the subconscious sense that Richard is poised in perfect stasis between will to resign and will to remain king.[95]

'Performance is a kind of will', but Richard's performance is a kind of unwilling will. It is true that, having handed over the crown, he calls himself a traitor to have given it with his 'soul's consent' (4.1.249), but beforehand he had never once expressed his free consent to pass it. His 'I will undo myself' (4.1.203) is not so much a statement of his volition, as a prediction of his future action. His statement 'I'll give, and willing too; / For do we must what force will have us do' (3.3.206–7) equivocates the voluntary nature of his actions. As far as we know, Elizabethan playgoers were never permitted to witness the politically incendiary deposition scene on stage. Certainly they never saw an authorized version in print. Despite this, the fact of the deposition was plain enough from the play, and it was plainly puzzling. Part of the puzzle was to know if human will had forced the transfer of the crown or whether everything had unfolded according to the will of God. The question was intensely relevant to the question of who should succeed to the English crown after Elizabeth, and the related question of the mode by which the next monarch should succeed. In breach of the traditional rule of primogeniture, Henry VIII's will had sought to oust the Scottish line descended from his elder sister Margaret in favour of the descendants of his younger sister Mary Tudor. Elizabeth ignored her father's testament and confirmed the traditional mode of descent by consanguinity and primogeniture. She designated James VI of Scotland to be her successor, and though he had 'a hereditary claim no stronger than Bolingbroke's', it was at least a plausible hereditary claim. Elizabeth therefore 'spared the land the spectacle of a Monarch being designated by purely human agency'.[96] When Shakespeare wrote *Richard II,* it was politically prudent to leave the question open as between succession by tradition and succession by testament. The weighty question of will and descent was left in the playgoers' hands and in the balance of their minds – on this side one argument, and on that another.

This seems an appropriate point at which to pass from *Richard II* to *King John.* Tillyard downplays the correspondence between *Richard II* and *King John*, but this is because he was determined to demonstrate the unity of *Richard II* and *Henry IV.* He argued that between *Richard II* and *King John* 'the connexions are fitful and unimportant'.[97] I will argue, to the contrary, that the plays are in many substantial respects twinned; and not only because they are among a small group of Shakespeare's plays that are entirely in verse, or because they appear adjacent to each other (*King John* first) in the First Folio, or because they were both written around the same time.[98] The more important fact is that *King John* and *Richard II* resonate with each other and amplify each other through such shared thematic concerns as testamentary will, succession, inheritance, tradition and trade. The two plays also correspond in the ways these themes are realized through such performative attributes as staging, physical gesture and touch.

The key question posed by *King John* is essentially the same as that posed by *Richard II.* As Robert Lane puts it, *King John* asks 'to what extent should the prince be able to dispose of the Crown as if it were his/her own property, thereby superseding the historically sanctioned rules of succession?'[99] Swinburne correctly summarizes the legal orthodoxy when he writes that

'It is unlawfull for a king to giue awaie his kingdome from his lawfull heires',[100] but the orthodoxy had certainly been by challenged by the pretensions of Henry VIII's testament (supported by statute, see Chapter 1) and, as we observed in relation to *Richard II*, the position remained doubtful and dramatically potent throughout Elizabeth's reign.

The traditional rules of succession by blood supported Arthur's (John's nephew's) claim to the throne by virtue of his being the surviving legitimate son of John's elder brother Geoffrey, Duke of Brittany. John disputes Arthur's claim, and when he observes 'There is no sure foundation set on blood' (4.2.104) Shakespeare might be implying, beneath the more obvious sense of blood in battle, that an estate established on lineal descent of blood is less secure than one established by a strong political will. Arthur is a somewhat weak-willed creature, quite unlike his mother Constance but rather like Richard II. He even resembles Richard in talk of graves ('I would that I were low laid in my grave' [2.1.164]) and in his precipitous descent from a castle wall. In Arthur's case, his descent is an immediate fall to his death. The text tells us that 'th' inheritance of this poor child' is a 'little kingdom of a forced grave' (4.2.97–8). (Recall that Richard traded his 'kingdom for a little grave' [3.3.153].) If this is what becomes of Arthur's weak will and his claim based on inheritance by descent, perhaps John was right to suppose that a claim based on will is superior to one based on blood.

In terms of direct and prior lineage, John's title is not so well supported as Arthur's, but it has its props. One is John's 'strong possession' of the crown; another is the support of the people; a third is the testamentary will of his elder brother Richard I; and a fourth is the fierce support of his mother Elinor (of Aquitaine). As for the first prop, Elinor confides in John that she suspects that he relies on 'strong possession' more than his 'right' (1.1.40). It may be that possession cannot confer moral 'right', but the position in law was, and remains, that possession confers a presumption of formal entitlement. This is why King John can challenge the citizens of Angiers with the question 'Doth not the crown of England prove the king?' (2.1.273). John's argument was an old one, as William Camden confirmed in his *Annales of the reign of Queen Elizabeth*: 'The Lawes of England many yeeres agoe determined ... That the Crowne once possessed, cleareth and purifies all manner of defaults or imperfections.'[101] We noted earlier that Shakespeare's King Henry IV was confident on his deathbed that his son's possession of the crown would quietly settle the title that had hitherto been questionable. This was an important principle for the Tudor dynasty, for it relied upon the crown's peaceful descent to Henry VIII to settle the title that his father Henry VII had acquired through war. Shakespeare includes essentially the same theme in *King John*. John had acquired the crown laterally by act of will, but when John dies Philip the Bastard expresses the hope that John's son, Henry, will succeed by traditional vertical (lineal) descent:

PRINCE HENRY
At Worcester must his body be interr'd;
For so he will'd it.
BASTARD Thither shall it then:
And happily may your sweet self put on
The lineal state and glory of the land!
To whom, with all submission, on my knee
I do bequeath my faithful services
And true subjection everlastingly. (5.7.99–105)

Regarding the second 'prop' in John's support, which is the support of the commoners, John argues that if the crown does not prove him king then 'I bring you witnesses, / Twice fifteen thousand hearts of England's breed' (2.1.274–5). John's reliance upon commoners to bear witness echoes Bolingbroke in *Richard II*, who had issued the instruction 'Fetch hither Richard, that in common view / He may surrender' (4.1.156–7). Bolingbroke, fortified by the commons, looked to God to bless his possession of the crown. Robert Parsons, an early modern commentator, saw something similar at work in the reign of the historical King John. He wrote that Arthur sought 'to remedy the matter, by warr, yet it semed that god did more defend [the] election of the common wealth [in favour of John], then the right title of Arthur by succession'.[102] The third prop supporting John was the will of Richard I. This was of prime importance to the historical King John (Holinshed records that the will had purported to assign to John 'the crowne of England, and all other his lands and dominions'),[103] but Richard's will is passed over only fleetingly and obliquely in Shakespeare's play. No doubt 'Richard I's will gave the succession dispute in *King John* a direct relevance to the Elizabethan debate',[104] but Shakespeare did not focus on historical detail to the detriment of drama. Regardless of what he knew about the testament of Henry VIII, the Acts of Succession and the Statute of Wills, Shakespeare's instinct for dramatic tension led him to focus on battles between the wills of the living rather than upon the documented will of the dead. When Elinor opposes Constance and Arthur with the claim 'I have a will', Shakespeare elides the fact that she is referring to the will of her son King Richard I. Constance's reply – 'Ay, who doubts that? a will! a wicked will; / A woman's will; a cank'red grandam's will!' (2.1.193–4) – puts the focus firmly on the living will of Elinor (and of her son John) as the main dramatic opposition to Arthur's claim.

In *King John* and *Richard II*, Shakespeare invites us to question the capacity of individual will to determine the destination of the crown and of other landed estates. To respond to that invitation involves nothing less than to question an individual's capacity to depart from tradition. *King John* poses the question in the opening scene in which the king adjudicates upon the testamentary will of the deceased gentleman Sir Robert Faulconbridge. The primacy and prominence of this testamentary trial indicates Shakespeare's intent to make contested will a central *agon* of the play. Lane points out that the testamentary episode 'is wholly Shakespeare's invention', there being no reference to a testament in the earlier play *The*

Troublesome Reign of King John which supplied Shakespeare's play in other respects.[105] In the opening scene, Shakespeare's King John performs the role of the participatory witness and judge. He is the testamentary 'third party standing by' who plays the part that is necessary to fulfil the dramatic action of the two protagonists (see Chapter 1). The dispute between them concerns their entitlement to succeed to the Faulconbridge estate. On one side is an elder son fathered by Richard I but born to the wife of Faulconbridge. On the other side is the younger son of the same mother, but this one fathered by Faulconbridge. The younger asserts the testamentary wishes of the deceased Faulconbridge. He claims to be entitled to 'My father's land, as was my father's will' (1.1.115). John rejects that claim and instead recognizes the rights of the elder son. He employs the then standard, and dehumanizing, proprietary reasoning that applied to a child born to a woman within wedlock, which was to recognize the husband's entitlement to the 'calf bred from his cow' (1.1.124).[106] The upshot was that the elder Faulconbridge, though acknowledged to be the bastard son of Richard I, was adjudged to be the legitimate son of Sir Robert. Thus Philip Faulconbridge, called the Bastard, was held to be heir to the Faulconbridge estate. John explains to the younger son that 'Your father's heir must have your father's land' (1.1.129). In dismissing the will of Faulconbridge and favouring the traditional mode of descent by inheritance, King John was obeying the law as it was prior to the 1540 Statute of Wills, but it was nevertheless somewhat hypocritical to do so when he had himself taken the crown by will despite Arthur's better legal claim by blood. The hypocrisy does not lie, as Lane suggests, in the fact that King John depended upon the will of Richard I.[107] The historical king did, but Shakespeare's king did not. In the play, John's decision to oppose individual will in the Faulconbridge dispute is hypocritical, not because John's title rests on the testamentary will of Richard I, but because John's title rests on the living will of John, supported by the living will of his mother Elinor.

In *Richard II*, the initial scene of the king on his high throne and the central scene of Richard '*on the Walls*' (stage direction 3.3.62) is succeeded later in the play by the commoners on the high walls of London who look down on Richard and Bolingbroke (5.2). In *King John*, the opening scene of the king on his high throne arbitrating between the two sons of Faulconbridge is followed in the next act by the scene of the citizens of Angiers installed high '*upon the walls*' of their city (stage direction 2.1.200) arbitrating between King John and King Philip of France. At this point 'the stage picture is divided significantly both horizontally and vertically, with the English and French either side of the stage, and the Citizens centrally and above'.[108] As in the opening scene, the conflict before the walls of Angiers is between traditional lineal succession and individual will, but the subject matter of the issue between King Philip and King John concerns nothing less than the proper descent of the English crown. The citizens who look down on the debating kings are not mere passive bystanders, but observers of an active and participatory sort. To express their role in testamentary language, we can say that they are not mere witnesses but judges who are called upon to observe the trial or probation of John's will – in other words, to decide in testamentary mode if his will has 'passed probate'. If not, the default rule of lineal descent should determine the outcome in favour of Arthur and the French king. The progress of the play from the first scene to this has the effect of passing judicial authority from monarch to commoner. That progress naturally culminates in the passing of judicial authority from the citizens on stage to the citizens in the audience. Thus 'Shakespeare provokes precisely what the Crown's policy precluded – the exercise of critical judgment on the part of his audience – casting them as participants in the process of determining the successor'.[109]

Modern playgoers are also invited to participate as judges,[110] although we may 'feel that, like the citizens of Angiers, we cannot adjudicate between the claims'.[111] The question put to the citizens of Angiers, and hence to the playgoers, is not a straightforward dispute between traditional inheritance and testamentary will. On the side of traditional inheritance is the default mode of lineal succession according to descent by blood – which order of descent was assumed to have been ordained by divine providence of priority and gender at birth. Advocating this side of the argument on behalf of Arthur, King Philip appeals to 'God and our right!' (2.1.299) and asks John: 'How comes it then that thou art call'd a king, / When living blood doth in these temples beat, / Which owe the crown that thou o'ermasterest?' (2.1.107–9).[112] In similar vein, Arthur's mother Constance complains that Elinor is a 'monstrous injurer of heaven and earth!' (2.1.174) for denying 'The dominations, royalties and rights / Of this oppressed boy: this is thy eld'st son's son' (2.1.184–5). The words 'o'ermasterest' and 'oppressed' both connote the revolutionary overthrow of God's order and imply that John, in wrongfully assuming a height not ordained by God, has turned the true king into a 'subject' – literally someone thrown-under (*sub-jactus*). The language of over-mastering and over-pressing evokes the image of the king trodden underfoot, which was so powerfully employed in *Richard II*. Indeed, King Philip makes express the connection between 'tread' and the subjection of Arthur and the justice of his claim: 'For this down-trodden equity, we tread / In warlike march these greens before your town' (2.1.241–2). 'Equity', in the sense used here, means the divinely ordained descent of the crown.[113] The word imports a sense of substantial truth and justice that differs from formal appearance. John's title is based on the legal formality of physical possession and (obliquely) upon the form of Richard I's will. Philip claims that despite John's formal or apparent title, Arthur's title is the one supported by the divinely ordained default rules of descent. When King Philip later turns traitor against Arthur, Constance turns Philip's own use of 'tread' against him. She complains that fortune 'with her golden hand hath pluck'd on France / To tread down fair respect of sovereignty' (2.2.57–8). In this we hear her complain that tradition has been downtrodden by the levelling tread of trade. It is a note that resonates with *Richard II*, but also with the passage in *King John* in which the Bastard delivers his famous commentary on 'commodity'. In that speech, he likens the distorting effect of commodity on the world to the distorting effect of a bias (weight) on a bowling ball (2.1.574–80). In his plays, Shakespeare usually employs the word 'commodity' in the economic sense of the word. (The phrase 'profitt and comodytye' even appeared in his deposition in the dispute over the dowry to the marriage of Stephen Bellott to Mary Mountjoy.[114] This followed his role as 'an agent, a go-between, a broker' in securing that marriage.)[115] In *King John*, the Bastard's usage emphasizes commodity as 'exchange-value'.[116] He should know, for he had exchanged his own feudal inheritance for 'adventure capital on the international battlefield'.[117] The Bastard helps the playgoers to see the mercantile reality of the peace brokered between King John and King Philip, which had been sealed by the marriage of John's niece Blanche to the Dauphin together with 'Full thirty thousand marks of English coin' (2.1.530).[118] The Bastard alerts us to the fact that 'Angiers finally opens its gates, not to its rightful king but to a bargain'.[119]

King Philip had Arthur in hand when pleading his traditional right: 'Lo, in this right hand, whose protection / Is most divinely vow'd upon the right / Of him it holds, stands young Plantagenet' (2.1.236–8), but King John had tried to take Arthur in hand by force of will: 'Arthur of Britain, yield thee to my hand; / And out of my dear love I'll give thee more / Than e'er the coward hand of France can win: / Submit thee, boy' (2.1.156–9). In the event, the two kings cut a deal that rendered Arthur irrelevant and they sealed it by the joining of their hands. The scene has been called '[p]erhaps the most graphic illustration of the symbolic power invested in the early modern handclasp'.[120] The business handled between the kings, mirrored in the handfasting of Lewis and Blanche (2.1.532–3), engages the playgoers to handle the matter in their minds. The papal legate will soon be persuaded to approve the kings' bargain, but initially he cautions 'Philip of France, on peril of a curse' to 'Let go the hand of that arch-heretic' (3.1.191–2). The legate will later say that John, having seized Arthur, holds a 'sceptre snatch'd with an unruly hand' (3.3.135). (Compare Henry IV's deathbed confession that the crown 'seem'd in me / But as an honour snatch'd with boist'rous hand' [*2H4*, 4.5.190–1].) Philip initially resists the legate's request to part hands that have been 'newly knit ... newly join'd in love' (3.1.226, 240), and at first he refuses to 'Unyoke this seizure and this kind regreet?' by snatching 'palm from palm' (3.1.241, 244), but he inevitably relents. Only when John makes his peace with the papal legate is the pact between the kings confirmed. In *King John*, the matter of tradition, which should be handed down inviolate, is handled like the stuff of trade. As in *Richard II*, even the physical crown is handed over. For Shakespeare, the most significant event of the reign of King John was not the signing of Magna Carta, but the surrender of the crown to the papal legate and his receiving it back again 'as a vassal of the Pope'.[121] John's 'Thus have I yielded up into your hand / The circle of my glory' (5.1.1–2) receives the reply of the papal legate: 'Take again / From this my hand, as holding of the pope' (5.1.2–3). When John hands the crown to the Pope and receives it back, he claims that he does so in a manner that is 'but voluntary' (5.1.29). This confirms that the transfer is part of a free-will bargain, and yet it is the sort of foolish exercise of free will that merely serves to produce new subjection. (For discussion of this species of foolish will in Shakespeare's comedies, see Chapter 3.)

The bargains in *King John*, and the many other evidences of John's self-will, collectively demonstrate the same shift from handed-down tradition to hand-to-hand testamentary trade that we witnessed in *Richard II*. Queen Elinor employs testamentary language when she invites the Bastard Faulconbridge to pursue his will and abandon his inheritance to the younger Faulconbridge: 'wilt thou forsake thy fortune, / Bequeath thy land to him and follow me?' (1.1.148–9). His response – 'Brother, take you my land, I'll take my chance' (1.1.151)

– leaves us unsure, as the broker Bolingbroke left us unsure, whether to choose chance is to choose the path of self-will, or to commit the lottery to the hand of God. The Bastard's preference for 'chance' is in one respect the commercial preference of a merchant venturer, but it is also, etymologically speaking, a preference for whatever may fall from on high. Elinor's use of the word 'fortune' is similarly ambiguous in the way it confuses notions of traditional inheritance with merchant commodity. What we are really seeing when we see a shift from tradition to trade (and, by the same token, from tradition to testament) is not unlike the shift from status to contract that Sir Henry Maine observed in the ancient world;[122] it is not a neat paradigm shift, but a dramatically significant change in emphasis. Elizabethan playgoers would have taken different sides in the drama and appreciated Shakespeare's questions differently according to the perspectives of their own cultural, and specifically religious, traditions. It has been said, for example, that during Shakespeare's lifetime 'the Catholic sin of usury' became 'the Protestant virtue of banking'.[123] One person's tradition is another person's trade.

The key witness to the wills and deeds in *King John* is the Bastard Faulconbridge. He is 'a surrogate for a particularly arch kind of spectator'.[124] This is perhaps especially clear in Scene 2.1 in which he provides a running commentary on the contest conducted between the kings before the citizens of Angiers on their high walls. At the conclusion of that scene, the Bastard is left alone on stage to deliver his soliloquy on commodity. The scene can be appreciated as an extended metatheatrical exercise in the art of persuading the playgoers to identify themselves with the citizens of Angiers. Some of the metatheatrical references will seem obscure to us now, including King John's reference to 'the sky that hangs above our heads' (2.1.397) and Lewis's reference to 'the vaulty top of heaven / Figur'd quite o'er with burning meteors' (5.2.52–3), but Elizabethan playgoers would have incorporated this into their appreciation of a playhouse ceiling that was both the natural sky and the ceiling of the stage 'heavens' (i.e. the underside of the 'hut' projecting over the inner stage, which was decorated with comets and other celestial forms). Other metatheatrical references are blatant, as for example where the Bastard observes: 'By heaven, these scroyles of Angiers flout you, kings, / And stand securely on their battlements, / As in a theatre, whence they gape and point / At your industrious scenes and acts of death' (2.1.373–6). The play's (politically dangerous) success in the endeavour of securing the playgoers' imaginative participation might explain the strange change mid-scene from 'Citizen' to 'Hubert' in the First Folio's designation of the spokesman for Angiers. The change might have signalled 'a sense of political decorum' and specifically a 'reluctance to grant a significant role to an unnamed, untitled figure who speaks for a body of the king's subjects'.[125]

It is fitting that we should end with the practical business of the theatre. When Shakespeare referred to it as the 'two hours' traffic of our stage' (*RJ*, 1.prologue.12), we can be sure that one sense of the 'traffic' he had in mind was the commercial offering that his performing company made to the paying playgoers. His use of the word in the other nine plays in which it appears is always in a merchant or monetary context. In *1 Henry VI*, reference is made to a royal marriage made 'in traffic of a king' (5.3.164). In *Macbeth*, he expressly pairs traffic with trade to emphasize their shared capacity to subvert traditional hierarchy. Hecate, Queen of the Witches, objects that her underlings (the 'weird sisters') have taken business into their own hands, and insists on her position at the top of the hierarchy (*Mac*, 3.5.4).

Even clearer from the context is that Skakespeare was using 'traffic' to refer to on-stage dynamics of dramatic exchange between the players themselves. The word 'traffic' probably derives from the Vulgar Latin **transfricare* ('to rub across'), the original sense of the Italian verb being 'to touch repeatedly, handle'.[126] The traffic of the stage is the trade business of handling and handing on. Occasionally, it is the handing on of props such as crowns and rings and parchments: '[m]uch like coins and other units of currency, hand props testify by their size and portability to an open potential. They can be variously possessed, traded, lost, found, concealed, and evaluated.'[127] Gesture also plays its part in this stage traffic or trade. Since ancient times, rhetoricians have appreciated the need to combine gesture and word in the process of conveying meaning. For the ancient orators and their early modern counterparts, rhetoric was the 'open palm' to logic's 'closed fist'.[128] Even during everyday speech, the gestural move from grasping to letting go, for example by relaxing and opening up a fist, frequently signals a handing over of the power of speech.[129] The business of Shakespeare's stage was the urgent traffic of 'two hours' and lines were sometimes handed over so briskly that they rubbed up against each other. A single ten-syllable line of verse might be trafficked between parts as if the words were an object too hot to handle. A good example appears in *King John*, in the scene in which Hubert threatens to burn out Arthur's eyes with a hot brand:

HUBERT Young boy, I must.
ARTHUR And will you?
HUBERT And I will. (4.1.40)

For all the talk of 'will' in that exchange, there is a clear sense that neither party is willing to hold the horrible thought for long. A scene such as this demonstrates one of the key demands made upon all theatrical performance: if the playgoers are to be moved, the drama must be full of moving energy and drive. When actors trade words and gestures and objects on stage it will be for nothing if there is no passing on of what I will term the performative 'urge'. The word 'urge', from the PIE root **werg-* ('to work', 'to do' or 'to perform'), usefully combines the theatrical sense of practical production ('dramaturgy') with the theatrical sense of spiritual ceremony and dance (as in the Greek '*orgia*'), as well as the sense of speed ('urgency') and thrust ('energy') and the sense that all parts ('organs') work together in the performance. Lag on stage is like 'the law's delay' (*Ham*, 3.1.71); it does not feel 'just'. Stage action feels fairer when it shows the humanity of swift and lively exchange between the players. The playgoers will be caught up in the current of the drama when the treading of the boards, trading of hands and trafficking of words is done 'trippingly' (*Ham*, 3.2.2). To return to this chapter's theme of 'dust', we can say that stage action should be like legal action in the popular 'Court of Piepowders'. This ad hoc court was required to be present at medieval and early modern markets and fairs and was first named because merchants and market-goers would find justice done as 'speedy' there 'for the advancement of trade and traffic, as the dust can fall from the foot' (French: 'pie poudre').[130] Sir William Blackstone called it 'the lowest, and at the same time the most expeditious, court of justice known to the law of England'.[131]

One of the rehearsal exercises employed by the Royal Shakespeare Company calls for a circle of actors to pass a pulse round the group with a clap of their hands – one actor clapping to give, and the next, facing, clapping to receive. Allocating the players a line from a passage of text, the exercise is repeated with each actor speaking their line before handing on to the next actor to speak theirs. The individual actor should not speak their line as if it stops with them. The breath must not be allowed to drop off at the end.[132] Borrowing the legal vernacular of *Richard II*, we might say that the actor should not neglect or 'waste' the energy of the speech, but that it must be kept up and passed along. Cicely Berry notes that there are many clichés for this: 'keep the ball in the air', 'pass on the baton', and so forth.[133] She advises that syllables should be differently weighted and that the 'key' is to 'perceive the thought as movement'.[134] Thus the practical traffic of the stage is a sort of trade in metaphysical currency; a discharging from hand-to-hand, and mind-to-mind, of the precious cargo of a question, an idea and a will. The treasured thought, expressed in word and movement and gesture and breath, should not be wasted or dropped or thrown down. It must be handed on. It then becomes something more than it could have been in a single mind or in one person's hands. The creative trade of hands fills it up with values that economic grasping would hollow out. It becomes a communal and artistic artefact that can be passed from the stage to be handled by the playgoers. The playgoers will feel the frisson of its touch. They will encounter its weight, and it will move them. This sort of traffic is Shakespeare's stock-in-trade, and it is part of the legacy he hands on to us.

3

Worlds of will in *As You Like It* and *The Merchant of Venice*

As You Like It is Shakespeare's most obviously testamentary play. Juliet Dusinberre calls it 'the most dynastic of all Shakespeare's comedies'.[1] From the first line, the formal terms of a last will establish the tension from which the dramatic action flows. The play is therefore testamentary in the technical legal sense. *As You Like It* is also peculiarly testamentary in the broader sense in which this book uses that term, for the play calls the audience as witness to a governing will and the performance is constituted by communal approbation or 'probate'. The identity of the play's 'testator' – the author of the governing will – we do not learn until the end, for it is a rule of comedy that we should learn nothing until the end, and even then wonder if we are still fools.

The play begins with Orlando complaining to old Adam (the faithful family retainer) that his eldest brother, Oliver, has not given him his due under the will of their late father, Sir Rowland de Boys:

> As I remember, Adam, it was upon this Fashion bequeathed me by will but poor a thousand crowns, and, as thou sayst,

> charged my brother on his blessing to breed me well; and there begins my sadness. (1.1.1–4)

That speech concludes with Orlando's own statement of will: 'I will no longer endure it' (1.1.22–3). He repeats the exact same phrase when they are joined by Oliver. To him, Orlando protests:

> My father charged you in his will to give me good education. You have trained me like a peasant, obscuring and hiding from me all gentleman-like qualities. The spirit of my father grows strong in me, and I will no longer endure it! Therefore allow me such exercises as may become a gentleman, or give me the poor allottery my father left me by testament; with that I will go buy my fortunes. (1.1.62–70)

Express use of the word 'testament' is unusual in Shakespeare's plays, appearing only eleven times in total. It appears twice in *As You Like It*, which, matched only by *Henry V*, is the most in any play. The second occurrence comes when the 'melancholy Jaques', weeping over the wounded deer, says 'thou mak'st a testament / As worldlings do, giving thy sum of more / To that which had too much' (2.1.26, 47–9). This is a literal reference to the tears that the 'sobbing deer' has needlessly added to a forest stream, and it is a figurative reference to such testamentary schemes as the fee tail male, a form of entail under which the eldest son, having received most favour while his father was alive, receives most wealth in his father's will.[2] Jaques's lament might also make oblique reference to the merchant Antonio, who in *The Merchant of Venice* gave a sum of more to one who had too much. Having already loaned money to Bassanio with little hope of seeing its return, Antonio loaned more when Bassanio urged him to shoot a second arrow to find the first one lost (1.1.148–50). Further echoes of Antonio in Jaques's scene are the lament to the 'sequestered stag' in terms of its being a 'poor and broken bankrupt' (2.1.33, 2.1.57) and (more tentatively) the bleeding hart (an arrow is present or implied, and Antonio's 'pound of flesh' is a bleeding heart). This is not to say that the original playgoers would have noted any allusion to Antonio, but merely to suggest that Shakespeare had Antonio in mind as he formed the melancholy Jaques. 'Sequestered', meaning 'set-apart' from the main body, perfectly describes both Jaques and Antonio. The latter even marked himself out in a related (albeit ovine) image as a 'tainted wether of the flock' (4.1.113) (compare *Tit*, 2.3.75). The word 'sequestered' was used to indicate a religious or political state of excommunication, but it also had a technical meaning in law. In William West's *Symbolæography*,[3] in the section immediately preceding the section on 'pledging and gaging' (recall that Bassanio was 'gaged' to Antonio),[4] we learn that 'sequester' was the title for the 'indifferent man' who held money in dispute between parties to a suit.[5] The notion of indifference is most pertinent to Jaques's role as bystander and witness in *As You Like It*, on which more will be said later. The merchant Antonio is every inch the sort of 'worldling' that Jaques has in mind. By his own account, Antonio holds 'the world but as the world … / A stage, where every man must play a part' and his 'a sad one' (1.1.77–9). The sentiment is echoed in Jaques's commonplace observation that 'All the world's a stage' (2.7.140). Jaques is in many respects a curiously reflective character. Not only does he reflect Antonio and cause us to reflect on Antonio, but he also has his namesake in the play in the peripheral form of the second son of Sir Rowland de Boys.[6]

The pairing of the melancholy Antonio and the melancholy Jaques is just one respect in which *The Merchant of Venice* is a natural partner to *As You Like It*. Another significant point in common is the fact that testamentary will drives the dramatic action in both plays. In *The Merchant of Venice*, it all starts with a testamentary provision in Portia's father's will – the one that requires her future husband to pass the test of choosing the correct casket from the three alternatives. That testamentary provision directly binds Portia, and in turn it indirectly binds Bassanio to Antonio, and Antonio to Shylock. (It even binds Shylock to his kinsman Tubal, but little is made of that.) Shylock's will to enforce the bond, which only becomes dead-set when he loses his daughter Jessica to her Christian lover, Lorenzo, parallels the testamentary power of Portia's father's will. Towards the end of the trial scene (4.1), Shylock relents and would release Antonio from the bond, but Portia will not then let him go. She holds Shylock to the letter of the law and thereby performs a type of delayed revenge upon her own father's testamentary control. The circle of bondage to will remains intact, but Portia positions herself as the one who spins the circle round. Indeed, her determination to bind Bassanio to the love token of her ring may be said to perpetuate the same cycle of bondage to will that her father had started.[7]

Another feature that the two plays have in common, and one which provides a focus for this chapter, is the distinction in each play between two worlds. That basic distinction is now a commonplace feature of critical commentary on the plays.[8] My contribution is to seek to understand the two worlds as distinct worlds of will, and to understand them in performative terms as worlds in which different modes of will are performed through contrasting acts of will. In *As You Like It*, the protagonists flee from a courtly world to the country world of forest and field. In modern performances, the two worlds of *As You Like It* are sometimes starkly contrasted through variations in set design, and through the characters' modes of dress, speech and movement.[9] It can also be effective to represent the two worlds as 'mirrors of each other rather than complete opposites'.[10] In *The Merchant of Venice*, the differences between Venice and Belmont, between the city world and the island world of fantasy, are less clear-cut. In Polly Findlay's production (RSC, 2015), set designer Johannes Schütz preferred to emphasize their similarity. Golden mirrors acted as the floor and back wall throughout the entire play, creating continuity between Venice and Belmont. The action of both moneyed worlds, the faces of the fee-paying playgoers, and the props and other stage materials were always reflected in gold. The continuity of the two worlds, and the constant exchange between them, was further enhanced by the swinging pendulum of a large metallic globe which, as unthinkingly repetitive as economic activity, moved hypnotically back and forth near the back wall of gold. Which is the world of law here and which of love, which the world of hierarchy and which of horizontality, is never perfectly clear. Portia's question, 'Which is the merchant here, and which the Jew?' (4.1.170) expresses something of the comedic confusion between the play's twinned worlds, even as it plays on a great deal else.[11] Michael Billington complained in his review of Findlay's production that the set 'fails to anchor the play in any specific location',[12] but the visual blurring of the worlds is arguably a strength. The many textual references to music in Belmont suggest that sound would have been a strong marker of location in the original Elizabethan production. (Music most certainly marked the distinctiveness of the forest world of *As You Like It*, for the play text demands that the forest should be filled with songs.) In Findlay's production, Marc Tritschler's music infused Belmont with the music of St Mark's Basilica.[13] If the Venetian city world of the play is a legal and mercantile world 'still deceived with ornament' (3.2.74), the contrasting sound world of Belmont cautions us to judge by the ear – not as the goddess Justitia does, by putting on a blindfold (the ear can be deceived by a 'flattering tongue' [4.1.172]), but by trusting to sight and sound together.[14] Reliable witness to theatrical performance calls for the ear to take critical note of the eye and for the eye to be overseer of sounds. What Thomas Wilson wrote in *The Arte of Rhetorique* is now trite psychology: 'when a man bothe heareth and seeth a thing … hee doth remember it much the beter.'[15]

The opening line of *As You Like It*, with its reference to the 'fashion' of the formal testament, introduces the unreliability of ostensible forms as a theme that runs through the entire play, most notably when the male actor representing the female character Rosalind is disguised as the male character Ganymede and impersonates the female character Rosalind (4.1.105). It has been observed that *As You Like It* 'is a play about convention, and the different conventional worlds in which each of the characters' lives are defined by the characters' dress'.[16] Yet such dress definition as there is merely serves the deeper dramatic purpose of disturbing formal expectations. Portia's (dishonest) disguise as a young male lawyer triumphs over the law and form of dress in a way that mirrors her (possibly dishonest) triumph over the law and form of her father's testament by marrying her true love Bassanio. In *As You Like It*, the success of Rosalind's complex cross-dressing mirrors the triumph over testamentary 'fashion' and form that is hoped for from the opening line of the play.[17]

Talk of costume as stage property brings us to property in another sense: the very significant issue of property as a legal, social and political concern. The settlement of title to land, and the disposition of proprietary benefits in land and other assets, is obviously one of the prime concerns of testamentary performance in law. It is also a major concern of *The Merchant of Venice* and *As You Like It*. Gervinus was overconfident in his ability to distil each of Shakespeare's plays to a single idea, but it is nevertheless noteworthy that *The Merchant of Venice* was for him a play in which 'the intention of the poet ... was to depict the relation of man to property'.[18] This is comparable to *As You Like It*, in which 'modulations of the rhetorical and poetic convention of the *locus amoenus*' ('pleasant place') can be said to 'explicate a nexus of property issues'.[19] The 'pleasant place' of *As You Like It* is the Forest of Arden, and it is interesting to note that between 1598 and 1600, around the time that the play was taking final form, Shakespeare was bound to Arden by a very particular type of proprietary nexus.[20] James Shapiro has suggested a connection between the play and Shakespeare's contemporary interest in litigation to recover lands that his grandfather, Robert Arden, had bequeathed to his mother, Mary Arden, but which Shakespeare's father had mortgaged to Mary's brother-in-law Edmund Lambert as security for a loan. The Chancery suit *Shakespeare* v. *Lambert*,[21] which had been commenced to redeem the Arden legacy, entered a significant phase between June and October 1599, and Shapiro conjectures that Shakespeare would have visited Stratford (hence also the Forest of Arden) at that time to 'sift through documents' and 'contact potential witnesses'.[22]

The connection between testamentary will and comedy is not an obvious one – like Shakespeare's King Richard II, we associate 'talk of wills' more readily with 'graves, of worms, and epitaphs' (3.2.143, 140) than with any matter of mirth – but the nature of the connection I have in mind can be quite simply stated. It is that comedy lies in the possibility of escape from a world of subjection to the will of another into a world of freedom to express a will of one's own. There is comedy when the escape succeeds and comedy when old bondage is willingly exchanged for new. The stubborn will of a powerful person can subject others to an obstacle of seemingly immovable weight: a father's will might be set against his daughter; a husband's will set against his wife; a creditor's will might be set against his debtor; an elder brother might set his will against a younger. Where such a will is settled by the formal last testament of a person it becomes utterly irrevocable at the moment that person dies, and becomes in that moment an object intractably opposed to the free will of those subject to it.[23] The testamentary will of a deceased person seldom features in Shakespeare's comedies – the will of Sir Rowland de Boys in *As You Like It* and the will of Portia's father in *The Merchant of Venice* ('the will of a living daughter curbed by the will of a dead father' [1.2.23–4]) are rare instances. What is more common is the performance of a will so stubborn and having such a bearing on the estate of the one subject to it that it may be said to exert a testamentary force. We are concerned here not only with the 'wills of the dead', but also with 'dead wills' – that is, with wills that are dead-set. Shylock's wilful insistence upon his bond for a pound of flesh is of this sort. Shylock's bond is not testamentary in any technical sense, but his settled resolution to enforce the bond, sealed with 'An oath, an oath ... an oath in heaven' (4.1.224) is his attempt to produce the same species of terminal irrevocability that is normally achievable only by a will and testament, and only then upon the testator's death. By conceiving his oath to be in heaven, Shylock purports to render the bond irrevocable as if it were his testament and he were already dead. (Shylock's wilful resolution is in this respect comparable to the 'Firm and irrevocable ... doom' [1.3.80] pronounced by Duke Frederick in banishing Rosalind from court.) The Jacobean tragedy *King Lear* provides another example of a living will expressed with fatal finality, and much has been written on Lear's attempted threefold division of his domain and its possible relation to inheritance laws and customs.[24] The examples of Shylock and Lear show that self-will stubbornly imposed upon oneself frequently accompanies the tragedy of self-will imposed upon others, but will stubbornly imposed upon self can also be the starting point for comedy. In *Much Ado About Nothing*, for example, we have a comic volte-face in Benedick's firm resolution to remain a bachelor. His stubbornness establishes the static state against which the moving powers of the poet's rhetoric can be displayed to best dramatic effect.

Antonio eventually makes a fatalistic concession to Shylock's pursuit: 'Let me have judgment, and the Jew his will' (4.1.82). The line comes at the end of a speech in which Shakespeare uses a type of rhetorical '*gradatio*' or ladder to emphasize the stubbornness of Shylock's stance. Beginning 'I pray you, think you question with the Jew' (4.1.69), Antonio's speech moves down grades of hardness from 'pray you' to 'think you' to 'stand' to 'bid' to 'forbid' to 'anything most hard' to 'than which what's harder – / His Jewish heart!' (4.1.78–9). That rhetorical question, which is suitably hard to pronounce, is answered in the concluding words 'his will' (4.1.82). The steps leading down to the hardness of Shylock's will are confirmed by a second ladder running up through the speech from 'beach' to 'height' to 'mountain pines' to 'high tops' to 'heaven'. These twin examples of rhetorical *gradatio* follow immediately after Shylock's rhetorical *anticategoria* ('Hates any man the thing he would not kill?' [4.1.66]) and his *metastasis* ('What, wouldst thou have a serpent sting thee twice?' [4.1.68]), and therefore contribute to the rhetorically rich opening of the rhetorically intense trial scene.

In Shylock's case, his rhetoric establishes his stubbornness,[25] but stubbornness is more usually the starting point from which the moving arts of rhetoric proceed. Without stubbornness to overcome there can be no rhetorical triumph. When the banished duke in *As You Like It* animates the dumb material of the Forest of Arden with lively metaphors (e.g. 'Sermons in stones' [2.1.17]), he is congratulated on his ability to 'translate the stubbornness of fortune / Into so quiet and so sweet a style' (2.1.19–20). In other words, he is congratulated on overcoming the stubbornness of nature with rhetorical art, and specifically with his sweet (that is 'persuasive')[26] rhetorical style and his use of the rhetorical trope of 'translation' (Latin '*translatio*'), which we refer to by the Greek word 'metaphor'. Metaphor is etymologically that which connects one place to another as a bridge does, thereby allowing one to ferry ('phor') across ('meta') the sense one is trying to convey. Metaphor usually carries over an abstract value in concrete form, as, for example, 'Time's ... sickle' (Son 116.9–10). As metaphor bridges worlds with words, so worlds can be connected by all aspects of a theatrical performance, including dress, props, movement of the characters from one place to another, and the continuity of dramatic character despite translocation. Duke Senior might be considered one long, extended metaphor for the very concept of connection between distinct worlds. That the whole play is a metaphorical translation and translocation between worlds is unintentionally amplified in the coincidental fact that its title contains two classic signals of simile: the 'as' and the 'like'.

The wilfulness of Oliver, the eldest brother in *As You Like It*, draws strength from tradition (as discussed below, the scheme established by the last will and testament of his father created a traditional hierarchical scheme), from his superior social status (as eldest son) and from his strict insistence on his legal entitlement under his father's will (in which latter respect his wilfulness resembles Shylock's insistence upon the strict terms of his bond). Oliver oppresses his younger brother Orlando by aligning his own will with the letter of their father's formal testament, while neglecting its spirit. In response, Orlando opposes Oliver's oppression through recourse to other terms expressed in his father's will, and through recourse to his father's spirit, the strength of which he feels is within him. All this talk of oppressive will suggests a scene more tragic than comic, but in Shakespearean comedy tragedy must be present in order for comedy to be appreciated; 'tragedy is always there, *felt*, if not seen'.[27] Comedy celebrates the expression of free will in the face of the tragic possibility of will's oppression. In many of Shakespeare's comedies, including *As You Like It*, escape takes the form of actual physical flight to a new domain – typically from court to country. The trajectory of this escape can be conceived as escape from a hierarchical scheme of social status to a horizontal plane of communal relations; from a traditional scheme in which power and property is handed down, to a scheme of trade in which assets pass horizontally from hand to hand contractually.[28] As we saw in Chapters 1 and 2, distinctions between tradition and trade are not drawn like axes on a graph. The boundaries between them have been permeable throughout history, but the point is that there is a polarity to be played with.

Orlando's response to the formal hierarchical strictures of his father's formal settlement, as enforced by Oliver, is to seek 'some settled low content' (2.3.68), and this, at the horizontal level of fellowship, is what he finds in the Forest of Arden. Orlando is not the only victim of oppressive will in *As You Like It*. The wilful act by which Duke Frederick usurped his brother has incidentally deprived Rosalind of any interest which she might have anticipated in the estate of her father, the banished Duke Senior. In a fleeting but significant moment at the start of the play, the promise of comedic upheaval, which we first see in Orlando's rebellion against his brother, is confirmed in the voluntary undertaking Celia gives to Rosalind. By the terms of that undertaking, Celia will restore Rosalind's estate to her when (should events so transpire) Celia receives it on the death of her own father, the usurping Duke Frederick: 'what he hath taken away from thy father perforce, I will render thee again in affection' (1.2.19–20). When Celia makes this offer of her own free will, we are reassured that oppressive will allied to hierarchical power will not win the day.

Passing from legalism to love, from the domain of grasping to the domain of grace, is not an easy journey. It is the hard journey of a good life. The comedy of the journey is to be found as much in the attempt as in the hoped-for joyous outcome. Indeed, the trials of translocation from tyranny to fellowship may demonstrate a defining dynamic of the form we call comedy, for it is, in essence, a translation from a lesser existence to a greater.[29] It is world-changing. It is life-changing. We laugh when we watch a comedy because as we witness the characters passing from one world to another, we experience vicariously (what we could not the first time) the experience of being born. Or again, comedy makes us laugh because when we witness the characters 'crossing over', we experience vicariously something of the liberating, hopeful and heavenly possibilities of death without the trauma and loss of actually having to die.[30] With comedy we only 'die laughing'. When we witness testamentary will, we cannot ignore the shadow of tragedy, but we can also observe the essential human comedy of the testator's attempt to impose his will over death and future life, even though he must be an outsider to both.

In several of Shakespeare's plays, the stubborn will of a ruling male is the direct cause of female flight, but Orlando's flight is in response to the tyranny of an elder son who seeks to enforce his rights over a younger. Orlando acknowledges that, as the first-born son, Oliver has superior status by the 'courtesy of nations' (1.1.41–6),[31] but despite this acknowledgement of the privilege of primogeniture, and although Oliver insults Orlando with the feudal 'villain', Oliver's right is not based on the traditional status that comes from being his father's first-born legitimate son. Oliver's entitlement to his father's land is based on his rights under his father's testamentary will. Shakespeare elides the technical distinction between inheritance and will, presumably because for purposes of the drama it makes little difference to the oppression that Orlando feels. Shakespeare's choice to use the will of Sir Rowland de Boys to establish an entail in favour of the eldest male (so as to produce a similar scheme of hierarchical priority to that which the contemporary default rules of inheritance would have produced according to the feudal rule of primogeniture) is a significant point of departure from his 'sources'. Literary precedents for *As You Like It* preferred to explore the dramatic power of testamentary will to depart from the feudal scheme, whereas Shakespeare explores the folly of will that perpetuates primogeniture and the feudal hierarchy. Shakespeare's choice was a thoroughly contemporary one. As Richard Wilson puts it, 'Shakespeare's generation fashioned their unprecedented self-autonomy on a unique opportunity to restrict the freedom of their heirs'.[32] Indeed Shakespeare's own will attempted to create a form of entail in favour of male descendants of his eldest daughter (see Chapter 6). Wilson argues that, by means of the entail, the '*lateral* network of social affiliations and obligations, was abandoned for a new documentary and legal system of transmission, focused on selected *lineal* descendants'.[33] This is an accurate analysis at the particular level of the entail, but the more general trend in the period following the 1540 Statute of Wills was from the lineal (vertical) to the lateral (horizontal), from testamentary will constrained by the hierarchical strictures of feudalism (as Henry VIII had tried to reassert them) to testamentary freedom to dispose of land.

Thomas Lodge's *Rosalynde* is a precedent for several aspects of Shakespeare's play, including its testamentary theme.[34] Lodge, a second son who had been excluded from his father's will,[35] has the father in *Rosalynde* show atypical favour to the youngest of his three sons. In making this choice he was looking at least as far back as such traditional stories as the fourteenth-century *The Tale of Gamelyn*, in which the dying father attempted to persuade his fellow knights to take the unusual step of holding his estate equally between his three sons, regardless of their ages. Shakespeare's petty tyrant, Oliver, is also an elder brother lauding it over a younger, but in this case the elder is merely insisting (too strictly, too wilfully) upon what is his by the express terms of his father's testament. As a 'merchant' playwright in the city of London who became in course of time a gentlemen and performer at court, Shakespeare was familiar with the obstacles and opportunities presented to the second and lesser sons of the nobility and gentry. He must have had many friends and acquaintances in that social stratum. One we know of is Thomas Russell esquire,[36] who was named as 'overseer' to Shakespeare's will.[37]

The forest fellowship of *As You Like It* presents Shakespeare's London playgoers with a mirror image of themselves, or – setting aside the differing social strata represented in the hierarchy of the playhouse seats or 'stands' – a vision of what they might become. In the Forest of Arden, at the common level of the earth, we see representatives of all strata of society living a communal existence as 'co-mates and brothers' (2.1.1). Juliet Dusinberre makes the important point that in the forest the 'exiled courtiers ... are ... liberated from hierarchy'.[38] Orlando's flight from the court to the Forest of Arden, and that of Rosalind and Celia, have counterparts in the flight of Shylock's daughter Jessica to the fantasy island of Belmont in *The Merchant of Venice* and, we might add, in the flight of Hermia from the court of Athens to a nearby wood in *A Midsummer Night's Dream*. Each escapee takes flight with a companion. Fellowship is their destination and desire. The physical descent of Jessica from a casement window (recall Rosalind's 'will'-full claim that women's wit 'will out at the casement; shut that and 'twill out at the key-hole; stop that, 'twill fly' [4.1.151–2]) to the level of the stage represents the move from hierarchical to horizontal; from locus to platea, to use Weimann's terms (see Chapters 1 and 2). By the same token, Jessica transfers herself from the world of her father's tradition to the merchant world of free trade. This transfer is represented materially in the fact that Jessica's descent from the casement is accompanied by a casket of cash liberated (stolen) from Shylock. Daughter and ducats descend together. The young escapees in Shakespeare's comedies flee from subjection to a paternal or paternalistic will that derives its power from traditional social hierarchy. In *A Midsummer Night's Dream*, the will of Egeus that bears down upon his daughter Hermia is expressly confirmed by a direct decree from higher up the social hierarchy. Theseus, Duke of Athens, warns her: 'fair Hermia, look you arm yourself / To fit your fancies to your father's will' (1.1.119–20). The advice to 'arm' has at least a double sense. It can be understood as an invitation to Hermia to contain herself, as if fitting herself within the protective (albeit restrictive) armour of her father's will. It can also be understood as an invitation actively to take up arms against her own fancies, and therefore to 'fit' in the synonymous early English sense of 'fight'.[39] In both senses there is a notion of struggle or wrestling between self-will and the will of her father. Her response, as we know, was to prefer flight to fight. In *As You Like It,* Orlando also flies, but not before he puts up a physical fight.

There are three scenes of physical wrestling early in *As You Like It* and they combine together to emphasize the dramatic tension inherent in the play's major motif of 'wrestling with will'. Orlando is involved in two of the three bouts of physical wrestling. His first bout is in the opening scene, in which he grapples with Oliver in the garden. The setting suggests something of Eden and legendary conflicts between biblical first-born sons and their younger brothers.[40] Orlando wrestles Oliver into making a significant express concession to Orlando's will:

OLIVER Let me go, I say.
ORLANDO I will not till I please ...
OLIVER Well, sir, get you in. I will not long be troubled with you; you shall have some part of your will. I pray you leave me. (1.1.61–2, 72–4)

The second bout of physical wrestling in the play, reported by the courtier Le Beau, is not seen on stage. The usurper, Duke Frederick, has a prize wrestler in his pay. Charles the Wrestler is the 'general challenger' (1.2.162) who will fight all-comers that dare to grapple with him. Le Beau reports to Celia and Rosalind, and therefore to the playgoers, that Charles the Wrestler has recently defeated the three sons of a certain old man. The report is included in the play in part to heighten the playgoers' concern that Orlando, himself one of three sons, might shortly suffer a similar fate.

LE BEAU There comes an old man and his three sons –
CELIA I could match this beginning with an old tale.
LE BEAU Three proper young men, of excellent growth and presence –
ROSALIND With bills on their necks: 'Be it known unto all men by these presents.'
LE BEAU The eldest of the three wrestled with Charles, the Duke's wrestler; which Charles in a moment threw him, and broke three of his ribs, that there is little hope of life in him. So he served the second and so the third. Yonder they lie, the poor old man their father making such pitiful dole over them that all the beholders take his part with weeping. (1.2.113–25)

The 'old tale' to which Celia refers is not a reference to Lodge's recent work, but to the older tradition of folk tales, alluded to earlier, in which:

The youngest son triumphed, like Jack the Giant Killer, over a strongman, a wrestler, joined a band of outlaws in

> the forest, became their king, and with the aid of an old servant of his father, the wily Adam Spencer,[41] in the end had his revenge on his brother and got his rights.[42]

Le Beau's report of the defeat of the old man's three sons prompts a witty response from Rosalind in which she incidentally advances the play's thematic concern with legal formality. Her phrase 'With bills on their necks: "Be it known unto all men by these presents"' is more than a pun on Le Beau's use of the homonym 'presence'. Rosalind is alluding to (indeed translating) the phrase '*noverint universi per presentes*' which appeared in the first line of legal deeds in the early modern period (see also *Tim*, 5.1.12). This Latin line did not appear in wills, so it is not testamentary in the technical legal sense of the word, but it is testamentary in the more substantial sense that it calls upon communal (indeed universal) witness to the parties' formal act of will. In contractual bonds, the line typically took the form '*Noverint universi per presentes me* [name of first party] *teneri et firmiter obligari* [name of second party]', which indicates that the first party is 'held and firmly bound' to the second. Andrew Zurcher notes that this wording has 'obvious resonance when the metaphorical obligation is pictured by a wrestling'.[43] We may observe in passing that it also resonates with the bond world of *The Merchant of Venice*, where, in relationship after relationship, 'The law hath yet another hold' (4.1.343).

The climactic third bout of physical wrestling, the second of the two that Orlando participates in, occurs when Orlando takes up the general challenge thrown down by Charles the Wrestler. Oliver, who has advance notice of Orlando's intention to wrestle Charles, does not seek to dissuade Orlando from the venture. Indeed Oliver sees in the bout an opportunity to bring a convenient end to his own struggle with Orlando. The language that Charles uses in conversation with Oliver in advance of the bout seems to pun on the language of credit and debt, notably where the words 'credit', 'acquit' and 'tender' appear in successive lines (1.1.120–2), and later where Charles promises 'I'll give him his payment' (1.1.150). In the mouth of a professional wrestler who is both a mercenary and a servant who must act 'altogether against' his 'will' (1.1.128), the mercantile language evokes the tension between feudal tradition and merchant modernity that runs through the play. In the event, it is Orlando who is victorious. This triumph over the duke's wrestler, together with Orlando's success in his grapple with Oliver, foretells that in due course Orlando will overcome the will of the usurping duke and the will of his eldest brother. Orlando's victory in his physical struggles therefore represents in microcosm the contemporary struggle between the feudal, hierarchical tradition and the emerging modern agency of 'free will' (which is the language used in the first section of the 1540 Statute of Wills; see Chapter 1). The stage representation of Orlando's success in that struggle must have played well to Shakespeare's London playgoers, many of whom were second and younger sons of nobles and gentlemen who had come to London to seek and pursue mercantile opportunities or to acquire a professional trade or profession.[44]

Orlando's wrestling with will is an individual's struggle, but it also represents the struggle of will as a social struggle – a wrestling between two sociopolitical world views. There is, furthermore, a sense in which Orlando's struggle to express his will against the forces of tradition is a battle against the forces of fortune. Helen Gardner, paraphrasing Suzanne Langer, describes comedy as 'an image of life triumphing over chance'.[45] Fortune is very obviously a feature of the new world of trade, but it is also a feature of the old world of tradition. Indeed, such accidents as being born first, male and legitimate were foundational of feudal hierarchy. Sir Rowland de Boys could have employed the power of his testamentary will to counter these forces of fortune, as the fathers did in *The Tale of Gamelyn* and in Lodge's *Rosalynde*, but instead he exacerbated the accidental status of Orlando's birth by the small legacy he left Orlando in his will. The use of the word 'allottery' (1.1.69) to describe that small legacy hints at the sometimes capricious, somewhat random or fortuitous quality of the free exercise of testamentary will.

The alignment of forces of tradition and fortune in opposition to Orlando's will can be compared, somewhat broadly, to a wrestling with the divine will. Joseph S. Jenkins identifies the account of Jacob wrestling with the divine being (Gen. 32) as a defining instance of human struggle with the will of God, and he connects this to theatre and the 'comedic power ... of audience pleasure generated by young love's foiling of the senex'.[46] Jenkins devotes an entire chapter on *The Merchant of Venice* to that theme, but makes no reference to *As You Like It*. With its wrestling scenes and overt concern with testamentary will, this play would appear to offer an excellent case – perhaps a supporting case – for his thesis. Its omission might indicate how hard it is to conceive a triumph over the divine will in terms of comedy (if indeed such a triumph is conceivable in any terms).

More likely territory for comedy is the battle of wills that takes place between lovers. Sometimes the lovers are wilfully opposed to each other, at least to begin with. *The Taming of the Shrew* and *Much Ado About Nothing* are exemplary. Frequently though – and *Much Ado* is exemplary of this also – the comedy lies in the fact that the apparent battle of will is really a sham and when it comes down to it, self-will is easily overthrown. When Benedick and Beatrice spar, there is much ado about their opposing wills, but really there is nothing in it. In *As You Like It* there is not even a pretence of struggle. Juliet Dusinberre observes that in the course of the play 'gentleness is allowed to overcome force, just as the weaker wrestler (Rosalind) is allowed to overcome Orlando'.[47] It is equally the case, as Rosalind admits, that Orlando overthrows her; and the funny thing is that both their wills are mutually and instantly overthrown. The lovers are defeated in a comedic draw as if each had been thrown down even as each threw the other down. Orlando's private confession that his 'better parts / Are all thrown down' (1.2.238–9) is immediately followed by Rosalind's aside to Celia, 'my pride fell with my fortunes', and her compliment to Orlando: 'Sir, you have wrestled well and overthrown / More than your enemies' (1.2.243–4). In a play that juxtaposes serious bouts of physical wrestling to grand themes of struggle against oppressive will, one has to laugh to see how easily and effortlessly lovers' wills are thrown head over heels.

Charles the Wrestler stands (and lies) as a living symbol of conflict between the courtly world of feudal tradition and the emerging modern world of horizontal hand-to-hand trade. It is therefore appropriate that he should be the first person to present us with a picture of the world of brotherhood that the exiled duke has established in the Forest of Arden in opposition to the oppressive hierarchy of the court. Charles relates the report that Duke Senior 'is already in the Forest of Arden and a many merry men with him, and there they live like the old Robin Hood of England' (1.1.109–11). Charles's 'like' conjures up the metaphorical or allegorical sense of parallel or alternative worlds. The 'already' might suggest a temporal sense of concurrence – a 'meanwhile' – but Charles goes on to say that Duke Senior and his band of exiles 'fleet the time carelessly' (1.1.112–13). The temporal is not as important as the topographical, and this, Helen Gardner has suggested, is a feature typical of Shakespeare's comedies: 'comedies are dominated by a sense of place rather than of time.'[48] The courtier Le Beau expresses something of this topographical (and also something of a 'testamentary') sense after the bout with Charles, when he expresses the prophetic hope that Orlando will fare well 'in a better world than this' (1.2.273). Sherman Hawkins identifies two distinct types of topography in Shakespeare's comedies.[49] He does not assert 'will' as a defining distinction between them, but 'will' is clearly part of Hawkins's thinking; thus he depicts the world of the 'city' (following Shakespeare's frequent practice of eliding the distinction between 'city' and 'court') as a world in which the governing will is the individual will of a powerful person, typically a duke or paterfamilias, aligned with a traditional hierarchical social structure:

> The city is conceived as a close-knit community of families where marriage is a matter of social and even civic import, where parental will has the force of law, where the duke himself may be called upon to discipline a rebellious son or daughter.[50]

The forest world of *As You Like It* is quite different. It presents a fellowship in which individuals associate according to their free will; at least that is part of the fantasy of the place. The truth (the playful 'truth' of the drama) is that no member of the forest fellowship is truly free. Hawkins was not the first commentator to suggest a strong association between physical place and social space for self-expression. Inspired by such lines as Celia's 'Now go we in content / To liberty and not to banishment' (1.3.134–5), C. L. Barber observed that:

> The Forest of Arden, like the Wood outside Athens, is a region defined by an attitude of liberty from ordinary limitations, a festive place where the folly of romance can have its day.[51]

As You Like It is a very foolish and a very wilful play. It contains 'over sixty references to "fool", "folly", "foolish" and associated morphemes'[52] and the phrase 'I will' occurs frequently. It is precisely the folly of turning free will into new bondage that supplies the comic 'punchline' in *As You Like It* and many other Shakespearean comedies. The very title of *As You Like It* (as with the '*What You Will*' subtitle of *Twelfth Night*) tells us that Shakespeare is inviting his early modern, or emerging modern, playgoers to observe the comedic folly of self-will and, if they will, to observe it in themselves.[53] Hawkins stresses that the folly of romance is consummated in marriage and that this completes a dramatic 'movement' from oppressive (usually paternal) 'wilfulness' to 'new freedom' expressed 'in the voluntary "bond" of wedlock':[54] 'The marriage in which comedy ends is both freedom and bond, the fulfilment of the individual will and the nexus of a new social order.'[55] The movement in *As You Like It* is from a hierarchical domain of will to a horizontal social settlement. This is amply demonstrated when, one by one, the parties in the forest fellowship repeat their 'will' to be bound by Rosalind's scheme (5.4.5–25); a scheme which she promises will 'make all this matter even' (5.4.18). The future tense 'I will' was the performative speech act of the Elizabethan marriage contract in *verba de futuro*. The corresponding performative speech act in *verba de presenti* was the 'I do'.[56]

The scheme that Rosalind has in mind has more than a hint of horizontal hand-to-hand trade about it, as the words 'compact' and 'bargain' especially confirm. Her reference to 'matter' that may be made 'even' (5.4.18) suggests a materialist claim to be able to control social relations as if they were stuff to be conjured with. This is the sort of magic that law, including testamentary and inheritance law, claims to perform through such fictional constructs as 'money' and 'property'. Rosalind's use of the word 'even' conveys the sense of even-handed commercial dealings and marriages that join individuals as even-numbered pairs. The reference to even matter also conveys a material sense of level ground, echoing the earlier speech act – 'Well, this is the forest of Arden' (2.4.13) – by which she had identified the boards of the stage with the horizontal domain of the forest.[57] Both senses of 'even' – the topographical and social – are present when the god Hymen sets his seal on Rosalind's success with the declaration that 'earthly things made even / Atone together' (5.4.107–8). In one sense, Hymen's intervention supports Northrop Frye's suggestion that in Shakespearean comedy 'the renewing power of the final action lifts us into a higher world, and separates that world from the world of the comic action itself'.[58] In another sense, Hymen's masque is a very worldly affair. Not only does it incorporate popular and festive modes of wedding celebration into the play, but it also confirms the contractual sense that permeates Rosalind's horizontal hand-to-hand arrangements. The god's language is heavy with the language of bargain and bond (5.4.126–8, 140,

142). Ultimately, Hymen's intervention 'confirms conservative structures – marriages, political restitution, the return to the court'.[59] That a god – the very essence of hierarchy – should be the one to set a seal on the successful pursuit of human 'freedom' heightens our awareness that the forest ideal of freedom is actually a foolish fantasy. It is even possible that the masque was added as part of the re-drafting of the play for the occasion of a wedding attended by James I.[60]

Given the original social context of Shakespeare's plays, it was inevitable that when the comedy concluded, those left on top would be those with a vested interest in maintaining traditional hierarchies of social status. Gender distinctions may be 'played with' in Shakespeare's comedies, and in none more so than in *As You Like It*, but distinctions in social status are 'absolute'.[61] Despite the 'dressing up' in *As You Like It*, nobody dresses 'up' the social scale. Indeed, it has been observed that no character in any of Shakespeare's plays is ever shown to 'disguise up' willingly.[62] Duke Senior is content to see, at the end of the play, that all parties have been reinstated 'According to the measure of their states' (5.4.173). Shakespeare immediately has him reassert the playful illusion of social equality: 'Meantime, forget this new-fall'n dignity / And fall into our rustic revelry' (5.4.174–5), but the duke fools nobody. The playgoers will plainly see that the play has concluded with confirmation of the traditional scheme.

The romantic notion that marriage seals the end of the drama is a joke, and Shakespeare, even by the experience of his own life, knew it. When a woman married in Shakespeare's day she escaped one set of social constraints only to bind herself within another. The law confirmed the constraints and to some extent created them, and they were nowhere more strong than in the domain of property law and testamentary disposition. Henry Swinburne explains that a 'Maried woman ... can not make her testament of any ... lands', because 'so soone as a man and a woman be married' the wife's 'goods and cattels personal ... and also the catteiles reall, if he ouer liue his wife; belong to the husband'.[63] When the female characters in Shakespeare's plays fly from the fetters of a father's will, they usually end up in a state of (supposedly) voluntary – that is, willing – contract to the will of a husband. Out of the frying pan into the fire; or, to borrow a metaphor from *As You Like It*, 'from the smoke into the smother' (1.2.276). The joke is on the men too. They fly to the forest like birds escaping the cages of court, only to lock themselves in love and the bond of wedlock. Of course all the players in The Lord Chamberlain's Men who first performed *As You Like It* were men bound together in a common commercial and artistic enterprise. Within the group some were proprietorial sharers and some were more senior than others, but in terms of wider society they were largely all of a level. Technically that level was the level of a nobleman's servant. The players of The Lord Chamberlain's Men were a band of brothers but they were bound by more than brotherhood. Just as the bond of wedlock has a binding legal status that goes beyond the bonds of love and the joining of hands, so the leading players in the dramatic company were bound to each other by bonds under which they assumed a contractual commitment to their shared enterprise. *Henslowe's Diary* records, for example, that on 6 August 1597 the player Richard Jones was bound to Henslowe's company, The Admiral's Men, by a bond of assumpsit: 'a sumsett of ii^{d} to contenew & playe with the companye of my lord Admeralles players.'[64] Assumpsit was a cause of action arising as a result of a party's promise or undertaking. It arose, in other words, when a person 'assumed' some obligation. Promises giving rise to assumpsit were frequently oral and unconfirmed by any writing and, as such, were more akin to flexible commercial deals than to, say, the very formal indentures and articles by which boy actors were apprenticed to the company.[65] Players' bonds fettered the freedoms of the players subject to them, but there is no doubt that their freedoms were fettered voluntarily. Bondage to a playhouse represented opportunity, with the expectation that more would be gained than lost through it. Players' bonds were therefore akin in this respect, at least from the male perspective, to marriage and mercantile bonds. Even hireling players would willingly bind themselves formally and financially to the opportunities afforded by a playhouse fellowship. Andrew Gurr cites the example from *Henslowe's Diary* of hired men who were 'prepared to furnish bonds of £40 to guarantee their stay with their company'.[66]

The typical bonds of Shakespearean comedy are marital bonds and bonds of friendship. In early modern England, such bonds frequently had a financial dimension. Marriage certainly had something of the market about it. Rosalind plays wittily on this a number of times throughout the play, most memorably in her advice to Phoebe: 'Sell when you can, you are not for all markets' (3.5.61). At the point of taking Orlando to be her husband, she says: 'I might ask you for your commission' (4.1.128). We wonder if she is talking love or gold, for earlier she had spoken of love and gold as if they were interchangeable means to 'buy entertainment' (2.4.70–1). This interchangeability of love and money as motives for entertainment might be a metatheatrical joke between the players and between the players and the paying spectators. More seriously, it indicates the deep folly of reducing human values to the stuff of economic handling. Regarding the play more optimistically (perhaps too optimistically), we might see the possibility of liberation in the fact that the forest women are astute to the 'trade' potential of their bridal hands. It is the women who speak in these terms. Celia says 'we shall be the more marketable' (1.2.95); Phoebe talks of her idol in terms of property 'marked ... / In parcels' (3.5.125–6), and of her love match as a 'bargain' (5.4.15). It is Phoebe, again, who, to excuse her silence in the face of Ganymede's insults and to retain her right to make a future response, expresses a principle of commercial law in the phrase 'omittance is no quittance' (3.5.134) – 'quittance' being the cancellation of a debt by formal receipt of payment.[67] ('Aquittance' is also the process by which executors are discharged from liability after the proper execution of their duties.)[68]

The progress from traditional bonds to trade bonds in *As You Like It* is an example of the inconclusive conclusion that typically brings Shakespearean comedies to an end. It is not so much an ending as a cyclical return to a renewed beginning, for, as the play tells us, 'There's no news ... but the old news' (1.1.94–5). Helen Gardner emphasizes the place of marriage in the cyclical scheme: 'The great symbol of pure comedy is marriage by which the world is renewed, and its endings are always instinct with a sense of fresh beginnings.'[69] She concludes that '[a]t the close of a tragedy we look back over a course which has been run: "the rest is silence"', whereas '[t]he end of the comedy declares that life goes on: "Here we are all over again"'.[70]

The comedic 'here we are all over again' is very clear in *A Midsummer Night's Dream*, where it resides in a progress from the courtly domain of governing will to the magical woodland realm and back again to the traditional hierarchies of court. Hermia's and Lysander's acts of will are not validated until the will of Theseus, Duke of Athens, overrules the will of Hermia's father, Egeus. Comparable to Hymen's intervention in *As You Like It*, the duke wreathes the lovers' supposed triumph with a reassertion of traditional hierarchy: 'Fair lovers, you are fortunately met: / ... / Egeus, I will overbear your will; / For in the temple, by and by with us, / These couples shall eternally be knit' (4.1.170–4). Quince's 'prologue' to the playlet *Pyramus and Thisbe* in the final act confirms free will as the premise of the comedy: 'If we offend, it is with our good will. / That you should think, we come not to offend, / But with good will' (5.1.108–10). This might also be a pun on Shakespeare's name. If so, it exploits the comedy inherent in the fact that, metatheatrically speaking, the play, as all of Shakespeare's plays, begins and ends with the authoritative will of its author.

The comedic conclusion of renewal through nothing new can also be seen in the outcome of *The Merchant of Venice*. Antonio's first folly of pledging his flesh in bond for Bassanio is reiterated in the final scene in Faustian form when he expresses willingness to pledge his soul in bond for his friend.[71] At the start of the play Antonio says 'I am to learn' (1.1.5), but in the end he learns nothing. In *The Merchant of Venice*, the three pairs of lovers (the pairing of Antonio and Bassanio is another conversation) take each other's hands in the trade of betrothal and marriage and go round in circles just as gold circulates hand-to-hand in Venice. Foolish games played with the lovers' gold rings symbolize the folly that turns their freedoms full circle into marriage bonds and marriage bands.[72] Only Jessica's ring, which Shylock received from her mother when he was a bachelor, and which Jessica would have inherited from Shylock had she not stolen it from him, does not feature in the foolish games. It is an heirloom and as such is the stuff of tradition and should not be the subject matter of trade. It is rumoured that Jessica sold it, but whether that rumour is true we do not learn. What matters is that Shylock believes it. For him there can be no reconciliation or renewal, and therefore no comedic ending. Jessica's triumph of free will through the trade of love means defeat for Shylock's tradition. His error had not been to respect tradition, but, having lost the power to align his will to his traditional status as paterfamilias, his mistake had been to attempt to sublimate his will into a trade bargain with a quality as binding as if it had been his testament and he were already dead. Shylock's error is akin to that alluded to in a song penned by the melancholy Jaques in *As You Like It*. It is the error, or folly, of one who acts a 'stubborn will to please' (2.5.47). The duke's description of Shylock as a 'stony adversary' (4.1.3) is one that Shylock would have had no desire to deny. This error of stubbornness leads to tragic results, as shown in the examples of *Richard II*[73] and *Julius Caesar*.[74] Whereas the comic characters in *The Merchant of Venice* continue to run in circles, Shylock follows the trajectory of tragedy as Helen Gardener defines it. His is a 'course which has been run'.[75]

The comedic 'here we are all over again' of *As You Like It* resides partly in the move that turns forest freedoms into new fetters of marriage and mercantile bonds, and partly in the possibility that, for all its apparent communal horizontality, the world of forest and field actually contains old hierarchies in new forms. When Rosalind employs the shepherd Corin to act as her estate agent, he still conceives himself in feudal terms. He styles himself her 'faithful feeder' (2.4.98), which, as well as punning on the fact that he will feed sheep and be fed by Rosalind, also confesses his status as feudal vassal or 'feodar'.[76] Corin's inferior status is confirmed from the moment Touchstone introduces the court exiles to him as his 'betters' (2.4.6). 'Having lost common use rights to property, Corin accepts that his best lot is to work for a kinder master';[77] thus Rosalind's dealings with Corin exemplify the fact that '[p]roperty is the medium through which the characters understand and exercise ... their social relationships'.[78] Property conversations hold out the possibility of individual agency – even estate agency – but in the end the supposedly free world of forest and field perpetuates the feudal property- (and specifically land-) based hierarchies it pretends to oppose.

The comedic 'here we are all over again' is also to be found in the ultimate return of key characters to the world of court, city and traditional civic order. Oppressive individual wilfulness has been separated from the traditional hierarchical structures of social power – hence Duke Frederick and Oliver, having accepted the error of their ways, resign their status – but the traditional structures are not rejected outright. Instead, peace and progress is assured by placing new wills in old positions. Harmony for the early modern mind was not to be found in the absolute triumph of either tradition or trade, but in a balance, even a playful tension, between horizontal and hierarchical, at the place where new will meets the old world. So, in the end, Duke Senior retakes his rightful place at the pinnacle of society and Oliver purports to pass his estate to Orlando.[79] What the middle brother, Jaques, made of Orlando's advancement we can only guess, but therein lies the potential for a comedy sequel about another brother wronged. Even the melancholy Jaques, the unwilling player and constant observer, shows some willingness to vary the mode of his melancholy. He resolves to give up the world and worldlings for the liberating bondage of the religious life. Whether he carries through with that resolve, or is persuaded otherwise when he meets Duke Senior in his cave, we will never know. There is a good chance that he returned to court with the rest of them, for what would Jaques be without spectators to his melancholy performance? Comedy 'demands the co-operation of another mind', namely the mind of 'the audience'.[80] Indeed no theatrical drama is complete without the cooperation and complicity of witnesses. Witnessing is the part of the performance that integrates the act to the community as a whole, and thereby affirms, authorizes, validates and 'approves' it as performance. Theatrical performance, being 'testamentary performance', needs witnesses and it needs to pass probate. When people approve a performance with their applause, even the prevailing hierarchies of social status must yield to the democratic clamour of clapping.

In *As You Like It,* Jaques plays the part of witness. We see this, for example, when he secretly observes Touchstone with Audrey the shepherdess and undertakes to act as witness to their marriage. He also enjoins the playgoers to be his fellow witnesses, as for example through his asides when Touchstone woos Audrey. When Jaques calls Duke Senior's forest fellowship like 'fools into a circle' (2.5.52), he simultaneously calls for the participation of the playgoers who have already been summoned (but not authoritatively summonsed) into the circle – the 'wooden "O"' (*H5*, 1.prologue.13) – of the playhouse. Immediately after calling the 'fools into a circle', Jaques proceeds to say that if he cannot sleep he will 'rail against all the first-born of Egypt' (2.5.53–4). In this we can hear Shakespeare playing to the second, and lesser, sons in his London audience. Jaques's most celebrated contribution to the play is, of course, his 'seven ages' speech, which begins with his most famous lines: 'All the world's a stage, / And all the men and women merely players' (2.7.140–1). Whether or not this sentiment also featured on the sign or flag outside the Globe theatre,[81] it has the effect of incorporating the playgoers as Jaques's fellow witnesses to the performance. They are, as Juliet Dusinberre writes, 'participants' in the play.[82] She observes that *As You Like It* 'demonstrates a sophisticated awareness of stage space, of audience interaction with the players, and of the players themselves as spectators of their own play'.[83]

Jaques is not the only character to bridge the divide between players and playgoers. His most celebrated speech was actually inspired by Duke Senior's own observations on the same theme: 'Thou seest we are not all alone unhappy. / This wide and universal theatre / Presents more woeful pageants than the scene / Wherein we play in' (2.7.137–40). Jaques is, however, much more akin to the audience than the duke, because Jaques, like the audience, is sequestered from the main action. He stands on the stage, but he is set aside. His asides to playgoers emphasize this. Jaques's quality of being set aside to function as a bridge between player and playgoers can also be emphasized in physical aspects of the performance, for example by locating him on a spur of staging intruding into the pit of the playhouse, as occurred for significant parts of his performance in the 2015 production at Shakespeare's Globe (Blanche McIntyre, 2015). C. L. Barber cited a testamentary precedent for this in his chapter 'The Alliance of Seriousness and Levity in *As You Like It*':

> Although both Jaques and Touchstone are connected with the action well enough at the level of plot, their real position is generally mediate between the audience and something in the play, the same position Nashe assigns to the court fool, Will Summers, in *Summer's Last Will and Testament*.[84]

Barber goes on to make the point that this 'enabled the dramatist to embody in a character and his relations with other characters the comedy's purpose of maintaining objectivity'.[85] That word 'objectivity' is key. Jaques can perform as an objective witness because he has no material interest in the matter at hand. He contrasts himself with Touchstone, the courtly and 'material fool' (3.3.29) who becomes emotionally and physically embroiled in the country world. Jaques is an objective bystander and (as a distinguished lawyer wrote more or less contemporary with the play) '[i]t is often seene, that a stander by seeth more than he that plaieth'.[86] Jaques is not a tragic figure who lacks will, but a comic figure who is positively unwilling. His speech is not passive, but has the performative power of a speech act. In the testamentary moment of his departure from the world, when he resolves to join Duke Frederick in holy orders, Jaques confers a series of bequests on those who will remain in it (5.4.182–91). The words spoken to Duke Senior are: 'You to your former honour I bequeath' (5.4.184). 'Bequeath' is the potent word, for to be-quoth is the magical speech act that speaks one's world into being and speaks one's being out of the world.

Many of the characters in *As You Like It* appeal to the audience and amuse them. The courtly clown Touchstone even manages some moments of testamentary profundity, as in his threat to the young man William by which he summarizes the entire rhetorical, testamentary and translational (that is translocational) essence of the play: 'I kill thee, make thee away, translate thy life into death, thy liberty into bondage' (5.2.53–4). That said, the only character who matches Jaques's sublime capacity to straddle the play world and the world beyond is Rosalind. Edward Berry observed that 'Rosalind becomes in a sense a figure for the playwright himself, a character whose consciousness extends in subtle ways beyond the boundaries of the drama'.[87] Juliet Dusinberre concludes the introduction to her Arden edition of the play with some thought-provoking reflections on the 'authorial power invested in Rosalind'.[88] Dusinberre suggests that Rosalind's 'movement out of the drama into the theatre reminds the audience that they too are actors on a stage from which there is no easy exit'.[89] Where might these observations lead if we take seriously the testamentary theme of the play and its exemplary status as an instance of testamentary performance? One answer is that as the actors are the executors of the play's governing will, and Jaques and the playgoers are witnesses who affirm and constitute the reality of the governing will, so we can regard Rosalind as the embodiment of the will, or, to speak more properly, say that Rosalind is the testator (or testatrix) of the play. She has a testator's quality of being simultaneously present and absent in the world. That quality is beautifully dramatized when Orlando, not realizing that Rosalind is standing next to him disguised as Ganymede, addresses 'her that is not here nor doth not hear' (5.2.104). Rosalind has all the qualifications necessary to be the testator of the testamentary performance of the play. She is in the world but not in it. She exercises a governing will. She is a landholder (almost her first act upon entering the forest was to purchase a cottage). Most important of all is the fact that she has the power of be-queathing, which is the capacity to utter speech acts with something like the power of magical spells. This is the power – the world-making power – of creating by saying. Rosalind expressly acknowledges that since the age of three she has conversed with a 'magician' and developed a power to 'do strange things' (5.2.58–60). Possible literary allusions aside, the 'magician' may be Shakespeare's personification for Rosalind's (and hence his own) creative wit. When she says 'I say I am a magician' (5.2.69), the statement itself is a speech act of self-creation. Jaques has something of Rosalind's power to conjure with words, as his 'Greek invocation' (2.5.52) proves, but whereas Jaques is the play's 'unwilling', Rosalind is its 'will'. Rosalind's distinctive capacity for speech acts even extends to directing the speech acts of others, as when she instructs Celia: 'You must begin: "Will you, Orlando –"' (4.1.119), and directs Orlando: "You must say: "I take thee, Rosalind, for wife"' (4.1.125–6). That scene of a playful, sham marriage presents this intriguing question about performance: if, as here, the correct parties utter the correct words with the necessary substantial intent ('will') but in a false or fabricated form, what element is lacking to make the performance 'real'? The same question can be asked of speech acts in law. Suppose that a panel of the UK's most senior judges were assembled in the Supreme Court building, and suppose that they heard full argument on a hypothetical but realistic set of facts and applied the relevant law and passed a fully reasoned and considered judgment on those facts. Would the outcome be 'real' law? If not, what element in this performance renders it 'moot'? The answer seems to lie in the lack of communal consent derived from a community of witnesses who will approve the performance as authoritative. The actors and the witnesses know that reality is in suspense.

As the speaking will of the play, Rosalind is its testator. She might have been called its 'testatrix', but ultimately it is the play's male author who endows her with his will and authority. In her epilogue, which is the only known instance of Shakespeare bestowing that honour on a female part, she boasts 'My way is to conjure you' (epilogue.10–11). Who is boasting here: Rosalind or Shakespeare? It is significant that the opening lines of Rosalind's epilogue expressly call upon us to look back to the prologue: 'It is not the fashion to see the lady the Epilogue, but it is no more unhandsome than to see the lord the Prologue' (epilogue.1–3). The word 'fashion' appeared in the first line of Orlando's prologue. Its repetition here, at the formal ending of the drama, affirms the play's comedic concern with the unreliability of external forms. Rosalind also repeats technical testamentary language that was used in the prologue. The 'charge' placed upon Oliver by the will of Sir Rowland de Boys is translated into the 'charge' placed by Rosalind upon the female and male playgoers in turn (epilogue.11–13). The prologue introduced the will of Sir Rowland as the will within the play. The epilogue confirms the (nearly) anagrammatic Rosalind (Sir'o'land) as the will that is both within the play and beyond it – both here and 'not here' (5.2.104). Rosalind becomes, then, a sort of surrogate for the author. William Shakespeare is the governing will of all the worlds of this play, and why should he not, in this play of all plays, disguise himself as a woman? In various places and in a variety of ways, Will Shakespeare seems to appear before us in this play set in the forest of his home county of Warwickshire. (The courtly world of the play is intended to feel French, but the Forest of Arden belongs to Warwickshire, not to the Ardennes.)[90] Perhaps he even appears in that incongruous moment of dialogue between Touchstone and William in the first scene of the final act – the one in which Robert Armin, the trained goldsmith who first played Touchstone, asks the young William 'Art rich?' (5.1.25). As always when we wrestle with Shakespeare's authorial will in his plays, we find that, like Rosalind, he is here and not here.

What we witness at the end of *As You Like It* is not the performance of free will unfettered, but free will that voluntarily enters into new bonds. This is the last laugh. The crux of the comedy does not lie in the conclusion of a complete crossing over, as from life to death, but rather in the fact that, cross and re-cross life's stage as we will, we will never be free so long as we live. This is not only because, at the start and end of our lives, and regardless of our will, we must have what Jaques calls our 'exits' and 'entrances' (2.7.142) (compare *KL*, 4.5.174–5), but also because, unless we are to live like Jaques in melancholy solitude, we must live bound to other souls by our common society and common humanity. Exposure to the seasons caused Duke Senior to complain that he could 'feel ... the penalty of Adam' (2.1.5), but the true curse of Adam is our own human nature. It is in our social nature that we cannot live a full life alone and yet cannot live a fully free life with others. Thus all life is bondage and we must carry the curse of Adam on our back wherever we go, just as Orlando carried the 'venerable burden' (2.7.168) of Adam to the fellowship in Arden. It is sometimes said that Shakespeare himself played the part of that old man.[91] How appropriate that 'will' should be the burden. When we witness Shakespeare's comedy, we witness escape from the will of an oppressor to a more happy will. Not a free will unfettered, but one that willingly bears the burden of fellow travellers in the hope of friendship and love. When we see the hand-me-downs of traditional hierarchy become the hand-to-hand of trade, we may be witnessing legerdemain. It may be that we are material fools to be conjured with. It doesn't matter, so long as we put our hands together when the comedy ends.

4

'Shall I descend?': Rhetorical stasis and moving will in *Julius Caesar*

'Friends, Romans, countrymen, lend me your ears' (3.2.74).[1] The opening words of Antony's funeral oration exemplify what the rhetorician Thomas Wilson called 'a plaine beginning' wherein 'the hearer is made apt to giue good eare out of hande'.[2] This type of 'plaine beginning' has a history in English drama going back at least as far as *The Castle of Perseverance* (c. 1420), where the prologue contains the second flag-bearer's 'Farewel, fayre frendys, / That lofly wyl lystyn and lendys'.[3] Antony delivers his opening words (in rhetorical terms his 'exordium') from what Shakespeare calls 'the pulpit'. He addresses the plebeians down on the stage, but the groundlings in the playhouse yard, sharing the inferior aspect of the stage citizens, must have felt that Antony was delivering his rhetoric directly down to them.[4] All classes of playgoer are incorporated into the performance. So when Antony addresses the 'gentle Romans' (3.2.73), Shakespeare is speaking to the gentlemen playgoers and to any who, like the poet, had the will and social ambition to climb up to gentility.[5]

Antony's speech also speaks to playgoers of the highest social standing, and by the end of it they had cause to stir uneasily in their seats.

To the Elizabethan playgoer, Antony in his 'pulpit' was in the familiar place of preacher. Brutus likewise. What kind of preachers were they? We might characterize Brutus as a sort of Puritan. From the first scene it is clear that the men of his faction disapprove of ceremonial holidays and the sanctification of Caesar. In this they share the Puritans' objection to Roman Catholic ceremony and saints' days. Brutus's followers also object to the threatened crowning of Caesar and insist on the removal of robes and diadems from his public statues. What Brutus fears is a crown coupled to the caprice of individual 'will' (2.1.17). 'Will' was a particular concern of Protestantism during Elizabeth's reign. Calvin, following Luther, believed that individuals have no free will to reject God if he chooses ('elects') them, but that humans are morally responsible for their own acts of will.[6] Calvin's rejection of astrology chimes with Cassius's advice to Brutus that the 'fault ... is not in our stars / But in ourselves' (1.2.139–40). The conspiracy of Brutus and Cassius can be understood in Calvinist terms as their taking responsibility for their own willed acts in resistance to the will of Caesar. Antony, in contrast, is no Puritan. In his forum speech he speaks of Caesar as Roman Catholics speak of saints: prophesying that the people would 'dip their napkins in his sacred blood, / Yea, beg a hair of him for memory' (3.2.134–5). The historical Antony was the holder of high priestly office in Rome, but Shakespeare's play presents him as something like an altar boy to Caesar's Roman Catholic priest. Antony plays his part in the ceremonial rites of Lupercal as Caesar directs him – 'When Caesar says "Do this", it is performed' (1.2.10).

If these are the respective natures of Brutus and Antony as Shakespeare presents them, does he give them rhetorical language appropriate to their character? Clearly not. One of Shakespeare's masterstrokes is to lend Antony a style and an argument that should properly belong to Brutus. Antony employs a congregational style and argument in order to promote the quite contrary cause of Caesar and the crown. ('A crucial point of contention between Anglican conservatives and Puritan reformers was whether a clergyman's authority came from above or from below, from the crown or from the congregation.')[7] Antony makes much of the fact that on the feast of Lupercal, he three times offered Caesar a crown, which 'he did thrice refuse' (3.2.98), but he conceals the fact (revealed by Casca [1.2.241])[8] that Caesar's true desire was to take it. Outwardly Antony acknowledges the authority of the people, but he hides the crown in his heart. In contrast, Shakespeare makes the supposedly 'congregational' Brutus rely upon the inappropriately aristocratic virtue of his own high 'honour'. As the historical Brutus rested his ultimate claim to honour on the merits of his ancestor Lucius Junius Brutus who had expelled the kings from Rome,[9] so Shakespeare's Brutus bases his claim to honour on his status as a patrician within the traditional social hierarchy. To early modern ears, this undermines his congregational cause and his pretension to be a man of the people. Writing in 1579, William Harrison equated the Roman patricians with the English nobility.[10] Brutus further damages his Calvanist credentials in the eyes of the playgoing 'congregation' by asserting human favour as the basis of his honour. For Calvin, 'anything in profane men appearing praiseworthy must be considered worthless'.[11] (Compare Henry V's 'if it be a sin to covet honour' [*H5*, 4.3.28].) By the same token, Brutus offends the ethos of the early modern Neostoics, for, as Guillaume DuVair wrote in 1598, we should not look to others to honour us since that 'doth no way depend of our willes'.[12] The Neostoics were reacting to the commonplace notion that honour is the 'reward due to virtuous action'.[13] Brutus resorts to this commonplace when he purports to honour Caesar because he was 'valiant' (3.2.25–6).

Brutus demands that the 'base' plebeians should 'honour' him because of his superior status. Instead of demanding 'Believe me for mine honour' (3.2.14–15), he might have fared better if he had said 'Honour me for mine acts', or better still, to have left his honour out of it. Antony takes a very different approach. He commences his address to the plebeians with 'humble talk to win their good wils'.[14] Shakespeare has Brutus speak in prose and Antony in verse. In a play that is only five per cent verse, this is clearly a considered choice. At first sight, prose might seem to enhance Brutus's credibility with the commoners, given Shakespeare's known practice of allocating prose to lower status speakers, but Brutus's prose speech gives no sense that he has the common touch. Instead, his prosaic style makes Brutus seem cold. It confirms the perception that Brutus is employing rhetoric 'by the book', with its calculated logic and formal schemes (*isocolon, parison, antithesis* and *chiasmus* all figure prominently).[15] Mark Antony's more naturalistic verse speech achieves the early modern rhetorical ideal of hiding the art and it serves to emphasize the essential humanity that connects him to Caesar and the citizens.[16] Shakespeare has Brutus fall into the trap of promoting a coup by the nobility, leaving the way clear for Antony to feed, and to feed off, the forces of popular uprising.[17] Antony succeeds because he wields the popular will, and at the conclusion of his forum speech he wields it tangibly in the form of Caesar's sealed testament. The assassins had manifested their bloody hands and stained swords. Antony brandishes the will marked red with Caesar's seal.[18] Antony tantalizes the citizens with talk of their legacy under it: 'Let but the commons hear this testament – / Which, pardon me, I do not mean to read' (3.2.131–2). This rhetorical device of *paralepsis* or *praeteritio*, a species of irony, serves to increase interest in the very thing that is purportedly downplayed. In Thomas North's 1579 translation of Plutarch's *Lives*, Antonius reveals the content of Caesar's will before he reveals Caesar's bloody mantle.[19] In Shakespeare's drama, suspense is sustained. The mantle is examined, the corpse is disclosed (an event not recorded in Plutarch) and only at the last, when the citizens have been stoked to mutinous fervour, does Antony restrain them just long enough for them to hear the terms of the will: 'To every

Roman citizen he gives, / To every several man, seventy-five drachmas. /… / Moreover, he hath left you all his walks, / His private arbours and new-planted orchards' (3.2.234–9).[20] This is a popular will indeed.

The unveiling of Caesar's corpse relates to 'the play's interest in vesting and divesting of power'.[21] Equally potent is the unfolding of the will, especially in the way it speaks to key sociopolitical concerns of early modern England, for it reveals the commoners' vested interest in financial resources, physical spaces and political discourse which had hitherto been the preserve of a privileged elite. The outcome of Antony's oratory in Shakespeare's play is the same as in North's Plutarch: 'his words moved the common people to compassion' and they 'fell presently into such a rage and mutiny, that there was no more order kept amongst the common people'.[22] Like Bolingbroke in *Richard II*, Antony opens a 'purple testament' of blood. Crucially, though, and in true Elizabethan style, there is no outright rejection of monarchy. Indeed, one of the plebeians responds to the reading of the will with the exclamation 'O royal Caesar!' (3.2.237). The word 'royal' appears in only one other place in the play: in Antony's description of Caesar spoken by Antony's servant at the scene of the assassination (3.1.127).

What action might suit Antony's most famous phrase 'Friends, Romans, countrymen, lend me your ears'? The first action, especially important in a rhetorical performance, is to assume an appropriate posture and demeanour. Before he spoke a word, Ray Fearon's Antony (Gregory Doran, RSC, 2012) commenced with a suitably humble downwards countenance and slightly stooped stance. What next? Should the actor stand still or walk? What gesture should accompany the spoken words? Should the actor gesture with his hands? The action should be something suitable to the logical sense of the line, but the action (or inaction) accompanying the exordium of an oration should also be suitable as an introduction to the themes of the speech as a whole. The appropriate choice will vary according to the medium. The close confines of the Elizabethan theatre and Shakespeare's references to 'pulpit' and 'coffin' suggest the intimacy of a church funeral service. Gestures might be correspondingly contained. In cinematic renditions, the dynamics can be quite different. Marlon Brando's Antony spoke from the rostra in the noisy forum and had to shout down the clamour with 'lend me your ears' (Mankiewicz, MGM, 1953). Charlton Heston's Antony (Burge, Commonwealth United Entertainment, 1970) shifted in the forum scene between public oration and private conversation and his attempt to integrate these contrasting approaches perhaps comes across as a somewhat precarious balancing act. Don Kraemer supposes that in the forum scene Antony 'deploys rhetorical strategies perfected by Demosthenes'.[23] Demosthenes was one of the great orators of ancient Greece. The Vatican Museum in Rome contains a statue of the man which is missing its hands and therefore stands as a symbol of the harm that is done to rhetoric by the removal of manual gesture. Rhetoric is too frequently regarded within the academic's study as if it were only concerned with the short journey from brain to mouth and back again. A full appreciation of rhetoric's true capacity to touch us and to move us requires us to attend to the whole body. That effort should include attention to the hands.[24] Peter Ure summarized the forum speech in *Julius Caesar* in terms that merit repetition:

> The speeches are deeds done, in a society which is shown as moving and being moved primarily by the power of words, or, rather, by the arts of the orator, words accompanied by the proper and revealing gestures ... with words men strike through each others' armour and at each others' wills.[25]

Even when rhetoric is described as an art of speech, it is inevitably concerned with handling matter, and is frequently described using 'manual' terminology. Consider the opening paragraph of Thomas Wilson's treatise:

> *Rhetorique* is an Arte to set foorth by vtteraunce of words, matter at large, or (as *Cicero* doth say) it is a learned, or rather an artificiall declaration of the mynd, in the handling of any cause, called in contention, that may through reason largely be discussed.

For good or ill, rhetoric is an art of 'handling' or manipulation, and in this play Antony is the arch manipulator.[26] Shakespeare has Antony manipulate the playgoers through props and gesture and through his feel for verse. Antony even uses Caesar's corpse as a prop in his rhetorical performance and thinks of his ally Lepidus merely 'as a property' (4.1.40). Casca is the conspirators' counterpart to Antony when it comes to active exploitation of stage properties. Casca was the first assassin to stab Caesar and he was the only Roman to draw a weapon before the assassination.[27] He enters Scene 1.3 with his sword drawn after an encounter with a lion and, in another scene, he points his sword to the sun (2.1.105). In the same scene, he indicates a correspondence between the physical Capitol and Caesar's lofty status, at which moment it would be appropriate to point to the lords' rooms or to the gallery ('balcony') aloft the stage (2.1.106–10). It is in Casca's words as he stabs Caesar that Shakespeare most clearly shows his appreciation of the expressive power of gesture: 'Speak hands for me!' (3.1.76).[28]

'Friends, Romans, countrymen, lend me your ears.' As an experiment, let me invite you, the reader, to deliver Antony's famous line. For this you will need to stand up and put the book down. Or the book could be held in the left hand to replicate in a small degree the way that the Roman toga weighed down the left arm and restricted its movement.[29] Consider how you will vocalize Antony's line and what actions you will use to accompany the words, bearing in mind that an over-literal correspondence between word and action might not be the best choice. A discerning actor or director might choose to generate dramatic interest by deliberately resisting or disrupting the most obvious correspondence between word and deed. That point can be illustrated with the line 'Something is rotten in the state of Denmark' (*Ham*, 1.4.90). How would Hamlet 'suit the action to the word' (3.2.17)? Perfectly correspondent action might prompt the actor to walk across the stage and to stop on the word 'state' in order to emphasize that word's static connotations, but the better choice might be the opposite one of starting in a static position and to commence walking on the word 'state' in order to emphasize the expressed sense that the state is rotten. To take another example involving the word 'state', it seems suitable that Mark Antony's servant should, like Caesar's static corpse, lie prostrate at the feet of the conspirators when he refers to 'hazards of this untrod state' (3.1.136). Clearly there is no single right answer to such performative choices, but deeper attention to Shakespeare's words in their context will expand the possibilities and improve the chances of choosing something more suitable. Before we conjecture a suitable action for Antony's famous opening line, we should bear in mind Harley Granville-Barker's belief that Shakespeare's verse was his chief means of emotional expression and that 'when it comes to staging the plays, the speaking of the verse must be the foundation of all study'.[30] This suggests that one gestural option is to be guided by the metre of 'Friends, Romans, countrymen, lend me your ears', by which I mean its syllabic structure. (Seymour Chatman writes that '[t]he only important question for metrics is "How many syllables are there?"'.)[31] We can see that Antony's line is arranged into two distinct syllabic groups: the first six syllables followed by the final four. The 'end' sound in the first and seventh syllables marks the start of each of the two syllabic groups. The striking structural pattern of the first six syllables resides in the swelling sequence of one syllable, two syllables and three syllables. I am not the first person to notice this,[32] and at least one editor has noticed that the gradation of the syllabic groups from smallest to largest is suited to the expanding sense of the sequence 'friends' to 'Romans' to 'countrymen'.[33] Antony's intimate style makes one think when he talks of 'Romans' that he is referring not to the whole Roman Empire, but to the people of Rome to whom he is directly speaking. Thus 'friends' is the smallest and nearest group; 'Romans' is a bigger group suggestive of the ambit of the whole city; and 'countrymen' denotes the largest group and the ambit of the entire country. The first three words therefore produce 'a special and subtle case' of 'ascending tricolon'.[34] What makes it special is that Antony achieves a kind of expanding emphasis without any actual ascent. The expansion is horizontal, not vertical. The three opening words are 'on the level' and this is because Antony is 'appealing to his crowd on a human level'.[35] What has not been noted before is how this expansive effect corresponds with the expansive sense of the word 'ambition', which is a key word in Brutus's complaint and Antony's response, and how the four syllables of the second part of Antony's line reverse the expansive effect of the first six syllables by turning expansion into intimacy. Before elaborating this, it should be noted that the spatial sense of Antony's address might have been more obviously apparent to an Elizabethan audience than it is to us, for Shakespeare's playgoers would have been attuned to hearing 'Rome' pronounced 'room',[36] hence the pun 'Now is it Rome indeed, and room enough' (1.2.155).[37] One wonders if Thomas Wilson's advice on opening an oration was echoing in Shakespeare's head: 'by no meanes better shall the standers by knowe what we say, and carie awaie that which they heare, then if at the first we couch together, the whole course of our tale in as small roome as we can.'[38] It is certainly significant that Antony's soliloquy over the corpse of Caesar in the previous scene had primed the playgoers to associate the dead Caesar with spatial confinement rather than expansive ambition. Antony had invited the association through his use of the rhetorical figure of *asyndeton* (the contraction of speech through the omission of conjunctions): 'Are all thy conquests, glories, triumphs, spoils, / Shrunk to this little measure?' (3.1.149–50).

Before deciding on the gesture that will accompany Antony's first line (and let me stress again that there are almost as many valid alternatives as there are actors), it is not enough to note significant metrical patterns. It is also necessary to appreciate the verse metre in the context of the whole speech, and this requires us to relate the syllabic structure to the argument that Antony employs to oppose Brutus's claims. Brutus presents two key justifications for his actions. First, that Caesar was ambitious and for that reason deserved to die. Second, that he (Brutus) is honourable and for that reason deserves to be respected. Antony's opening line of speech is his initial effort to undermine the first of Brutus's claims. The line swells physically as ambition does – one syllable, two syllables, three syllables; and it swells conceptually as ambition does – from friends, to Rome, to the whole country. An atmosphere of ambition having been thus established, it is swiftly undone by the two short pairs of syllables that express the friendly intimacy of 'lend me your ears'. The spatial contraction is confirmed by Antony's metonymic use of the small organ of the 'ear' to represent the hearers' whole attention and perhaps (synecdochally) their whole selves. Let us ask the question again: what gestural action might accompany Antony's line? Is there anything more suitable than to start with one's hands held close to one's chest; to open them out a little on the monosyllabic 'friends'; to open them wider on the two syllables of 'Romans'; to open them to their full lateral extent on the three syllables of 'countrymen'; and, finally, to draw the hands in again to the heart with the words 'lend me your ears'? As the ambit of Antony's arms and the sense of his words swell wider and wider, his initial gesture might seem to suggest that he is ambitious and thereby lend support (by reason of Antony's association with Caesar) to Brutus's argument that Caesar was ambitious, but when Antony's arms are drawn in again to the heart, the sense of ambition is replaced by a sense of humility and intimacy. The cumulative gestural effect of the outward expanse of the first six syllables and the inward gathering of the last four is to produce the action of an embrace.[39] The overall effect is that Antony's opening line preemptively answers with a subconscious 'no' a question that he will posit later in his speech with reference to Caesar's counduct: 'Was this ambition?' (3.2.98).

Building on the syllabic subtleties of the opening line, Shakespeare goes on to employ the verse metre throughout the opening passage of Antony's forum speech to produce an embodied effect that will confirm the playgoers' subconscious rejection of the charge of ambition. The effect I am referring to derives from Shakespeare's ingenious use of short lines every time the word 'ambitious' appears. *Julius Caesar* is 'a play notable for its experiments with short lines',[40] but Shakespeare's inventiveness with Antony's 'ambitious' lines has hitherto been overlooked. Shakespeare's Antony's thirty-four lines of speech from 'Friends, Romans, countrymen, lend me your ears' to 'And I must pause till it come back to me' are mostly of ten syllables in length and many, including the last line, can bear a regular iambic stress. Only five of the thirty-four lines are missing a syllable and each of those hypometrical lines ends with the word 'ambitious'.[41] In what follows, I want to explore the potential significance of this fact, but first I need to defend the 'fact' against editors who have suggested that the 'ambitious' lines should be filled out to ten syllables by stressing the word 'ambitious' tetrasyllabically ('am-bish-ee-us').[42] I can't recall an example of an actor adopting that practice and it would surely sound highly artificial and pompous if any did. It is possible that in the original Elizabethan pronunciation the word was sometimes pronounced with four syllables, but Shakespeare's other plays supply example after example to indicate that if 'ambitious' is pronounced strictly within the metre it will be pronounced trisyllabically.[43] In *Julius Caesar*, the only use of 'ambitious' outside the forum scene is in Casca's line 'Th'ambitious ocean swell, and rage, and foam' (1.3.7). This line is ambiguous as to syllabic length, but the contraction 'Th'ambitious' might imply that the line has been deliberately shortened to bring it within the standard pentameter. If so, 'ambitious' would be trisyllabic. A further clue to the fact that Shakespeare intended to make the 'ambitious' lines in the forum scene seem short compared to their neighbours is the fact that there are only four over-length ('hypermetrical') lines in this whole passage of speech and two of these come immediately before an 'ambitious' line. This alerts us to the fact that something unusual is at work in the metre. The first line concluding with the word 'ambitious' is immediately preceded by a twelve-syllable line; which is the longest line in the entire passage. Another 'ambitious' line is preceded by an eleven-syllable line. This combines with the missing syllable in the 'ambitious' lines to exaggerate the discomforting sense that something is lacking in those lines.

Whatever the original pronunciation might have been, it is clear that a modern actor should pronounce 'ambitious' trisyllabically. Trisyllabic pronunciation produces an under-length ('hypometrical') line that engenders an embodied sense that is directly contrary to the literal sense of the word 'ambitious'. To be ambitious is to seek a wider and larger ambit of power and influence, but in Antony's speech the lines ending 'ambitious' are the most humble lines of all in terms of syllabic extent. As a result, those lines ring false. The missing syllable also gives the audience space in which to connect their embodied sense of disquiet with Brutus's claim that Caesar was ambitious. The pause gives just enough time to sense that Brutus was lying. The doubt is felt limbically before it is thought logically, by which I mean that the doubt flows primarily from an embodied sense of lack. This turns satisfaction into dissatisfaction. The poetic strictures of metrical verse are in some sense artificial, but one cannot be reminded too often that the rhythmic quality of poetic metre has a natural appeal almost in spite of the art. Part of its appeal is the fact that the two syllables of a metrical 'foot' echo the beating of the human heart. This is true of all disyllabic metrical feet, but the iambic foot has a special resonance. The cardiac cycle produces a number of sounds, but the human ear can detect two dominant beats: the so-called 'lub-dub' pairing. This sound is comparable to the iambic foot of an unstressed syllable followed by a stressed. Antony stokes the citizens' subconscious unease by setting up a natural rhythmic expectation through regular iambic pentameter only to snatch it away in the repeated hypometrical 'ambitious' lines. Alongside this subconscious sense he strikes his hearers' conscious sense with express doubts concerning Brutus's claim: 'Did this in Caesar seem ambitious?'; 'Ambition should be made of sterner stuff'; 'Was this ambition?' (3.2.91, 93, 98). For good measure he even reminds them, again repeatedly, that Caesar's ambition is not a fact but something that Brutus 'says' and 'Hath told' (3.2.87, 94, 99; 79).

Shakespeare's excellence as a poet is to a great extent an excellence in knowing how to manage the embodied feel of words. Perhaps Shakespeare is advertising his own poetic awareness when he has Cassius say to Brutus 'what should be in that 'Caesar'? / Why should that name be sounded more than yours? / ... / Sound them, it doth become the mouth as well. / Weigh them, it is as heavy' (1.2.141–5), and yet he might also be presenting Cassius as one who can only appreciate words instrumentally – politically rather than poetically. Caesar voiced this suspicion when he called Cassius 'a great observer' who 'looks / Quite through the deeds of men' and 'loves no plays' (1.2.201–2). If there is a part of Shakespeare in Cassius, it is the part of the pragmatic businessman and not the poet's part. Brutus is the only one of the conspirators who makes express reference to 'business' – notably in reference to the conspirators' 'bleeding business' (3.1.168), which he also terms their 'ventures' (4.3.222) – but it is Cassius who moved the 'bargain' (1.3.120) and 'enterprise' (1.2.297; 1.3.123; 3.1.13, 16) of Caesar's assassination. Eventually the private bargain will take Cassius to the tent of Brutus where the pair haggle on the theme of hands itching for gold (4.3.10–11). The mercantile scene can be appreciated as a potted version of *The Merchant of Venice*, in which Cassius plays the part of Antonio: beginning 'a-weary of the world', then bearing his naked breast to a dagger, and finally (having failed to transfer gold) announcing 'I ... will give my heart' (4.3.94–103).

At the assassination, we hear the dispassionate tone of the 'great observer' in Cassius's metatheatrical musings: 'How many ages hence / Shall this our lofty scene be acted over / In states unborn and accents yet unknown?' (3.1.111–13).[44] Cassius is the dramaturge of the conspirators' performance. He is not only a 'great observer' of the political scene, but also one who assembles others to act as witnesses ('Messala: / Be thou my witness that against my will / … am I compelled' (5.1.72–4)). He also has a dramatist's instinct to know that Brutus should not permit Antony to take the stage in Caesar's funeral. Cassius chooses Brutus to direct and star in the conspiracy because he can be relied upon to draw a favourable audience. The fact that Brutus 'sits high in all the people's hearts' (1.3.157) was a feature calculated to enhance the 'lofty' nature of the assassination. Brutus's chief mistake is that he plays the part too well and depends too much on his high status when he demands 'respect to mine honour' (3.2.15) and rests his credit on it ('Believe me for mine honour' [3.2.14–15]). As a strategy to enhance the ethos of his rhetoric, it backfires horribly. Antony not only casts doubt upon the honour of Brutus, but he also employs every aspect of his performance to subvert Brutus's founding assumption that honour is indeed a virtue. What if honour could be characterized as haughtiness? Brutus's confession that he 'rose' against Caesar (3.2.20), and the assertion of his status as a high-born patrician, would then serve only to distance him from the sympathy of the plebeians. In the assassination scene, Brutus and each of his fellow conspirators literally 'rises' from a kneeling position to stab Caesar.[45] Ray Fearon, playing Antony in Gregory Doran's Stratford production (RSC, 2012), described the conspirators as 'all honourable men' with a suitable upwards gesture that was effective in emphasizing Brutus's remoteness and haughtiness. Keith Michell's Antony (BBC, 1979) made a similar upwards gesture, followed swiftly by a downwards gesture to the corpse on the words 'in Caesar's funeral'. Shakespeare almost certainly knew Wilson's *Arte of Rhetorique*, but he needed no manual to tell him the strategy of judicial rhetoric by which 'We shall get fauour by speaking of our aduersaries ... if we report vnto the Iudges that they beare themselues hault'.[46]

There is no virtue in altitude, but it is a cultural and rhetorical commonplace to regard 'up' as good and 'down' as bad. As a rule of language it seems inviolable. We can no longer hear 'superior' as a value-neutral term. Heaven is up, hell is down; the high-born are the social betters of the base-born; things are looking up when they improve and there is a downturn when they worsen. Shakespeare's greatest rhetorical achievement through the course of Mark Antony's funeral oration is to turn this rhetorical and cultural commonplace on its head. Antony is a pragmatist and only takes the revolutionary route because Brutus insists so strongly upon the honour associated with his high social status. Antony's tactic in defeating Brutus's claim to honour is not to contradict Brutus, but instead to emphasize honour's haughty, hierarchical aspect and the contrasting merits of a lowly position. We can see this technique in operation at every turn of his oration, starting with his rhetorical commonplace 'The good is oft interred' (3.2.77). The dead are down but Antony sees their physically inferior status as a basis for dignity, not disgrace. Antony lays the body of Caesar on the floor of the forum, at the level of the common people and below the level of the 'pulpit' (Shakespeare's version of the Roman 'rostra').[47] In contrast, Brutus sets himself up. Not for the usual fall, but for the failure of being too far exalted above the plebeians. Even before he utters a word, Brutus physically distances himself from the people by taking the high ground of the pulpit. Antony will succeed if his oration can amplify the perceived distance between the humble level of the citizens and the high level of Brutus and the honourable patricians. I do not agree with Ernest Schanzer's suggestion that Brutus's refusal to lower his speech to the level of the plebeians is a 'compliment to their intelligence';[48] it is rather a sign of Brutus's arrogance. So too is Brutus's self-referential style, with its oft-repeated 'I', 'Brutus', 'me', 'myself' and 'mine'.[49]

The cue for Brutus's forum speech, spoken by one of the citizens, contains clues to three flaws in Brutus's rhetoric. The single line 'The noble Brutus is ascended. Silence' (3.2.11) confirms that Brutus is known for his high social status, that he takes the high ground (assumes superiority) and that he will not allow the people free expression. So it proves as his main passage of speech ensues. It begins with a repeated demand for silent audience: 'Be patient till the last' ... 'hear me' ... 'be silent, that you may hear' (3.2.12–14). The last line – 'I pause for a reply' (3.2.33–4) – pretends to open an opportunity for critical response, but it is unconvincing and no citizen feels free to speak. Brutus puts the plebeians firmly in their inferior place. He asks: 'Who is here so base, that would be a bondman? ... so rude, that would not be a Roman? ... here so vile, that will not love his country?' (3.2.29–34). Brutus is in no doubt that the commoners are base, vile and rude; he only questions the degree of their ignobility. As Brutus asks these questions, he employs the formal rhetorical ornament of alliteration – 'base/bondman', 'rude/Roman' and, more subtly, 'vile/love' – so that his audience will be in no doubt that these are rhetorical questions. As such, they admit no response. Schanzer was mistaken to suppose that Brutus was 'skilful' when he 'blocked all further questions'.[50] Foreclosing questions might seem a good technique for winning minds in a logical debate, but it is no way to win hearts in a rhetorical endeavour. Brutus's rhetorical questions are reminiscent of Thomas Wilson's: 'what man I pray you, being better able to maintaine himself by valiaunt courage, then by living in base subjection, would not rather looke to rule like a Lord, then to liue like an vnderling?'[51] At first sight, Brutus appears to urge the people to something more than base subjection, but in fact he has no intention that they should 'rule like a lord'. By naming their inferior status he keeps them down and persuades them, in Wilson's words, 'not to seeke anye higher roume'.[52] Brutus employs rhetoric not to change the social settlement, but to confirm the existing order. The question of the rights and wrongs of Caesar's assassination was a standard one in the rhetorical exercise of *controversiae* (debates) and specifically in the exercise of *argumentum in utramque partem* ('argument on both sides') in the Elizabethan school curriculum, but Brutus attempts to silence even that question and to take it out of the hands of the common people. He informs them that the debate has already been carried out, fully documented and securely filed in the archives on the Capitoline hill: 'The question of his death is enrolled in the Capitol' (3.2.37–8). Brutus thus forecloses the school exercise of the *controversiae* by attempting to replace it with a rhetorical set speech or *suasorium*. Yet the very formality of Brutus's approach removes the sweetness that should give a *suasorium* its defining persuasive quality.

Having established a great distance of social status between his high-born honour and the citizens' low-born baseness, Brutus will have done Antony's work for him if Antony can demonstrate either that elevation is bad or that lowliness is good. He does both by all manner of rhetorical means: verbal, gestural and spatial. As Antony's 'Friends, Romans, countrymen, lend me your ears' commences his assault on the argument of Caesar's ambition, so his line 'The good is oft interred with their bones. / So let it be with Caesar' (3.2.77–8) begins his revolutionary endeavour to show that the virtue of goodness might be found below rather than above. Antony's servant had already signaled his master's intent when, in the preceding scene, he had performed a gestural *gradatio* by kneeling, then falling down and finally prostrating himself before the assassins (3.1.123–5). When Antony contrasts the goodness of the dead Caesar with the evil of the living ('The evil that men do lives after them' [3.2.76]), he is alluding to the living Brutus. This is apparent from Antony's palindromic 'evil lives' (evillive), which turns Brutus's own palindromic pairing of 'vile' and 'live' (vileliv) back against him. This correspondence will only be sensed on a subconscious level, but it is all the more powerful for that. Shakespeare 'was a very great psychologist'.[53] Having confirmed that Caesar is down at the level of the commoners and that Brutus is up,

Antony continues to the key point of his rhetorical strategy which is to contrast his own place with that of the elevated Brutus. Antony locates himself in the same lowly position as Caesar, the plebeians and 'the good'. The first line to do this is 'Here, under leave of Brutus and the rest' (3.2.82). 'Here' awakens the hearers' spatial awareness, so that when Antony announces that he speaks 'under' leave of Brutus, it will produce the sense that he is positioned down with the people. It will also confirm Brutus in the contrasting position of being up with the conspirators, both in terms of social status and (to anyone with an awareness of the topography of Rome) physically up on one of hills adjacent to the forum: most likely the Capitoline or the patricians' favourite, the Palatine. Antony confirms his own lowly position by locating himself 'in' Caesar's funeral (3.2.85), just as he will shortly locate his heart 'in' Caesar's coffin (3.2.107). The eleven syllables of the line 'My heart is in the coffin there with Caesar' produce an embodied metrical sense of surfeit to match the logical sense of a coffin crowded with one heart too many. So far, there is nothing in Antony's oration that Brutus would have objected to it if he had stayed to hear it. Antony even continues, in his next lines, to amplify the high honourable status of Brutus and his faction: 'For Brutus is an honourable man; / So are they all, all honourable men' (3.2.83–4). This elevation of Brutus is done, as we now know, so that Antony can locate himself in the contrasting place of being down with Caesar and the people. The subsequent line – 'He was my friend, faithful and just to me' (3.2.86) – in large part fulfils the hope of creating fellowship between Antony, Caesar and the people which Antony had begun to advance with the very first word of his speech, 'Friends'.

In Chapter 2, we observed how *Richard II* and *King John* employed structural features of the theatre to upset normal expectations of social status. In *Richard II*, the king descends from his castle wall into the lower court and the next time we hear of high walls they are populated with the citizenry of London looking down on the deposed king. In *King John*, the play begins with the king on his throne looking down in judgment on two of his subjects, but soon he will be one of two kings subjected to the judgment of citizens located on the high walls of Angiers. In *Julius Caesar*, Shakespeare again employs the physical hierarchies of the stage to symbolic effect, but whereas the early histories for the most part employed the simple medieval semaphore of higher as better and lower as worse, the more mature artist of 1599 does something more sophisticated. (He does so not only in *Julius Caesar*, but also in the near-contemporary *Hamlet*, where the ghost of the king descends to the cellarage below the level of the stage; see Chapter 5.) Through careful coordination of staging, word and action in *Julius Caesar*, and in the forum scene in particular, Shakespeare succeeds in turning the traditional rules of the rhetoric manual upside down. He performs a hierarchical inversion befitting a Rome in which 'Graves have yawn'd and yielded up their dead' (2.2.18). *Julius Caesar* is similar to *King John* in the way it employs physical stage hierarchy to constitute the commons as judge, but in *Julius Caesar* the revolutionary innovation is to place the commons-as-judge physically below the level of Brutus, who is – at his own invitation (3.2.16–18) – the subject of their judgment. Shakespeare's decision to place judgment at the ground level of the commoners rather than raise the commoners up to the high place of the battlements or rooftops was as revolutionary in the monarchical state of early modern England as it was in the republic of Rome. It is revolutionary because it is fundamentally democratic.

The dramatic inversion that Shakespeare achieves in the forum is energized by the fall of Caesar. The first three acts employ the classic tragedian's trick of raising the titular hero to a great height in order that he might fall. It has been observed that until the forum scene, 'Caesar is rendered in terms of great height; all other men in terms of even subterranean lowness'.[54] There is a highly effective portrayal of Caesar's trajectory in the film version of Gregory Doran's *Julius Caesar* (RSC, 2012). The moment of Caesar's fatal decision to leave his home to go to the senate is marked by his symbolic descent down a flight of stairs. His assassination is played out at the foot not of Pompey's statue, but of an electric escalator that stands static and defunct. Shakespeare's dramatic prowess is witnessed in the way he charges the rise of Caesar with potential energy that is not lost when Caesar dies. Shakespeare is able to store up the dramatic energy or 'urge' (see Chapter 2) within the stage properties of the coffin, the bloody cloak and the corpse, until it is powerfully discharged in Antony's funeral oration. It is discharged from Antony to the common people, in whom the force of Caesar's spirit becomes a violent overflow. Cassius had provoked Brutus to mutiny with talk of Caesar as a colossus and complained that 'we petty men / Walk under his huge legs and peep about / To find ourselves dishonourable graves /... we are underlings' (1.2.135–40). Originally, these words might have been spoken between the two large stage pillars that underpropped the overhanging 'heavens'.[55] There is an almost comic irony here, for Cassius, despite being the stage manager of Caesar's downfall, fails to foresee that if they are under the tyrant's legs they will inevitably find the graves they are looking for when they bring the full force of Caesar's greatness crashing down. Elsewhere, Shakespeare posits a clue to the gravity of a great man and the crushing power of rhetoric when one of the conspirators conjectures that by enlisting Cicero they might cause their less weighty qualities to be 'buried in his gravity' (2.1.148). Just as 'gravity' contains a portend of 'grave', so does the sequence in that scene of the words 'soil', 'grieved' and 'buried'.

The speeches of Brutus and Antony in the forum are quite distinct from their mode of speech elsewhere. It is as if the forum oratory was crafted as a self-contained rhetorical étude and then inserted into the main course of the play.[56] It is plausible to suppose that Shakespeare is here deliberately showing off his rhetorical art. Dorsch opines that 'If ever Shakespeare wished to show genius at work, surely it was in Antony's oration'.[57] Plutarch records that Antony moved the people, but does not record what he said. Shakespeare seems to have taken this as a personal challenge to produce a piece of exemplary rhetoric. Like a schoolteacher setting a rhetorical exercise, history set Shakespeare the homework to end all homework – nothing less than to write the speech that turned Rome from Republic towards Empire. To display his rhetorical étude to best advantage, Shakespeare places it at the very centre of the play and at the crux of the dramatic action.

'Friends, Romans, countrymen, lend me your ears' is as rhetorically rich as one can imagine any phrase to be. It demonstrates Shakespeare's regard for all five of the 'faculties' or 'canons' into which early modern rhetoricians divided the art of rhetoric following the classical model. Thomas Wilson wrote that '[a]ny one that will largely handle any matter, must fasten his mynde first of all, vppon these fiue especiall pointes'.[58] The reference to 'handle' hints that it is probably not by accident that there is one faculty for each digit of the rhetorician's hand. The first faculty is 'Invention' ('*inventio*'), which encompasses the substantial content of a speech and comprises the three major categories of artificial proof as Aristotle described them: 'logos' (logical argument), 'ethos' (the speaker's character) and 'pathos' (gaining the sympathy of the audience);[59] The second of the five faculties is 'Arrangement' ('*dispositio*'), which is the ordering of the elements of an oration; then 'Memory' ('*memoria*'), which is the ability to deliver an apparently unscripted speech; next 'Delivery' ('*actio*'; Wilson's 'utteraunce'), which is the 'framing of the voyce, countenaunce, and gesture after a comely maner';[60] and finally 'Style' ('*elocutio*'), which covers all formal and figurative elements of the speech. By moving 'Style' from the middle to the last place, my sequence differs in this one detail from the classical and early modern model for no better reason than to order them Invention-Arrangment-Memory-Delivery-Style. This produces the initialism I-A-M-D-S and therefore enables budding rhetoricians to encourage themselves with this thought: 'I AM DemostheneS'.

The key elements of the faculty of 'Invention' – logos, ethos and pathos – are all present in 'Friends, Romans, countrymen, lend me your ears'. Logos is inherent in the conceptual and syllabic expansion from friends to Romans to countrymen and in the logical meaning of each word. Ethos is evoked in the implication that Antony exhibits the civic virtues of friendship and patriotism and in the humility of his acknowledgement that the common citizen might have something of worth to 'lend' so great a general. Pathos, which is emotional sympathy or fellow feeling, is engendered by the suggestion that he needs the people to lend him attention as if they were patrons lending cash to a client. An imploring facial expression would be one effective way to enhance the emotional pathos of the line. Brutus the Stoic relies on his ethos as an honourable man, but he omits pathos from his strategy or includes it clumsily and unconvincingly. Instead of actually weeping for Caesar, Brutus merely documents his emotions with the words: 'I weep for him' (3.2.24–5). Brutus sheds no tears for Caesar, for his wife or for Cassius. Indeed, as Hapgood notes, his first weeping is for his own lost cause.[61] Antony, in contrast, uses pathos to full effect. The citizens appreciate Antony's enthymematic logos: 'Mark ye his words? He would not take the crown; / Therefore 'tis certain he was not ambitious' (3.2.113–14), but it is equally clear that his pathos has persuaded them. One of them notes that his 'eyes are red as fire with weeping' (3.2.116), which recalls Thomas Wilson's observation that 'a weeping eye causeth much moisture, and prouoketh teares'.[62] The next line – 'There's not a nobler man in Rome than Antony' (3.2.117) – confirms that Antony's attempt to communicate his ethos has been successful. Compared to Antony, Brutus lacks human warmth. He is not 'void of all sense and common feeling of humanity', but it is only a slight exaggeration to equate Brutus with Erasmus's caricature of the Stoic who 'sets up a stony semblance of a man'.[63] Brutus is emotionally detached when he says 'I pause for a reply' (3.2.33–4), whereas Antony is seemingly overcome with emotion when he utters the corresponding words 'I must pause' (3.2.108). In keeping with his reliance on the pathetic affect, 'Antony employs one of the most distinctive features of Arcadianism: *animation*'.[64] This is exemplified in the way he animates Caesar's wounds as 'dumb mouths' (3.2.218) and imagines Caesar's blood 'rushing out of doors' (3.2.177). In performance, it would be in keeping with their contrasting styles for Brutus to assume statuesque stillness in contrast with a more physically animated Antony.[65] The actor playing Antony might adopt the advice of the Roman rhetorician Quintilian, which was to demonstrate passion by gesticulating with such vigour that the toga falls from the shoulder.[66]

The faculty of 'Arrangement' is exemplified by Antony's opening line; not merely through the organization of the words within it, but also by the careful positioning of the line within Antony's oration as a whole. To pick up on just one aspect, it is notable that Antony's first word associates himself with the citizens as their 'friend' and that a few lines later he associates himself with Caesar in the same terms: 'He was my friend, faithful and just to me' (3.2.86). The effect of the arrangement is to imply a direct association of friendship between the citizens and Caesar that Antony will later express in the phrase 'you all did love him once' (3.2.103). Contrast the poor arrangement of the words in Brutus's opening line and his failure to fit the sentiment of the opening line within the arrangement of his speech as a whole. His error within the first line is to move from the political sphere of 'Romans' to the political sphere of 'countrymen' and then to the intimacy of 'lovers'. Like talk of 'love' on a first date, this is too much too soon. It is a politician's awkward attempt to match the soldier's (Antony's) easy reference to 'friends'. The flaw is even worse when considered within the arrangement of Brutus's speech as a whole. Having announced at the commencement of his speech that the people are his 'lovers', he reveals at its conclusion that he 'slew' his 'best lover'. It is almost as if he has forgotten his use of the word 'lover' in his *exordium*. If he will kill his best lover for the good of Rome, will he not slay his new lovers, the citizens of Rome, on much lesser ground?

The faculty of 'Memory' speaks for itself, for Antony's opening line is among the most memorable in all of Shakespeare's works. It holds the mind through the combined grip of its metre and its many rhetorical features. The faculty of 'Delivery' calls for suitable use of voice, including pace and pitch, and also of the silent pause (the *aposiopesis* or *interruptio*).[67] Gesture, movement and the handling of material stuff also contributes to Delivery or '*actio*'. Indeed, it is the rhetorician's notion of *actio* that eventually gave its name to the theatrical profession of acting.

The faculty of 'Style' is abundant in Antony's opening line. The tricolon of the first three words is one stylistic feature, the syllabic *gradatio* within those words is another, and both features are amplified by the trisyllabic nature of the third word. The assonance of 'en' in the final syllable of 'friends', 'Romans' and 'countrymen' further exploits the 'rule of three'.[68] The overall effect is surreptitious theft of the listener's 'ear' while purporting, by means of the 'lending' metaphor, to merely borrow it. Much more could be said, but perhaps the most obvious stylistic element in Antony's line is the reference to 'ears' itself. This exemplifies metonymy (in that 'ear' represents 'hearing'), but to the extent that it uses a part to represent a whole (*partem pro toto*) it also, as briefly mentioned earlier, has something of synecdoche about it. As the pound of flesh represents Antonio's entire self in *The Merchant of Venice*, so 'ears' betrays the fact that Antony is not really seeking to borrow a part of his audience but is actually seeking to take them whole. It follows that there is also a euphemistic aspect to the phrase 'lend me your ears', for what Antony is really saying is 'listen to me' or even 'give yourselves to me'.

Notice the contrast between Brutus's ill-judged use of the language of love with Antony's skilful arts of persuasion. The word 'persuade' should not be taken to imply the achievement of winning an argument, but should be understood as the art of enhancing speech 'through sweetness' ('per-sweet'). Persuasion and delight are inseparable. As Thomas Wilson describes it, the 'ende of Rhetorique' is 'To teach. To delight.

And to perswade'.[69] Sweetness is the spoonful of sugar that makes the medicine of good teaching go down. Wilson writes that 'to delite is needfull, without the which weightie matters will not be heard at all, and therefore him cunne I thanke, that both can and will ever, mingle sweete among the sower.'[70] Like a master confectioner, Shakespeare combines word, metre, action and the materiality of stage and theatre space in order to sweeten just enough to win hearts. This, rather than to win a logical argument, is his aim. No wonder Francis Meres praised 'mellifluous and honey-tongued Shakespeare' for 'his *Venus and Adonis*, his *Lucrece*, his sugared sonnets'.[71] The art he had honed in his stanzas transferred perfectly to the stage.

In *As You Like It*, Rosalind asks the age-old question: 'can one desire too much of a good thing?' (4.1.113–14) (compare *Ham*, 4.7.115–16). Shakespeare the poet knows, as Shakespeare the rhetorician knows, that when it comes to 'the taste of sweetness', 'a little / More than a little is by much too much' (*1H4*, 3.2.72–3). Thus when occasion called for it, Shakespeare exploited the effects of excess in order that 'surfeiting, / The appetite may sicken' and a sweet thing become 'not so sweet now as it was before' (*TN*, 1.1.2–8). Words are likely to be rejected if their sweetness is detected, thus Caesar rejects 'sweet words, / Low-crooked curtsies and base spaniel fawning' (3.1.42–3). Metullus misses the point when, his entreaty having failed, he asks 'Is there no voice more worthy than my own / To sound more sweetly in great Caesar's ear'? (3.1.49–50). Excess of sweetness is a major reason why Antony's repetition of the word 'honourable' turns the idea from sweet to sickly. Antony utters it eleven times in the forum scene. This excess, which includes the threefold repetition of 'Brutus is an honourable man', turns the sense of Brutus's honour from something that might have started sweet to something unpalatable. Thomas Wilson understood the dangers of excessive repetition when he observed that 'we cannot without refreshing, long abide to heare any one thing'.[72] By the time Antony adds the slight variant: 'sure he is an honourable man' (which casually effaces

Brutus to 'he'),[73] the citizens are already sick of the sentiment. The word 'sure' is really an elliptical question '[*are you*] sure?' The citizens not only reject Brutus's rhetorical claim to 'honour' but they start to doubt the quality of 'honour' itself. This doubt eventually leads them to entertain the hitherto unthinkable possibility that the conspirators 'were traitors: honourable men' (3.2.154). When one of the citizens says this, Antony knows that he has succeeded in throwing down the high status of honour. With high honour discredited (and with it, Brutus), Antony might now succeed in his ultimate aim of encouraging the lowly citizens to identify with the dignity of Caesar's low-laid corpse. Only now does Antony descend to the floor of the forum. He does not descend as of right, but with tactical humility he asks the citizens' permission: 'Shall I descend? And will you give me leave?' (3.2.160).

Antony's rhetorical action of descending is calculated to provoke in the crowd the equal and opposite reaction of rising up.[74] The aim of Antony's rhetoric all along, and of all rhetoric always, is to move others. Michael Mangan suggests that Shakespeare's forum scene is 'apparently static', but can actually be considered 'the most dynamic scene in the play, the one containing the greatest amount of movement'.[75] Mangan rightly locates the main movement 'in the hearts and minds of the listeners, the people of Rome',[76] but we have seen how Antony's gestural movements and his physical descent can also operate to enhance the moving impact of his rhetorical speech. The opening scene of the play provides the first clue to the rhetorical heart of the whole work. The meanest of the playgoers may be mere groundlings down in the playhouse yard, but the first scene of *Julius Caesar* alludes to their capacity to move and rise up. When Marullus berates the on-stage citizens with 'You blocks, you stones, you worse than senseless things! / O you hard hearts, you cruel men of Rome' (1.1.36–7), Shakespeare is here employing a commonplace metaphor of the populace as a stubborn stone which the politician is called upon to move through the power of rhetoric. In his funeral oration, Antony contradicts Marullus when he says to the citizens: 'You are not wood, you are not stones, but men' (3.2.143). Actually, Antony knows as well as Marullus that the people are stubborn blocks, but he knows much better than Marullus how to move them. This is clear when he makes the disingenuous statement: 'were I Brutus, / And Brutus Antony, there were an Antony / Would ruffle up your spirits and put a tongue / In every wound of Caesar that should move / The stones of Rome to rise and mutiny' (3.2.219–23). Daniell associates this with the passage in Luke's gospel that prophesies that stones will be animated in praise of Christ,[77] but the metaphor of stubborn wills being moved through rhetoric to advance the public good was a commonplace of classical and Renaissance thought. For example, in Horace's *Ars Poetica* we read that 'Amphion too, the builder of the Theban wall, was said to give the stones motion with the sound of his lyre, and to lead them – whithersoever he would, by engaging persuasion'.[78]

Horace's oeuvre was a staple of grammar school education in early modern England. Pupils were required to memorize it and mine it for rhetorical instances.[79] In *Titus Andronicus*, Shakespeare makes specific allusion to grammar school study of the *Odes* (4.2.22–4). Perhaps he had also encountered the quoted passage from the *Ars Poetica*. Certainly he was familiar with the myth of Orpheus who, like Amphion, had a supernatural ability to stir stones by the music of his lyre (*TGV*, 3.2.77–9). In *The Merchant of Venice* we are told (by Lorenzo) that 'the poet / Did feign that Orpheus drew trees, stones and floods' (5.1.80). The 'poet' referred to is probably Ovid,[80] but it might be Horace. What is beyond doubt is that Shakespeare was fully conversant with the allegorical sense that art moves stubborn hearts and minds as supernatural music moves stones. It seems equally clear from the depiction of the citizens in *Julius Caesar* that Shakespeare conceived them to be stones susceptible to the moving music of rhetorical speech. Caesar himself, who is likened to a statue or 'colossus' (1.2.135), is the play's only true fixture. Caesar takes pride in it:

I could be well moved if I were as you:
If I could pray to move, prayers would move me.
But I am constant as the northern star,
Of whose true-fixed and resting quality
There is no fellow in the firmament. (3.1.58–62)

Caesar's pride in the fixed and unmoving nature of his will is the pride that precipitates his fall. The conspirators conclude that if the statue of his will cannot be made to move, then his flesh must be made to bleed. When Antony uses Caesar's corpse and Caesar's testament as theatrical props to move the people, the metaphor is clear. Caesar, whose will was immovable in life, still has power to move others in death. Brutus, having inflicted violent force on the great stubborn object that was Caesar and Caesar's will, sets it in motion and cannot stop the motion until it is too late. Even Caesar's ghost, a symbol of Caesar's animated will, is moved to haunt Brutus (the idea of ghost as testator is considered further in Chapter 5). It is only with Brutus's own last breath, and his own last 'will', that he can say 'Caesar, now be still. / I killed not thee with half so good a will' (5.5.51).

Marvin Spevack notes that 'The word "constant" and its inflected forms "constancy" and "constantly" occur more often in *Julius Caesar* (eight times) than in any other work of Shakespeare's' and that '[i]t is also a frequent and crucial word in Plutarch'.[81] It is especially striking that Shakespeare gives it to Caesar three times in quick succession 'in his ironic and hubristic insistence on his "constant" position and attitude just a few lines before he is struck down'.[82] Shakespeare's theme of Roman constancy is partly attributable to the rise of Neostoicism in England in the 1590s, as evidenced by such publications as DuVair's *Moral Philosophie*, mentioned earlier, and Sir John Stradling's 1595 translation of Justus Lipsius's *Two Bookes of Constancie* (1584),[83] but the emphasis on stubborn standing is also attributable to the Elizabethan renaissance of classical rhetoric. In rhetoric, *stasis* denotes a fixed or stubborn truth-claim on which one takes a stand.

Stasis is a highly dynamic and contested state. It only appears to be unmoving because as one side pushes, so the other side pushes back with equal vigour. Hanns Hohmann likens rhetorical stasis to 'a stance taken in a fight' and 'even to civil strife itself'.[84] The civil question between Brutus and Antony epitomizes rhetorical stasis. Shakespeare would have known that the 'foundation' or 'principall point in euery debated matter' was 'called of the Rhetoricians the state, or constitution of the cause'.[85] The idea of the 'state' or 'statement' of the cause at issue in argument goes back to Aristotle.[86] In forensic rhetoric it became 'the State legall'.[87] The rhetorical state of stasis is also akin to the medical state of stasis in which the flow of blood is blocked. When Antony triumphs in the forum scene, the blood flows. The 'st' sound is an ancient, indeed a prehistoric, example of 'sound symbolism'.[88] It is a perfectly efficient physical expression of the very thing it stands for – which is movement coming to a standstill. In the 'st' sound, the swift flow of breath is stopped by tongue on tooth. No single line more clearly encapsulates the static connotations of the 'st' sound than Caesar's 'I am constant as the northern star' (3.1.60). The very next line ('Of whose true-fixed and resting quality') contains three 'st' sounds, two of which are not apparent until the words are spoken. The Proto-Indo-European root **stā-*, which gives us 'statute' and 'statue', also gives us the key words 'constancy', 'stasis', and the related 'stay' and 'stand'. Indeed, *Julius Caesar* can be appreciated as an extended rhetorical exercise of *figura etymologica* on the Latin verb *stare* ('to stand')[89] and on the theme of rhetoric's capacity to move the stones of Roman popular will.

We have noted that Caesar's constancy – the fixed nature of his will and his unmovable spirit – is confirmed by the statue metaphor. In performance the metaphor is in turn confirmed by stage furniture. Marvin Spevack observes that it 'has ... become customary to have a statue of Caesar on stage'.[90] He cites the example of a performance at the Festival d'Automne in Paris, 2001, 'in which Antony's forum speech received visual comments from a bust of Caesar that descended from the flies "upside down"' (befitting the upset state of Rome) and in which the 'small corpse of the emperor' was dramatically contrasted to Antony's references to 'great Caesar'.[91] It might be small, but Caesar's corpse has an iconic, statuesque quality on stage. As Peter Ure observes: 'With a short break, Caesar's corpse is visible on the stage for more than five hundred continuous lines: this is a play whose centre is most exactly a murdered human body.'[92] Michael Vale's set for Gregory Doran's Stratford production (RSC, 2012) incorporated a towering statue of Caesar which uncannily faced away from the audience and thus implied that all the action was taking place not only within Caesar's shadow but also behind his back. It thus had the effect of constituting the audience as complicit participants in the play's secret conspiracies and devices.

When the conspirator Decius Brutus[93] urges Caesar to leave home for the Senate house, Caesar states in the space of a few lines: 'Caesar will not come'; 'The cause is in my will'; 'I will let you know'; 'I will stay at home today' (2.2.68–82). Caesar's stubbornness is reinforced by the static quality of 'stay', a word that belongs to the Proto-Indo-European **stā-* set. 'Stay' appears, with 'stay'd' and 'stays', nineteen times in the play. Without seeking to stand anything weighty on the shaky evidence of word frequency, it may be observed that, with three exceptions (*TS*, *RJ*, *3H6*), nineteen occurrences is not exceeded by any other of Shakespeare's plays, and is exactly the same number as in Shakespeare's other 'statue' play, *The Winter's Tale*. Caesar's own will to stay at home contrasts with Antony's will to move the crowd by means of Caesar's testamentary will. There are twenty-two lines of text from the citizens' first call to hear Caesar's will: 'We'll hear the will. Read it, Mark Antony' (3.2.139) to Antony's 'Shall I descend? And will you give me leave?' (3.2.160). Within those twenty-two lines the word 'will' appears twenty times. This is a remarkably concentrated and sustained repetition of a key conceptual word. That this passage of intense usage culminates in Antony's descent to the forum floor is telling. This physical act purports to acknowledge the popular will and therefore performs, however insincerely, a form of democratic devolution to the people. It has a parliamentary parallel in the 1540 Statute of Wills; a very different act of will, but one that also performed, however reluctantly, a democratic gesture of testamentary descent.

More prosaically, the repetition of the word 'will' serves to heighten the sense of anticipation. It connotes desire, but it also implies a future happening. At the middle of Antony's long list of 'will' references, we find his line 'Will you be patient? Will you stay awhile?' (3.2.150). 'Stay' draws attention to the stasis of this scene. When a citizen demands 'We'll hear the will. Read it, Mark Antony' (3.2.139), Antony stalls. The 'st' sound in his next line enhances the sense of stasis: 'Have patience, gentle friends. I must not read it' (3.2.141). With that line Antony stokes up the citizens' anticipation through the rhetorical device of *paralepsis* (*praeteritio*), which draws attention to a matter by appearing to pass over it. He use the device repeatedly in relation to Caesar's will: 'It is not meet you know how Caesar loved you' (3.2.142); ''Tis good you know not that you are his heirs' (3.2.146). His audience can by now be in no doubt as to the contents of the will, but as yet Antony has not come straight out with it. Instead, as with Caesar's corpse, he keeps the will in plain sight but formally under wraps. The anticipation of revelation and release produces a build-up of tension like dammed blood that is ready to burst forth.[94] This is stasis in the medical sense of the word. Shakespeare subtly associates Antony's rhetoric with the issue of blood even from the moment Antony resolves to deliver the funeral oration:

> Into the market-place. There shall I try
> In my oration how the people take
> The cruel issue of these bloody men. (3.1.292–4)

Mark Van Doran suggested that 'there is as much real blood in "Julius Caesar" as there is in stone'.[95] There is, though, an intense flow of rhetorical blood, pumped along by the beat of Antony's verse. Antony says 'I am no orator' (3.2.210), but the irony of this claim is apparent when he lists the rhetorical skills he lacks and, in the process, demonstrates not only a detailed knowledge of the key elements of the rhetorician's art but great practical skill in using them: 'For I have neither wit, [invention] nor words, [style, logos] nor worth, [ethos] / Action, [gesture] nor utterance, [delivery] nor the power of speech, / To stir men's blood' (3.2.214–16). His speech is calculated to move the standing, static members of the crowd and to 'stir' their blood.[96] To achieve this, he repeats the elements of the sound 'stir' with increasing intensity until eventually uttering the word 'stir' itself so as to strike the conscious mind with the subconscious sense that has been welling up (I call this technique 'fractional inference', see Chapter 2):

> But ye[ster]day the word of Caesar might
> Have [stood again{st the wor}ld. Now lies he there,]
> And none [so poor to do him rever]ence.
> O ma[sters]! If I were disposed to [stir]
> Your hearts and minds to mutiny and rage (3.2.119-123)

Fuzier observes that the final line of this quote contains the palindromic sound sequence r-t-m m-t-r, but what he does not notice is that the fulcrum at the centre of this balanced line is the 'st' sound formed from the end of 'minds' and the beginning of 'to'. The line exemplifies the stasis that is produced by the opposition of equal forces and nothing could be more fitting, not only to the line but also to this pivotal speech and to the theme of the whole play, than that 'st' should stand at the middle of it. When we think so structurally there is always a risk that we will miss the more fluid aspects of Shakespeare's poetic art, so for balance we should note that as the consonants supply the structural staves of the line, so the vowel sounds fill them with music. In modern Received Pronunciation the sequence of vowels is: ore – are – a – ai – oo – ewe – i – ee – a – aay (or to use the English phonetic alphabet: ɔː – ɑː – æ – aɪ – uː – juː – ɪ – iː – æ – eɪ). Of the ten vowel sounds in this sequence, only the 'a' sound in 'and' is repeated. The variation in the vowels enlivens and energizes the structural scheme of the consonants. The secrets of Shakespeare's rhetorical and poetic genius are to be found in countless similar instances. It is as astounding to think that they were produced instinctively as to think that they were produced by craft.

When the purple testament is finally opened, after so much pausing and putting it off, the blood begins its inevitable flow. Antony's repeated 'st' sounds correspond to the repeated use of the same sound in the scene of Caesar's assassination. Caesar's last speech had been on the theme of his constancy, the last lines being 'That I was constant Cimber should be banished / And constant do remain to keep him so' (3.1.72–3). After the stage direction 'They stab Caesar', the 'st' sounds uttered by the conspirators voice the percussion of their blades. Brutus's (inconsistent) statements 'Fly not; stand still;' (3.1.83) and 'Talk not of standing' (3.1.89) frame Metellus's 'Stand fast together, lest …' (3.1.87). There are numerous instances in the lines that follow, including the threefold repetition of 'stoop' (3.1.105–11). Brutus's reference to 'dust' (3.1.116) is especially noteworthy for the hold that dust seems to have had on Shakespeare's dramatic imagination (see Chapters 2, 5 and 6). Julius Caesar and Alexander were paired lives in Plutarch, and in *Hamlet* they are paired in Hamlet's extended discourse on their dust (5.1.193–205), which includes the couplet 'Imperious Caesar, dead and turn'd to clay, / Might stop a hole to keep the wind away' (5.1.202–3). How fitting that dust should end up as a stop. Dust ends with the stopping sound 'st', and we all of us end in dust.

Garry Wills suggests that Antony's descent into the forum mirrors the move from 'head to heart, from mind to will, from scrutiny to action'.[97] Through Antony, Shakespeare is surely calling on the playgoers to be more than passive spectators. They are called to be active participants in the constitution of the play world and in the political world beyond the playhouse walls. Likewise in the assassination scene, 'an audience may well feel that it is not only witnessing but participating in a kind of ceremony'.[98] It is the participation and approval of the witnessing public that perfects the performance and gives it the testamentary power to last 'many ages hence' (3.1.111). The call to the playgoers to assume responsibility as participatory witnesses is repeatedly confirmed in the nature of the on-stage action and speech. Armed with dramatic gestures and physical props, Antony marshals his rhetorical forces to produce a massy, moving press of figures around Caesar's corpse. The release of pressure through mutiny, riot and bloodshed becomes inevitable. We have seen how Shakespeare uses special metrical effects in the 'Friends, Romans, countrymen' speech. We will now see that he employs another quite different metrical effect in the speech beginning 'If you have tears, prepare to shed them now' (3.2.167). Before we consider the metrical evidence, it will be informative to note that the speech follows Antony's descent onto the floor of the forum and is immediately preceded by five tightly packed lines spoken by the citizens and Antony: 'A ring; stand round', 'Stand from the hearse, stand from the body', 'Room for Antony, most noble Antony', 'Nay, press not so upon me; stand far off', 'Stand back; room; bear back' (3.2.161–6). We have already noted how the repetition of 'stand' intensifies the rhetorical stasis of the scene and how this generates dramatic potential through the sense of anticipated movement. This almost physically palpable sense of pressure or dramatic 'urge' is further enhanced by a metrical effect that mirrors the thick throng of figures on the floor of the forum. There are twenty-nine lines in this speech from the first: 'If you have tears, prepare to shed them now', to the last: 'Here is himself, marred as you see with traitors' (3.2.195). Of those lines, the vast majority are in regular ten-syllable pentameter. There are only four lines that are of irregular length and every one of those extends to eleven syllables. (Other lines are contenders to have eleven syllables, but depend for their inclusion on the inelegant trisyllabic pronunication of such words as 'Cassius' and 'envious' which in context are best pronounced disyllabically.) The four hypermetrical lines are as follows:

> You all do know this mantle. I remember
> ...
> For Brutus, as you know, was Caesar's angel.
> Judge, O you gods, how dearly Caesar loved him.
> ...
> Here is himself, marred as you see with traitors. (3.2.168–95)

Three of the four hypermetrical lines contain express reference to the citizens' knowledge, distinctively employed to produce the sense that Antony is calling for the commoners to share with him in bearing witness to the truth: 'you ... know', 'you know', 'you see'. No other line in this section of the speech carries quite this sense of unity in perspective between Antony and the citizens;[99] no other line carries so clear a call for collective scrutiny of the evidence on show. Hypermetrical lines 'pluck at our metrical attention';[100] here they summon the audience to witness and they call for their judgment. It is notable that when a citizen passed judgment on the first passage of Antony's speech, it was done in an eleven-syllable line: 'Therefore 'tis certain he was not ambitious' (3.2.114). As always, 'the additional syllable at the end seems a major element in the line's structure'.[101] The citizen's 'ambitious' line supplies the syllable that was missing from each of Antony's 'ambitious' lines in his funeral oration. It confirms that Antony was successful in putting across his argument on the question of Caesar's ambition.

Taken as a whole, then, Antony's speech has the effect of incorporating Antony, Caesar and the citizens as one body. In similar vein elsewhere, Antony, speaking to the citizens, equates 'the dead ... myself and you' (3.2.127). The line 'Then I, and you, and all of us fell down' (3.2.189) is especially effective in this regard. The expansion and sudden contraction resembles the conceptual and syllabic expansion and collapse of 'Friends, Romans, countrymen, lend me your ears'. Where that line produced the sense of an intimate embrace, this line produces a sense of emotional collapse. Antony's descent also produces community in another way, for in theatrical terms it represents a move to the level of folk or 'popular' drama.[102] To use Weimann's terminology (see Chapter 1), 'Antony moves from locus to platea'.[103] The play began in the stage space of the 'platea' that unites the streets of Rome with the streets of London.[104] Now, at the moment of Antony's descent from the pulpit, he descends to the street level and to the communal ground that Shakespeare has prepared for him. Whereas Brutus is uncomfortable in close proximity to the plebs and seemingly could not wait to quit them (hence his 'Good countrymen, let me depart alone' [3.2.56]), Antony gives the appearance of being much more at home in the press of the common people of Rome.

Now that the dust has settled on the rhetoric and the riot, we can allow ourselves to join the playgoers in reflecting on the scene as objective bystanders. The black cloth hanging as a curtain from the stage to the playhouse floor confirms that we are witnessing a tragic drama,[105] but as we join the groundlings in pressing up against the stage and its deathly drape, we are left puzzling this profound question of the play: 'whose tragedy is it?' The title of the play, *The Tragedy of Julius Caesar*, states the obvious answer, but all states in the play, especially those relating to the person of Caesar, are contestable and moveable. The title, like the title of *The Merchant of Venice*, might be a tease: 'Which is the merchant here, and which the Jew?' (4.1.170). If this really is the tragedy of Caesar, we are bound to ponder the nature of his tragic flaw. Brutus claims it was 'ambition', but we have seen that Brutus's claim suffers some serious rhetorical opposition. The more plausible candidate flaw is that Caesar was excessively stubborn. For a rhetorical poet like Shakespeare, whose drama relies upon his art to move, stubbornness must seem a chief vice. Shakespeare was also a philosopher of practical reasonableness in the Aristotelian mode. He understood, as contemporary lawyers understood, that will without flexibility must be opposed as one must oppose law without equity.[106] On this view, Caesar's tragic flaw is the same that makes *The Merchant of Venice* the tragedy of Shylock. However rational his justification for stubbornness (for Shylock, the chief justification was the rule of law), Caesar's fault (as Shylock's) was to take hubristic pride in the security of his cause and in his personal immovability. The justice of equitable moderation, or practical reasonableness, demanded that Caesar be (re)moved precisely because he set such store by his stubborn constancy and – to borrow an apt phrase – his 'inflexible will'.[107] The art of equitable moderation is akin to the art of rhetoric, which, according to Wilson, calls for the quality of 'movyng pitie, and stirring men to mercie'.[108] A marginal gloss in North's Plutarch praises the 'wonderful constancy of Brutus in matters of justice and equity',[109] but Shakespeare prefers to set the Stoic constancy of Brutus against the wilful constancy of Caesar. Antony, the Lupercalian runner, contributes a dramatic urgency throughout the course of the play and he moves passions, but he stirs the people to riot and not to mercy. He brings no equity to moderate the strict constancy of Caesar or Brutus. We must look to the playgoers, performing as witnesses and jury, to supply the moderating equity.

The play can perhaps be thought of as the tragedy of Brutus. Brutus's last stand is predicted in the encounter that brings the forces of Cassius and Brutus to a state of impasse:

CASSIUS
Stand ho.
BRUTUS
Stand ho. Speak the word along.
FIRST SOLDIER
Stand.
SECOND SOLDIER
Stand.
THIRD SOLDIER
Stand. (4.2.32–6)

In the immediate aftermath of the assassination of Caesar, Brutus uses the word 'stand' in reference to death in a way that is significant: 'That we shall die we know; 'tis but the time / And drawing days out, that men stand upon' (3.1.99–100). What makes it so significant is that it anticipates Brutus's own death and the words of Antony: 'This was the noblest Roman of them all: / … / His life was gentle, and the elements / So mixed in him that nature might stand up / And say to all the world, "This was a man!"' (5.5.69–76). The exact phrase 'stand up' appears in only one other place in the play, and it is Brutus who uses it: 'We all stand up against the spirit of Caesar, / And in the spirit of men there is no blood' (2.1.166–7). This bloodless line exemplifies stasis. The reference to stand and to the lack of blood in Caesar's spirit evoke an unnatural, even statue-like, absence of movement in the physical state of the man and in the state of the body politic. The line is naturally followed by the flow of 'Caesar must bleed' (2.1.170). When that resolution is enacted by Caesar's assassination, stasis momentarily turns to catharsis and even the statue 'all the while ran blood' (3.2.187), as Calpurnia's dream had forewarned.

In Shakespeare's account, Brutus runs himself through on his own sword. North's Plutarch gives two versions, one in which Brutus holds the sword and one in which Strato holds the sword. Shakespeare, in adopting the latter account, omits North's description of Strato as one with whom Brutus 'came first acquainted by the study of rhetoric'.[110] He does something better. Through the entire course of the play he depicts a Brutus who is impaled on the point of his own rhetoric. In the forum scene, Brutus wounds his own cause with condescending patrician rhetoric and Antony deals the deathblow by a sort of congregational rhetoric that properly belonged to Brutus. There is, then, a (presumably unintended) mirroring of North's 'double' account of Brutus's death: Brutus is impaled on the blade of his own rhetoric held both in his own hands and in the hands of another. Shakespeare's Brutus is a student of rhetoric, a Stoic and an actor (witness Brutus's direction to his fellow conspirators that they should disguise their intentions and 'bear it as our Roman actors do with ... formal constancy' [2.1.225–6]). All things considered, he seems too cold and calculating a character to have the heroism necessary to make him the intended tragic subject of this play. Mark Antony has a claim to be the hero of the play, but in *Julius Caesar* his trajectory is in no plausible sense 'tragic' (contrast his fall in *Antony and Cleopatra*).

The most plausible possibility is that *Julius Caesar* is the tragedy of Rome itself. As Jennifer Richards writes, Antony's rhetorical 'success represents the beginning of the end for the republic';[111] 'Antony wins, but Rome loses'.[112] Ironically it all starts to go downhill for the republic following Antony's descent into the forum – that most potent physical gesture of condescension to the people. Perhaps it was only ever a shallow showman's gesture. For all his rhetorical sweetness, Mark Antony does not truly seek to replace traditional hierarchy with popular will. A wise witness can see this truth hidden in Antony's words. The Antony who predicts that the people, having heard of their legacy under Caesar's testament, will 'dying, mention it within their wills, / Bequeathing it as a rich legacy / Unto their issue' and 'dip their napkins in his sacred blood' (3.2.134–8) is, in early modern terms, a man who, despite talk of wills and pretension to congregational Protestantism, is harking back to hierarchical traditions of dynastic inheritance and Roman Catholic hagiography. The success of Antony's rhetoric is that it captured the will of the Roman people. Its tragic failure is that the will of the people was never free.

5

'His will is not his own': Hamlet downcast and the problem of performance

Hamlet invites playgoers to appreciate performance and to look through it. The question in the opening line ('Who's there?') and the demand in the second line ('unfold yourself') can be delivered as a direct challenge to the audience.[1] In most modern theatres, where the audience literally sits in the dark, pitching this challenge to the shadows adds another depth of meaning. The invitation to the individual playgoer, which is sustained throughout the entire play, is an invitation to ponder their own identity and the forms in which they perform themselves on the social stage. When the ghost addresses Hamlet with 'lend thy serious hearing / To what I shall unfold' (1.5.5–6), it reminds the playgoers of the challenge charged to them by the opening lines. That Shakespeare is here speaking directly to the hearers in his audience is evident from Hamlet's response: 'Ay, thou poor ghost, whiles memory holds a seat / In this distracted globe. Remember thee?' (1.5.96–7). Gurr and Ichikawa suggest that a suitable gesture for Hamlet at this point would be for him to hold his head ('globe') in his hands.[2] As well as punning on the skull-as-globe,[3] the line seeks to include the playgoer who 'holds a seat' in the Globe theatre.[4] Throughout *Hamlet*, the playgoers' every sense is engaged to witness and judge Hamlet, but also to witness and judge with him. They see what he sees; and the evidence is not merely seen, but weighed and heard. The physicality of the playhouse and the material stuff of the stage action convey the weight and feel of the matter to be assessed, and Shakespeare's 'Words, words, words' (2.2.189) call throughout for a fair hearing. In what sense this is a 'legal' hearing, we will discover before the end.

Hamlet plays out within the full scope of the 'distracted globe' – joining the materiality of the skull to the shell of the theatrical space and to the minds within. My interpretation of *Hamlet* is sympathetic to critics who see in the play 'a purposeful combination of materiality and metaphysics',[5] and likewise a plausible combination of the 'material' and the 'supernatural'.[6] J. K. Harmer notes how the play establishes from the outset a 'structural isomorphism' between, on the one side, such external stuff as ghosts and, on the other side, 'mental objects on the inside – the stuff of introspective reflection'.[7] I take a broadly compatible approach, but I argue that Hamlet's introspection is not merely a looking into himself and into the core nature of human being, but specifically a looking down to fundamentals, root causes and base matter. It is the downcast nature of Hamlet's gaze – as much 'subspective' as 'introspective' – that connects his mind to matter. It leads him to such physically material, and yet metaphysical, conclusions as his statement that man is a 'quintessence of dust' (2.2.274). Harmer's observation that Hamlet (and by extension *Hamlet*) represents 'mental objects and mental voices ... as at bottom the same kind of thing as words and meanings and objects in the world'[8] is apt; the words 'at bottom' especially so. It points us to the mastery of metaphor that is the foundation of Shakespeare's art, wherein 'the Poet's eye ... Doth glance / From heaven to earth, from earth to heaven' (*MND*, 5.1.12–13). The downward pull of metaphysical matters and basic physical material plays out on stage like a force of gravity. We witness its effects in such signs as Hamlet's dishevelled dress – even the falling down of his socks (2.1.77). Hamlet might physically crumple to the ground on the phrase 'sinews, grow not instant old / But bear me swiftly up' (1.5.94–5) and on the phrase 'What should such fellows as I do crawling between earth and heaven?' (3.1.126–7).[9]

Hamlet's immediate response to his father's ghost is a material response. Speaking in terms of the practice of inscription or engraving, he resolves to 'wipe away ... all forms, all pressures past' (1.5.99–100). There are, though, at least two problems with his method for discharging that resolution. The first is that forms fascinate him even as he should be seeing through them. One example is the form of his father's ghost.[10] Horatio warns that the ghost might 'assume some other horrible form' (1.4.72), but Hamlet accepts the apparition at face value, taking 'the Ghost's word for a thousand pound' (3.2.278–9). Faces are a surface form that especially fascinate Hamlet. He dwells on the detail of faces numerous times throughout the play. He asks about the face of the ghost; derides Gertrude's false face; rivets his eyes to the face of Claudius (or purports to); reads an essay on the face of Polonius; notes the player's beard; and 'falls to such perusal' of Ophelia's face 'As 'a would draw it' (2.1.87–8). Students of the play can perhaps relate to Hamlet's preoccupation with surfaces, for as we attempt to look through the window of the performance we find that the theatricality of the play is 'etched in the glass itself' and cannot easily be wiped away.[11] The glass of the window of the performance is not transparent. It is more like Hamlet's 'mirror up to Nature' (3.2.22) in which we see reflected whatever facet of our own nature we bring to it. Our best hope of seeing the mind of the poet at work in the depths of the play is to approach the play in the nature of a poet, for '[a]s the eyes of Lyncaeus were said to see through the earth, so the poet turns the world to glass'.[12] If the first problem in Hamlet's method is that he focuses on surface forms instead of looking through them or wiping them away, the second and related problem is that his critique of surface forms leads him to keep them in mind even as he lifts them up to look under them. Thus Hamlet delves down, unfolding form after form in search of meaning, until ultimately unable or unwilling to discard the forms, he buries himself under the collective weight of what he unfolds. According to Gertrude, death involves 'Passing through nature to eternity' (1.2.73), but Hamlet embarks on an impossible attempt to find a way through human nature even as he lives. Poignantly, the play's only other usage of the word 'wipe' is Gertrude's 'Come, let me wipe thy face' (5.2.277), as she tends to her son for the last time. The tender gesture recalls care for an infant even as it prepares her son's body for the grave. To wipe away 'pressures past' – Hamlet's metaphor of erased writing or effaced engraving – stands for the wiping of the marks of memory, but far from removing mental impressions, the effect of Hamlet's inquisitive and philosophical delving is to pile the psychological pressure on. He engraves himself and he prepares himself for the grave. To put it prosaically, Hamlet thinks too deeply. He perceived that the ghost had prompted 'thoughts beyond the reaches of our souls' (1.4.56), but he nevertheless went in search of them.

How each of us delves *Hamlet*, and how deeply we delve, varies from spectator to spectator, student to student.[13] There are fashions in *Hamlet* scholarship and these forms must also be looked through and suspected if we are to achieve understanding. *Hamlet* is suitable for poetic, theatrical and scholarly appreciation, but it cannot be contained within the confines of any single theory. *Hamlet* is undeniably and unfathomably deep, but its 'depth' is not quantifiable as if it were a static dimension of the play. Its depth is a dynamic incident of the complexity of textual and performative interpretation. The dynamism flows from the fact that it is impossible to '*stand* and unfold yourself'. There is something inherently unstable in relations between 'forms of self', and especially between 'artificial' or 'nurtured' self and so-called 'natural' self, that makes it impossible to identify our identities with precision or to isolate the exact motives for our actions. Hamlet knows it – he ponders how man is 'infinite in faculties, in form and moving', in 'action' and 'beauty' (2.2.270–3) – but no sooner has he acknowledged this than he looks down again to the 'quintessence of dust' (2.2.274) that expresses humanity at its most materially basic.[14]

As the ghost encouraged Hamlet to seek the underlying sense of things, so too in a different way does Claudius. Claudius directs Hamlet to his ancestral roots when he reminds him that his 'father lost a father' and 'That father lost lost his' (1.2.89–90). He cautions Hamlet to play the 'survivor bound / In filial obligation' only 'for some term' (1.2.90–1), but Hamlet does not, and perhaps cannot, stop his downward search into the roots of his being. He searches beyond his human origins into such stuff as earth that lies at the very bottom of the 'chain of being' in the Elizabethan world picture.[15] Claudius, in contrast, is determined to rise. Even as he kneels in prayerful confession, his resolute 'Then I'll look up' (3.3.50) confirms a wilful refusal to be downcast. Hamlet delves down for truth, even if it be (in Polonius's phrase) 'hid indeed / Within the centre' of the earth (2.2.155–6).[16] Claudius looks to heaven, believing that in contrast with forms of justice below, 'above … the action lies / In his true nature' (3.3.60–2). Claudius's problem, try as he might to look up, is that he is continually dragged back down to the base level of his sin: 'My words fly up, my thoughts remain below' (3.3.97). His reference to his 'limed soul' becoming 'more engaged' by the very process of 'struggling to be free' (3.3.68–9) is a reference to a type of bird trap and therefore tells us that even in the midst of his adhering sin, he believes himself to be a bird destined to soar.[17] *Hamlet* contains a great deal of avian imagery, but it is Claudius's faction (or 'bevy' [5.2.166], to use the First Folio's avian term) that is most consistently likened to birds. Claudius is a peacock (3.2.276) and Osric, the 'lapwing' (5.2.165) whose name is rendered 'Ostric' (ostrich) in Q2, wears a fashionable round-topped hat that Hamlet calls an 'eggshell' (4.4.52, 5.2.165) and which might have had an ostrich feather flying from it.[18] Rosencrantz and Guildenstern's deceit will 'moult no feather' (2.2.261). It was an Elizabethan commonplace to associate feathers with false and vainglorious form, and Shakespeare had received the insult personally in a 1592 pamphlet that alluded to him as 'an upstart Crow, beautified with our feathers'.[19] Claudius was mistaken when he attributed his own avian attributes to Hamlet ('There's something in his soul / O'er which his melancholy sits on brood' [3.1.163–4]). The sense was right, but the image was wrong. Hamlet is a burrower, not a bird. He does not struggle to fly up, but labours to dig down. He would 'rather bear ... / Than fly' (3.1.80–1). Claudius has the classic flaw of reaching too high and, like Icarus, falls because of his desire to attain the sun.[20] In the character of Hamlet, who from the very outset thinks himself 'too much in the "son"' (1.2.67), Shakespeare invents the quite opposite tragic flaw of reaching too far down.

'Don't look down' is advice that is offered to Hamlet in a variety of ways at the outset of the play, although never expressly in those words. The notion of 'looking down' is ambiguous. It can mean that Hamlet appears to be downcast but also that he peers down. Both senses – the watched and the watching – apply to Hamlet. He is, in Ophelia's phrase, 'Th'observed of all observers, quite, quite down' (3.1.153). Hamlet's mother is the first to advise him not to look down, and she advises him in both aspects: his appearing and his peering. Opposing his dejected appearance, she urges 'cast thy nighted colour off' (1.2.68). Opposing the downward focus of his gaze, she counsels 'let thine eye look like a friend on Denmark. / Do not for ever with thy vailed lids / Seek for thy noble father in the dust' (1.2.69–71). In performance at this point we expect to see Hamlet's physical aspect downcast. As events transpire, the queen's advice to look up is undermined by the ghost of Hamlet's father speaking from the 'cellarage' below the stage (1.5.151). Hamlet's gaze, which was already down in the dust before the ghost appeared, is captured by the spectre and enticed even deeper down by the ghost's descent through the trapdoor.[21] The sequence of Hamlet's 'obsequious sorrow' (1.2.92) for his father is to follow him into the ground. When Polonius asks 'Will you walk out of the air, my lord?' Hamlet's reply is instinctively downcast: 'Into my grave.' (2.2.203–4). Hamlet's regard for grave matter proves prescient, and one can detect another clue to Hamlet's fate in the repetition of the obituary 'ob' sound in Claudius's 'obligation', 'obsequious', 'obstinate' and 'Of ... stubbornness' (1.2.91–4). Horatio speaks prophetically when he warns Hamlet that to follow the unreliable form of the ghost might cause him to fall into 'madness' and death (1.4.69–78). He anticipates that the mere act of looking down from the 'dreadful summit of the cliff' (1.4.70) might precipitate a fatal fall: 'The very place puts toys of desperation / Without more motive into every brain / That looks so many fathoms to the sea' (4.1.75–7).

Despite the warning, Hamlet looks down. He does so constantly and in a variety of ways. His instinct when he first hears of the ghost is to ask 'What looked he – frowningly?' (1.2.229), and right away he talks of 'hell' and of foul deeds rising from below (1.2.255). (The cellarage under the stage was 'the traditional theatrical location of hell'.)[22] This indicates that his 'prophetic soul' (1.5.40) had subconsciously suspected foul play before the ghost confirmed it. When Hamlet accuses Rosencrantz and Guildenstern of attempting to pluck 'the heart' of his 'mystery', he conceives the mystery in terms of something deep down within him: he calls their effort an attempt to 'sound me from my lowest note' (3.2.358). His downward gaze is frequently confirmed in the smallest material details, as when he employs the height of a shoe ('altitude of a chopine' [2.2.364]) to note that one of the travelling players has grown taller. When Claudius's agent Guildenstern (seemingly sharing his master's disposition to look up), says he is happy to be 'On fortune's cap' even though he is 'not the very button', Hamlet responds 'Nor the soles of her shoe' (2.2.224–5). Even in his opening scene, Hamlet fixes on the foot when he measures the passage of time by the age of his mother's shoes (1.2.147–8). Hamlet's connection between the base physical sole of the shoe and the most basic metaphysical essence of the soul is gritty with a sense of quintessential dust beneath it. Another sense in which Hamlet 'looks down' is his looking disapprovingly on Claudius's courtiers when they follow customary forms of drunken revelry. Describing them as 'soil' that take from 'achievements ... performed at height' (1.4.20–1), he focuses his disapproving gaze firmly downwards, as he does again in his sardonic promise to Horatio: 'We'll teach you to drink deep ere you depart' (1.2.174).[23] The spatial dimension of Hamlet's downward gaze is appropriately amplified by having him look down on the court from a physically elevated part of the stage structure, as occurred in the castle setting of Franco Zeffirelli's film (Warner Bros, 1990), in which Mel Gibson's Hamlet spies on the court from a gangway high above the hall.

Why does Hamlet look down? It is inevitable that the social elevation of a royal prince (and the prince's physical elevation on such fixtures as a dais or high table) would engender a downward gaze, but with Hamlet it goes much further than this. Before we pry into his psyche, it must be acknowledged that some critics object to this kind of inquiry on the ground that it attributes unwarranted reality to a fictional character. Such critics caution us not to confuse the reality of Hamlet with, say, the reality of Queen Elizabeth I. In response to that, one is bound to acknowledge that Hamlet and Queen Elizabeth belong to different orders of reality, but it is difficult to say which is the more real. Speaking personally, I have been more moved by Hamlet than by Queen Elizabeth and I have seen more Hamlets in the flesh than I have seen Queen Elizabeths in the flesh. If I had ever acted Hamlet I could say that I had been Hamlet, and that my Hamlet was as real to me as any Hamlet could be, and for that matter a good deal more real to me than any Elizabeth could be. In the world of performance, Hamlet is no less real than any of us; indeed, to the extent that Hamlet is the product of stage poetry, he is almost perfectly real in the world of performance, and certainly no less real than we are in our own performative worlds. A practical compromise might be to say that when we question Hamlet's psychology (even so far as to wonder if his melancholia would nowadays be diagnosed as medical depression), we are really using his case to question our own psychology and that of other real humans.

The simplest explanation for Hamlet's looking down is that the strange circumstances of his family and the royal court – what Horatio calls the 'very place' – have cast him down. Laertes recognizes that Hamlet's 'particular act and place' constrain his capacity to act (to 'give his saying deed' [1.3.24–5]). This, one imagines, might be enough to depress Hamlet and make him downcast. More subtle than mere weight of local circumstance is the possibility that his own intellectual curiosity has cast him down in the way it killed Hamlet's 'famous ape' (the one that freed birds from a rooftop and, climbing into their empty basket to 'try conclusions', fell and broke its 'own neck down' [3.4.192–4]). Curiosity in apes is one thing; in such a sophisticated mind as Hamlet's (supplied as it is by Shakespeare) it can turn into the sort of profound philosophical inquiry that might contribute to mental breakdown.[24] The best explanation for Hamlet's looking down (one not unrelated to the possibility of natural curiosity) may be 'habit', which he calls 'That monster Custom' (3.4.159).[25]

The notion that behaviour habituates nature was a feature of the early modern renaissance of Aristotelian thought. *The Nicomachean Ethics* informs us that 'moral virtue comes about as a result of habit' and 'that none of the moral virtues arises in us by nature'.[26] Erasmus distilled Aristotle's idea into the adage 'use is another nature',[27] which Shakespeare expresses in Hamlet's commonplace observation that 'use almost can change the stamp of nature' (3.4.166). It is on the basis of this that Hamlet advises his mother to 'Assume a virtue' so that the habit 'of actions fair and good' will 'put on' a new 'frock or livery' (3.4.158–63) (compare *TGV*, 5.4.1), but it is never clear that Hamlet is truly convinced by Aristotle's psychological theory. He hopes that performance practised might produce a new form perfected, but he suspects that repetitive practice might only produce callousness. This suspicion leads Hamlet to wonder if 'damned custom' has 'brazed' his mother with an external armour that is 'proof and bulwark against sense' (3.4.35–6). It may be implied that she has been brazed by her customary 'blush' (3.4.39; compare *KL*, 1.1.9–10). Even Ophelia is wounded by Hamlet's assault on blushers: 'I have heard of your paintings well enough. God hath given you one face and you make yourselves another' (3.1.141–3). The gravedigger is spared this rebuke. Hamlet attributes the gravedigger's callous handling of the matter of death to the simple fact of his familiarity with the work.[28] We can perhaps hear the son of the glove-maker speaking in the line 'The hand of little employment hath the daintier sense' (5.1.65–6). The notion that mode of life can remodel one's nature had its material counterpart in the belief that clothes make the man,[29] which was a classical idea revived in another adage of Erasmus: '*vestis virum facit*'.[30] According to Erasmus's adage, the adoption of a new external habit may reform the inner self.[31] This assumes that the 'inward habit of virtue is first materialized through the out-ward habit of robes and gloves',[32] but if habit can reform, it can also deform. This is the essence of Hamlet's suspicion of the cosmetic performances by which women make up their faces (3.1.110–12).

If it is not Hamlet's circumstances that make Denmark a 'prison' of deep 'dungeons', it may be that his habitually downcast 'thinking makes it so' (2.2.240–50).[33] The question is whether he is capable of thinking any other way. Richard Lovelace claimed that 'Stone Walls do not a Prison make, / Nor Iron bars a Cage; / Minds innocent and quiet take / That for an Hermitage',[34] but Hamlet's mind is not quiet and perhaps it is not innocent. If Hamlet seems less than convinced by Aristotelian belief in the reforming potential of human habit, it may be in part because he lacks the capacity to perform the practices that engender habit. His dejected behaviour seems rather to support 'the Augustinian-Protestant theory of the ineradicability of vicious habits (*consuetudines*)'.[35] In other words, it could be that Hamlet is downcast by a sort of addiction or compulsion. When the ghost sinks back down to its pit, Hamlet seems all too ready to sink with it. He makes an apostrophe to 'heaven' and momentarily resolves to rid his mind of 'baser matter' (1.5.104), but his almost immediate 'Meet it is I set it down' (1.5.107) betrays a compulsive return to the downward habit of his gaze. Granville-Barker argues that Hamlet surrenders himself to the ghost with the simple phrase 'I will',[36] but if he has a will to rise up in revenge, it is soon recaptured by his downcast compulsion. Not even a bracing sea journey to England can break his habit. On his return to Denmark, he shows an unhealthy fascination with graves and skulls and the basic matter of human being: 'To what base uses we may return, Horatio! Why may not imagination trace the noble dust of Alexander till 'a find it stopping a bung-hole?' (5.1.192–4). Again, Horatio warns him against excessive investigation: ''Twere to consider too curiously to consider so' (5.1.195), but Hamlet again ignores the advice and indulgently insists upon his deep inquiries (5.1.196–205). Paul A. Cefalu observes that 'Hamlet imagines persons to be constituted by behavior, custom, and dispositional states all the way down', which he attributes to the fact that Hamlet 'reifies and objectifies habits'.[37] Hamlet may be less like Aristotle's human who sets himself on the road to ethical improvement than he is like Aristotle's 'stone which by nature moves downwards' and 'cannot be habituated to move upwards, not even if one tries to train it by throwing it up ten thousand times'.[38] From such inanimate examples as stones, Aristotle concludes that 'nothing that exists by nature can form a habit contrary to its nature'.[39] *Hamlet* plays with the possibility that the nature of human being might be as intractable (as resistant to change through its own will and power) as an inanimate thing – even a thing like Yorick's skull.

Hamlet looking at the object of Yorick's skull is Hamlet contemplating himself as an object. Even as Hamlet lifts up the skull, he calls it 'chapfallen' (5.1.182) and thereby reveals that his thoughts are down even as the skull is up.[40] Hamlet's downcast aspect is inseparable from the general downward trajectory of the physical and metaphysical play world in which he lives. Hamlet cannot resist the world of *Hamlet* and *Hamlet* cannot resist the demands of the tragic genre. Hamlet's tragedy is not the Greek tragedy of one who rebels against the moral order, but the Christian tragedy of one who, conscious of the fallen nature of his 'too too solid flesh' (1.2.129) and being powerless to resist its downward pull to death, nevertheless achieves an ultimate triumph over the grave.[41] (The reader will note that I prefer the First Folio's 'solid' to the 'sullied' or 'sallied' of Q2, but all three alternatives – the human body conceived to be a solid burden or tainted by sin or something subject to attack – make essentially the same theological point about the fallen state of the flesh.)[42] Hamlet is burdened not by flesh alone, but also by the world (the Herculean burden of the 'Globe' is considered below), and by the devil. In his *De Servo Arbitrio* ('On The Bondage of the Will'), Luther asserts that the soul: 'has no 'Freewill,' but is a captive, slave, and servant, either to the will of God, or to the will of Satan'.[43] Thus when Claudius says that Hamlet's behaviour 'shows a will most incorrect to heaven' (1.2.95), he alerts us to a question which would have been of theological concern to the play's original playgoers: is Hamlet's downcast habit deliberately wilful or is it an inevitable feature of his human nature? Is it the case that 'Our wills and fates do … contrary run' (3.2.205) and that 'There's a divinity that shapes our ends, / Rough-hew them how we will' (5.2.10–11)?[44]

The question of will and fate (already discussed in Chapter 4) is about as deep and complex as one can imagine any question to be, for we cannot assume that natural acts and deliberate acts are necessarily distinct, even though jurists and moral philosophers frequently rely on such distinctions when they talk of 'responsibility' and 'fault'.[45] The possibility that nature produces our will and that our will produces habitual practices that in turn produce a new nature (a nature 'manner born' [1.4.15]) opens up an endless cycle of cause and effect. Rather than follow Hamlet along this perpetual path of philosophical inquiry we might content ourselves with an appreciation of the puzzle in all its defiant, unresolved complexity. There is no better first step to such an appreciation than to consider Shakespeare's own poetic ruminations expressed through Hamlet throughout the play. On the profound and vexed questions of fault and nature, habit and will, we will do well to attend to the following sentence, in which subclause after subclause delves down through layer upon layer of human forms and performances, to the very roots of character:

> So oft it chances in particular men
> That, for some vicious mole of nature in them,
> As in their birth wherein they are not guilty
> (Since nature cannot choose his origin),
> By the o'ergrowth of some complexion
> Oft breaking down the pales and forts of reason,
> Or by some habit that too much o'erleavens
> The form of plausive manners – that these men,
> Carrying, I say, the stamp of one defect
> (Being Nature's livery or Fortune's star),
> His virtues else, be they as pure as grace,
> As infinite as man may undergo,
> Shall in the general censure take corruption
> From that particular fault. (1.4.23–36)[46]

As a royal prince, there is a distinctive sense in which Hamlet is 'subject to his birth' (1.3.18) (a phrase found in the First Folio, but not in Q2),[47] but so, in a different degree, are we all. We relate to Hamlet because he is alike to us in being born to endure 'the thousand natural shocks / That flesh is heir to' (3.1.61–2). We sense that, for good or ill, nature stamps all of us with her livery from birth, but we sense equally that 'use' or 'habit' might re-dress us and 'almost can change the stamp of nature' (3.4.166). Some faults are 'hereditary', some 'purchased' (*AC*, 1.4.13–14). Hamlet's 'mole of nature' is an intellectual curiosity and habit of subspection that feeds and is fed by a philosophical and existential need to burrow down to the roots of his character. Our miner sets himself the impossible task of undermining his own mine, which is to say that he tries to understand the nature of his own mind with no tool but his own mind to do it. It is in this vein that Claudius attributes 'Hamlet's transformation' (the fact that neither 'th'exterior nor the inward man / Resembles that it was') to his state of being put 'from th'understanding of himself' (2.2.5–9). Looking back on his supposed 'madness' (5.2.210), Hamlet attributes it to 'Hamlet from himself' being 'ta'en away' (5.2.212). Hamlet's undermining of his own nature inevitably splits self from self. When his delving throws up outward signs in the form of surface eruptions they are not superficial, but, like molehills and birthmarks ('moles'), they are indicators of deep disruption.

This brings us back to the key question, which is to know if Hamlet looks down because it is his will to delve. This key unlocks the most profound question of all, which is to know whether the thing we call our will – even our free will – is really ours at all. Remove our inherited nature and the social nurture from our make-up and what will be left to show that our will is distinctively, exclusively and personally *ours*? All who witness a performance of *Hamlet* can ask this question of themselves as deeply as they like and they will find no satisfactory answer. In the case of Hamlet, Shakespeare poses the question as a statement: Laertes's observation that Hamlet's 'will is not his own' (1.3.17). We are bound to ask if Laertes is right. The most famous question of the play – 'to be, or not to be' – is both a question about 'self-slaughter' (1.2.132) and a question about the state of being,[48] but in both aspects it most 'puzzles the will' (3.1.79) not because it presents a choice that we are in any real sense free to make, but because it questions our very capacity for free choice. Will does not ponder the puzzle; will is the puzzle pondered. It follows from this that a meaningful way to appreciate the character of Hamlet is to consider not merely if his downcast melancholia and subspection is his choice, but also to ask whether his choice was free or an inescapable feature of his nature; in other words, to ask not only if his fault is his will, but whether his will is his fault. Hamlet may be said to incriminate himself when he opines that 'sense' reserves 'some quantity of choice' even in 'madness' and 'ecstasy' (3.4.70–3), but even if he is right, we still do not know what 'quantity of choice' equates to fault.

Hamlet is profound, but it is also playful. Indeed, *Hamlet* is profound in large part because it is play wrapped in play wrapped in play. The inventive layering of forms in *Hamlet* – even if they are taken to be a series of superficialities – creates profundity. From the 'Who's there?' of the first line to the 'shows much amiss' of the penultimate line, *Hamlet* plays with notions of form and performance. The best proof of this is the 'advice scene' (3.2.1–43) in which Hamlet advises the travelling players on the arts of theatrical performance. It is one of the most entertaining scenes of the play and, with the possible exception of the graveyard scene, its most playful. As the most consciously performative scene in Shakespeare's most profound play on the nature of performance, it is the most important guide in Shakespeare's entire oeuvre to appreciating the arts of performance. One might, with a suitable note of caution, even hear in Hamlet's words something of Shakespeare's own opinions on the art of theatrical acting. It is on that assumption that John Barton commences his *Playing Shakespeare* with a call to return to Hamlet's advice to the players.[49] The advice includes the passage that is a constant refrain of the present book:

> Suit the action to the word, the word to the action … the purpose of playing whose end, both at the first and now, was and is to hold as 'twere the mirror up to Nature to show Virtue her feature, Scorn her own image, and the very age and body of the time his form and pressure. (3.2.17–24)[50]

Scene 3.2, which contains the advice to the players, the players' dumbshow and their abortive performance of 'The Mousetrap' (otherwise known as 'The Murder of Gonzago'), is structurally the central scene of *Hamlet*. This demonstrates the centrality of acting as a concern of the play.[51] Shakespeare uses the scene, as he had used the central scene of *Julius Caesar*, to constitute an on-stage audience and by that device to draw in the playgoers to witness and to judge upon the 'argument' (3.2.132) or 'necessary question' (3.2.40) of the play. The fact that the leading players performing *Hamlet* in the Globe had so recently played *Julius Caesar* in the same theatre would have enhanced a sense of playful participation in players and playgoers alike.[52] When Polonius says 'I did enact Julius Caesar. I was killed i' th' Capitol. Brutus killed me' (3.2.99–100), it might be a metatheatrical nod to the fact that the actor playing Polonius had previously played Julius Caesar.[53] If so, it is reasonable to speculate that Richard Burbage – the actor playing Hamlet – had previously played the part of Brutus.

One effect of the advice scene is to make the playgoers aware of the very forms of performance that the illusion of theatre normally pretends to conceal. This effect is called in varying contexts 'metatheatrical' or 'alienating' or a means of 'breaking down the fourth wall'. Alerting the playgoers to the arts of performance can lead to a deeper appreciation of those arts and to a deeper inquiry into the meaning of the play. If the 'purpose of playing' is 'to hold as 'twere the mirror up to Nature' (3.2.20–2), it is also to let the playgoer see the frame of the mirror; in other words, to urge the playgoer to appreciate the arts by which nature is performed in the playhouse. Perhaps Shakespeare even invites the playgoers to see his hand holding the mirror up. We are used to focusing on the glass of the mirror, but when our attention is diverted to the frame, the familiar object seems strange to us. This is what Bertolt Brecht termed the *Verfremdungseffekt* (usually translated 'alienation effect').[54] Whether or not we are invited to see the actor behind Hamlet will depend upon the choices made by the actor and director in the particular production, but in general terms the playgoers are certainly invited to see Elsinore as a stage on which the characters are all acting. Thus Hamlet is 'essentially ... not in madness / But mad in craft' (3.4.185–6) and he resolves to 'bear' himself by putting 'an antic disposition on' (1.5.168–70). In this way, Hamlet's act becomes a form of burden to him. The secret of his father's murder is a burden of acting too, and not just to him. He stage directs the gestures of his friends lest they 'With arms encumbered thus' (1.5.172) betray that they too are carrying the burden of Hamlet's secret. His rival actor Claudius, who laments the 'heavy burden' (3.1.53) of his own secret sin, seems almost to see through Hamlet's performance, observing that Hamlet's speech 'though it lacked form a little, / Was not like madness' (3.1.162–3). Claudius supposes that Hamlet 'puts on this confusion' (3.1.2), but ultimately he is unsure if Hamlet's act is deliberate. He concludes that Hamlet, his 'brains still beating', might be distracted 'From fashion of himself' (3.1.173–4). The nature of Hamlet's possible distraction is something to which we will shortly return.

To 'perform' can carry the etymological sense of 'perfectly form', but no performance is perfect. To 'per-form' is better understood as a process of acting 'through form' (which is to say, 'by means of form'). The observer has the opportunity to probe the form with a suspicious eye and to approve the performance as 'proof' if it passes the test. It will 'pass probate' (to use legal testamentary terminology) if it satisfactorily deflects critical probing. For Brecht, the aim of the *Verfremdungseffekt* is to 'make the spectator adopt an attitude of inquiry and criticism'.[55] He supposed that this would require a degree of resistance to techniques designed to produce empathy, but it produces fellow-feeling of another sort insofar as it enlists the playgoers to join with the actors in appreciating the performance as an uncanny object of critical attention.

Hamlet has a practitioner's skill to act through forms and to see how others act through forms, but he also has a philosopher's concern to look through forms in search of deeper truth. The problem of performance for anyone who is both practitioner and philosopher – as the character of Hamlet is, and as Shakespeare is, and as each one of us is to some degree – is to know how to summon the will to act through the medium of external forms when one's deeper understanding convinces one that the surface forms of performance are merely superficial; being 'abstract and brief' representations (or misrepresentations) of something more complex and profound. Hamlet's dual disposition as practitioner and philosopher opens within him a chasm between action and contemplation. It is well understood that to lose one's will is to lose the power to perform, but it is equally true – and the example of Hamlet confirms it – that to lose capacity to perform will erode one's will. Hamlet loses his capacity to perform because he cannot reconcile his desire to perform (to express himself through forms and to create forms through action) with his desire to displace forms through his delving critique. It is this distraction – literally a pulling of the mind in two directions – that exhausts and incapacitates his will.[56]

It has often been said that Hamlet's tragic failure is his delay in acting.[57] I will return to that question, but for now we can note that he acts quickly enough where his will and instinct coincide. He readily thrusts his sword through the arras because in that instant the wall hanging obscures all human form and all human performance from Hamlet's contemplation. This is a rare moment when Hamlet's 'native hue of resolution' is not 'sicklied o'er with the pale cast of thought' (3.1.83–4). What Hamlet is powerless to do is to perform when confronted with disjuncture between form and substance, as, for example, when he beholds shallow shows of funeral and wedding rites or when he holds a skull. The image of Hamlet crouching graveside with the skull of Yorick in his hand endures in part because it is the picture of the mind stripped of all burdens but the burden of its own irreducible form and it is a picture of the human reduced to its final performance. This, together with his cynicism about make-up, explains why Hamlet jests that Yorick's mortal remains should visit 'my lady's table, and tell her, let her paint an inch thick, to this favour she must come' (5.1.182–4). The radical reduction of the human condition is uprooted and presented centre-stage and found still to be but a 'fashion i'th' earth' (5.1.188).[58]

The skulls and the ghost that rise up from the grave are memento mori; their rising up causes Hamlet to look down. Hamlet, following the trajectory of his mind's eye, becomes increasingly downcast and this process of being 'thrown under' constitutes him a tragic 'subject' in the most literal sense of that word. The price of understanding is that he finds himself conscious of the weight of the forms he stands under: the costume of customs, social forms of status and even the form of his own 'too too solid flesh' (1.2.129). The pressure of this burden weighing down on him drains him of the energy to act; the futility of performance drains him of the will to act. This is a new variation on the old idea that Hamlet is paralysed by a contemplative mindset. It is a variation that takes us to the heart of performance where the solid stuff of the stage world connects to the intangible stuff of the will.

Costume is some of the stage stuff that I have in mind. Shakespeare employs costume in *Hamlet* to play with connected and contestable ideas of form, habit, custom and proof. He also uses it to communicate the downward trajectory of the tragedy. So the ghost appears at first in armour 'cap-à-pie' (1.2.199) which is 'top to toe' and 'head to foot' (1.2.226), but as the play progresses he is stripped down and when he next appears before the audience he does so '*in his night gowne*' (3.4).[59] Despite its dubious spectral form, Hamlet considers the ghost of his father to have an integrity of form and substance that Claudius lacks. When Hamlet calls Claudius 'a king of shreds and patches' (3.4.99), it is because the stains and flaws in his nature have been dishonestly covered up. Hamlet even goes so far as to assert that the flawed substance of Claudius has been subsumed in, and therefore covered up by, his marriage to Gertrude. He calls Claudius 'mother' on the theological basis that 'Father and mother is man and wife. Man and wife is one flesh' (4.3.49–50) (compare *RJ*, 2.6.37). In doing so, he inverts the Elizabethan legal doctrine that considered the person of a married woman to be for most legal purposes, including landholding and will-making, to be subsumed within the legal status of her husband.[60] Elsewhere, Hamlet talks of Claudius as one who merely 'plays the King' (2.2.285) and says, in more sardonic tone, that 'The body is with the King, but the King is not with the body. The King is a thing' ... 'Of nothing' (4.2.25–6, 28). James Calderwood says that Claudius, who is never referred to in the play by name, gave up his self for the form of a king.[61] Another Q1 stage reference to dress is '*Enter Ofilia playing on the Lute, and her haire downe singing*' (4.5.20). Granville-Barker called it 'a genuinely Shakespearean stage direction' despite acknowledged doubts regarding the 'origin and value of Q1 as a text'.[62] For a woman's hair to be let down at court would be considered shockingly disordered and dissolute.[63] In *King John*, when Constance lets down her locks, King Philip is instinctively irritated (*KJ*, 3.3.68–72).

Before her own descent into distraction, Ophelia had reported the demise of Hamlet's dress. Ophelia had been sewing in her closet when she witnessed Hamlet 'with his doublet all unbraced, / No hat upon his head, his stockings fouled, / Ungartered and down-gyved to his ankle' (2.1.75–7). For a prince to dress with such disorder in court would have been shocking in the early modern period. For any man to appear at court without a hat to doff would have been 'offensive',[64] although it may be that Claudius implicitly licensed Hamlet to go un-bonneted when he acknowledged him to 'Be as ourself in Denmark' (1.2.122).[65] Hamlet impressed Ophelia as one 'loosed out of hell' (2.1.80). The progressive decadence of his dress is like that of the ghost that was loosed out of the 'hell' beneath the stage.[66] Late in the play, Hamlet writes to Claudius (in curiously formal mode, as the 'statists' do): '*High and mighty. You shall know I am set naked / on your kingdom*' (4.7.43–4). The line contrasts the high status of the dressed-up king with Hamlet's own dressed-down state.

The very stage was 'dressed' in Shakespeare's day. A skirt of black cloth hanging from the stage, concealing the 'cellarage' with its ghostly 'mole' and its mine of wooden props, would indicate that the play was a tragedy.[67] The state of the stage encourages a certain state of mind (the Globe becoming skull again). The 'state' of the stage was in fact the name of the wooden construct on which Shakespeare's stage kings sat. The metatheatrical conceit is that there might have been something materially 'rotten' in the stage furniture as well as something rotten in the state of Denmark and in the mind of its prince. Marcellus's 'Something is rotten in the state' (1.4.90) and Fortinbras's belief (conjectured by Claudius) that the Danish state is 'disjoint and out of frame' (1.2.20) follows Horatio's foreboding sense of 'strange eruption to our state' (1.1.68). Thoughts of state, and the appearance of the ghost, put Horatio in mind of the 'high and palmy state of Rome / A little ere the mightiest Julius fell', which saw 'the sheeted dead ... squeak and gibber in the Roman streets' (1.1.112–15). Here Shakespeare is recalling his recent production of *Julius Caesar*. We saw in Chapter 4 that 'stasis' was a special concern of that play. The idea of stasis that we explored there – of action stalled – is clearly significant to *Hamlet* too.[68] The challenge of the play's second line, it will be recalled, is to 'stand'. Hamlet's stasis – the state of deep distraction that produces his hesitation to act – is signalled in the way that Pyrrhus, played by the leader of the travelling players, stalls his sword in the air just before he takes his revenge on Priam (2.2.417). The hesitation is highlighted by 'weighty pauses at the line-ends' in the text.[69] There may even be an allusion to Hamlet's stasis or 'pause' when Hamlet complains (using a musical pun) that Guildenstern and Rosencrantz have presumed to know his 'stops' (3.2.357). Granville-Barker calls *Hamlet* 'a tragedy of inaction' and at 'the center of it is Hamlet, who is physically inactive'.[70] He has 'forgone all custom of exercises' (2.2.262–3), will not 'walk out of the air' (2.2.203) and, with his book, spends 'four hours ... in the lobby' (2.2.157–8). Hamlet's physical stasis began when he agreed to 'stay' in Denmark instead of returning to his studies in Wittenberg. Hamlet's body, spirit and will are paused, as if in Limbo. When Hamlet first hears about his fellow spirit in Limbo, the ghost, he naturally asks 'Stayed it long?' (1.2.235). Horatio misses a trick when he attempts to answer the question with a precise account of the number of seconds the ghost was present. A more pertinent response would have been to explain that, despite Horatio's repeated requests 'to stay', the ghost refused to be bidden.

The ghost leads us to the materiality of the world beneath the stage. There, beneath the surface of things, we encounter a rich seam of mining imagery that runs from the start to the end of the play.[71] In the first act, Hamlet calls the ghost 'old mole!' and 'A worthy pioner!' after its return to the cellarage under the stage. When Hamlet hears the ghost's voice call from below, perhaps from different points of the stage, he wonders 'canst work i' th' earth so fast?' (1.5.161). A 'pioner' (or pioneer) was a miner, especially one employed to undermine enemy positions during military operations (*H5*, 3.2.89; *Oth*, 3.3.349). Perceiving that Claudius and his faction are labouring to undermine him, Hamlet says ''tis the sport to have the enginer' (miner) 'Hoist with his own petard' (explosive mine) (3.4.204–5), and resolves to 'delve one yard below their mines / And blow them at the moon' (3.4.206–7). In the same scene, he goads his mother with talk of 'rank corruption mining all within' (3.4.146). To be a 'labouring pioner' (*Luc*, 1380) was heavy work. It is very likely that Hamlet is referring to pioneers and miners when he wonders: 'Who would fardels bear / To grunt and sweat under a weary life' (3.1.75–6). The rhetorical question has close counterparts in Wilson's *Arte of Rhetorique*, where Wilson asks 'Who woulde digge and delve from morne till evening? Who would travaile and toyle with the sweate of his browes?'[72] The word 'fardels' surely alludes to the sacks of earth excavated by miners.[73] If so, how apt it is to describe the burdens that Hamlet's deep delving has placed upon his back. The reference to 'fardels' comes in the 'To be or not to be' soliloquy, which conveniently leads to my next topic.

Hamlet's most famous soliloquy is not tied to particular characters or events in the play, and this is part of its universal appeal. It has the quality of a poetic, philosophical and rhetorical set piece that has been super-added to the dramatic action. Its studied rhetorical nature is confirmed by the fact that it begins with words seemingly inspired by Cicero's phrase '*esse aut non esse*' ('either be or not be').[74] We saw in Chapter 4 that the rhetorical set pieces spoken in the forum in *Julius Caesar* have the same quality of having been supplied to the drama in the form of pre-prepared rhetorical set-speeches. How much of Hamlet's soliloquy is directly inspired by such authors on rhetoric as Cicero and Thomas Wilson is a moot point. In a recent chapter that is as rewarding as it is brief, E. A. J. Honigmann notes impressive similarities between the soliloquy and Cicero's *Tusculan Disputations.*[75] He singles out such lines as 'For who would bear the whips and scorns of time' (3.1.69)[76] and 'But that the dread of something after death' (3.1.77).[77] Wilson's *Arte of Rhetorique* ponders substantially the same issues when it conjectures that 'the troubles before death being long suffered ... are worse a great deale, then present death it selfe can be'.

Jenkins cited the *Tusculan Disputations* as a classical source for the Renaissance commonplace identification of sleep and death which Shakespeare employs in the repeated phrase 'to die: to sleep' (3.1.59; 3.1.63).[78] Shakespeare describes the sleep of death as 'a consummation / Devoutly to be wished' and Honigmann hears in this an echo of Cicero's 'if sensation is obliterated and death resembles the sleep which sometimes brings the calmest rest, untroubled even by the appearance of dreams, good gods, what gain it is to die!'[79] If Shakespeare adopted this, he also adapted it. His imagination will not let him repeat the groundless assumption that death is a sleep without dreams, but leads him to wonder 'what dreams may come' (3.1.65). In the end, his 'rest is silence' (5.2.344), which might suggest a 'rest in peace' free of troubled dreams.[80] Cicero wrote the *Tusculan Disputations* when contemplating the death of his daughter. Did Shakespeare write 'to be or not to be' when contemplating the death of his son, Hamnet? Did somebody give Shakespeare a copy of the *Disputations* to console him when Hamnet died? This is pure speculation, of course, but if someone gave Shakespeare a copy, the obvious candidate is Richard Field, Shakespeare's childhood contemporary in Stratford-upon-Avon, who was the publisher of a recent edition of the *Tusculan Disputations*.[81] One obvious connection between Hamnet and Shakespeare's play is that Hamnet was an alternative spelling of Hamlet (in Shakespeare's will, his friend Hamnet Sadler is rendered 'Hamlett'), so *Hamlet* is a play about a father and his only son that bears the name of Shakespeare's only son. To complete the trinity we must add the ghost, and acknowledge that in the play the spectral presence is a dead father rather than a dead son. Any biographical allegory is inevitably imperfect.

Let us come back to Hamlet and the possibility of repose in death. Whatever rest might await him, as Hamlet delivers his soliloquy he is unconvinced that death will unburden him. It is true that Hamlet notes that a dead person is unburdened of certain layers of social and physical form – that they have a 'bare bodkin' (3.1.75) (have no hat) and have 'shuffled off this mortal coil' (3.1.66) (have shed their flesh as a snake sloughs its skin), and that unburdened one might hope to 'fly' to the next world – but when Hamlet contemplates the stripping away of all burdens of forms, even to the extent of a skull or mere dust, it seems only to add to his mental burden a material sense of the weight of mortal being (that 'too too solid flesh' again). He is morbidly fascinated by the matter of death and the material stuff of death. In this play, the force of gravity that drags Hamlet down is especially strong in grave matter. It should be borne in mind that Elizabethans understood gravity to denote weight long before Newton named the physical force, and to Elizabethan playgoers the connection between gravity and the grave would have been more apparent than it is to us, if only because 'grave' was then pronounced 'grav'.[82] The strong pull of the obituary object on Hamlet's mind adds to our sense that 'his will is not his own'.

There is an old line of criticism that conceives Hamlet's

plight in terms of his 'tragic burden'.[83] John Dover Wilson presents Hamlet as a character who is heroic because he withstands a weight of 'circumstance'[84] that 'would annihilate us'.[85] He argues that Hamlet is paralysed and unable to act under the combined mass of one burden added to another, culminating in the ghost's mandate and Hamlet's own doubt, but that he is never pulverized beneath the load: 'Thus he continues to support the burden, but is unable to discharge it. That, in a sentence, is "the tragical history of Hamlet, Prince of Denmark".'[86] Wilson acknowledges that Goethe attempted to summarize the play in similar terms: 'a beautiful, pure, noble and most moral nature, without the strength of nerve which makes a hero, sinks beneath a burden which it can neither bear nor throw off.'[87] Immediately preceding the line seized upon by Wilson, there is a line in which Goethe supplies an exquisite metaphor to assist our appreciation of the nature and underlying cause of Hamlet's burden. The metaphor is the metaphor of the jar and the root. The English translation communicates the pithiness of Goethe's analysis: 'There is an oak-tree planted in a costly jar, which should have borne only pleasant flowers in its bosom; the roots expand, the jar is shivered.'[88] By the logic of Goethe's metaphor, Hamlet is burdened not by the piling on of circumstances (as Wilson argues), but because, like a root, he has extended himself down into the depths of his own human nature. His omission to act in revenge is not attributable to paralysis (as Wilson argues), but to the fact that he is occupied with other activity: the activity of digging down. In conclusion, he is 'heroic' not because of his ability to bear his load passively (as Wilson argues), but because of his resolve to pursue the mystery of his being as far down as he can. In the end the endeavour shatters him, but however disintegrated might be the constraining frames of his life (his relationships with family, his lover and certain friends, to name a few), the integrity of his own endeavour remains intact. The jar shivers, but the root remains. Hamlet's endeavour is heroic not because it is justified or excusable in disinterested, independent terms (although it may have such justification and excuse); it is a downward endeavour that is heroic on its own terms in the way that striving upwards to the top of Everest is heroic: because the great challenge 'is there'. Hamlet is a pioneer for all of us.

The play contains numerous images that might have contributed to Goethe's picture of roots shattering a vase. The most obvious is the ghost's allusion to the roots on Lethe wharf. Hamlet's first response to the ghost's mission was to say that he would fly to his revenge 'with wings as swift / As meditation' (1.5.29–30). The ghost finds this apt, saying that Hamlet would be 'duller ... than the fat weed / That roots itself in ease on Lethe wharf' if he 'Wouldst ... not stir in this' (1.5.32–4). In the event, as we know, Hamlet's thought does not fly up on wings of action, but buries itself in rooted contemplation. More support for Goethe's image comes in Laertes' observation that human growth is a feature not only of the external forms of our flesh, but of the interior expansion of the mind and soul:

For nature crescent does not grow alone
In thews and bulks, but as this temple waxes
The inward service of the mind and soul
Grows wide withal. (1.3.11–14)

There is a sense with Hamlet that his mind and soul have grown too large to be contained by the forms of mortal life. Ophelia recognizes that in Hamlet a 'profound' thing 'did seem to shatter all his bulk' (2.1.91–2). In this instance the profound thing was merely a sigh, but the sentiment stands for the deep roots of his melancholy. Hamlet himself acknowledges that the 'o'ergrowth of some complexion' might end in 'breaking down the pales and forts of reason' (1.4.27–8), and some of Hamlet's lines spoken to the ghost give a prophetic sense of deep mental exploration and expansion bordering on the explosive:

Let me not burst in ignorance but tell

Why thy canonized bones hearsed in death
Have burst their cerements, why the sepulcher
Wherein we saw thee quietly interred
Hath oped his ponderous and marble jaws
To cast thee up again. (1.4.46–51)

The word 'burst' is here repeated three times. The second occurrence, confined between the other two, bursts out of the words 'bones hearsed'. It is closer, then, to the explosion of a miner's petard than to the slow action of inquiring roots, but both metaphors press the sense that Hamlet's pent-up mental pressure will lead to breakdown and violent expression.

The image of the unquiet ghost of a murder victim bursting from the grave is representative of truth breaking through surface forms and being thrown up from profound places. Claudius has cause to know, at least as well as Hamlet, that the performance of an attractive surface can be a cover for repellant substance. When Claudius utters the words 'we are pictures or mere beasts' (4.5.86) and asks if Laertes is 'the painting of a sorrow, / A face without a heart? (4.7.106–7), he might have been reflecting on himself, for he admits his skill in 'forgery of shapes and tricks' (4.7.88) and in the previous act he had confessed in an aside that a 'harlot's cheek beautied with plastering art' is not uglier than is his deed to his 'most painted word' (3.1.50–2). This associates him with Pyrrhus, the 'painted tyrant' (2.2.418), and the association is confirmed when Shakespeare has Claudius 'stand in pause' (3.3.42) before his attempt to pray, for (as noted earlier) Pyrrhus had paused (his sword 'seemed i'th' air to stick' [2.2.417]) on the verge of his taking revenge on Priam. Claudius's 'Pray can I not: / Though inclination be as sharp as will' (3.3.38–9) echoes the description of Pyrrhus as one who stood 'Like a neutral to his will and matter' and 'Did nothing' (2.2.419–20). Of course, in the matter of the pause – and incapacity to act on will – both Pyrrhus and Claudius point to Hamlet's famous 'pause': the so-called 'delay' in taking revenge on Claudius that led Hamlet to ask himself 'Why yet I live to say this thing's to do' (4.4.43). Numerous commentators have warned that we should not assume that Hamlet actually hesitated. Some have even claimed that there is 'no justification' in the text for saying that Hamlet lacked resolution.[89] Can such a view be reconciled with lines like the one just quoted? Without attempting that task of reconciliation, I will say that what I see in Hamlet is a pause that is in no way hesitant or lacking resolution. He suffers, rather, from a type of stasis produced when his lively mind confronts the immovable matter of his mortality and the human condition. This can be pictured as a dramatic conflict arising from the clash of equal forces pushing against each other, or, pictured yet another way, as the tension produced when equal forces pull away from each other that cannot break free. Stasis of this sort is not irresolution or hesitation, but it can look and feel that way. Of course it may be that the answer to Hamlet's question 'Why yet I live to say this thing's to do' lies in factors external to him. It may be that 'There's such divinity doth hedge a king / That treason can but peep to what it would, / Acts little of his will' (4.5.123–5). These are the words of Claudius, but like so many of his formal pronouncements, they serve to cover up the lie at the heart of the man. Claudius knows by the example of his own treasonous act of murder that these words cannot be true.[90]

Polonius acts as a sort of formal buffer between Claudius and Hamlet. Claudius is the ultimate target of Hamlet's revenge, but in the meantime Hamlet is content to whet the blade of his wit against Polonius. Indeed, he continues to poke fun at Polonius even after he has run him through with his sword. Polonius puts on forms of social grace and prolix speech and rules. He is a man of 'outward flourishes' (2.2.91), obsessed with the names of every formal genre of theatre ('pastoral-comical' and the rest [2.2.334–5]). He is a masked man who is curiously excited when the leader of the travelling players talks of the 'mobled' (the 'veiled' or 'muffled') queen (2.2.440–1). His advice to Laertes, whom he later spies on, is a manual of dishonest disguise and dissemblance. His code is concealment. What else can it be, if one must 'give thy thoughts no tongue' (1.3.58)? The only friend to be trusted is the bird in full plumage, not the 'new-hatched, unfledged' sort (1.3.64). When he advises against 'fancy' and 'gaudy' clothes, it is not because he thinks such forms to be false, but because he is committed to suppressing any genuine expression of individuality. He fears the honest voice by which 'apparel oft proclaims the man' (1.3.71). As a 'typical Elizabethan Machiavellian, Polonius wills evil ... His rhetoric mirrors his moral deviousness. Appearance has become his reality'.[91] When a Machiavellian is to his 'own self true', it must follow that he is then false to every man. Hamlet sees that Polonius is a 'great baby ... not yet out of his swaddling clouts' (2.2.319–20). It is fitting that Polonius, who is always under wraps, should meet his end hiding under cover of the arras and that Hamlet should be the one to probe through the pretence. Yet Shakespeare is generous even with Polonius. In death, his covers are removed and he is borne 'bare-faced on the bier' (4.5.160). He was never so honest in life. Hamlet receives no such mercy yet. As Hamlet lugs the corpse away, Polonius becomes just the latest formality to burden him.

Polonius is buried 'hugger-mugger'.[92] The play skips over his burial, and so will we. We will go straight to the grave of Ophelia. The reliable Q2 and First Folio agree that Laertes leaps into his sister's grave to embrace her one last time. An engaging and surprisingly lively debate has sought to determine whether Hamlet followed suit in this energetic show of passion. I suspect that he did, although whether he was in there with Laertes at the same time is more doubtful. Q1 contains the stage direction '*Hamlet leapes in after Leartes*' (5.1). This is the so-called 'bad quarto', but even if it is a mere 'memorial reconstruction'[93] based on the recollection of performances that the compiler had seen or played in, it might be expected to remember something as significant as a lead character leaping into the stage trap. Other evidence for Hamlet's leap is *A Funerall Elegye on the Death of the Famous Actor Richard Burbage who died on Saturday in Lent the 13 of March 1619*.[94] It contains the line 'Oft have I seen him leap into the grave'. The fact that the elegy elsewhere makes express reference to 'young Hamlet' crying 'Revenge!' for his father's death might suggest that the elegist is referring to an earlier Hamlet play, not by Shakespeare,[95] but the likelihood is that he is recalling Burbage's more recent performances in Shakespeare's celebrated play.[96] Shakespeare's Hamlet does in fact make oblique allusion to his father as he enters the scene and before he leaps into the grave. He declares 'This is I, / Hamlet the Dane' (5.1.246–7).[97] Granville-Barker doubts that Hamlet leapt. He notes that Q1 is 'very corrupt' at the point of the stage direction.[98] That may be true, but it is no evidence against Hamlet's leap. It might simply suggest that Hamlet leapt in at a different point. The leap would make sense if, for example, it were placed after: 'Dost come here … / To outface me with leaping in her grave? / Be buried quick with her, and so will I' (5.1.266–8). Laertes might have left the grave by this point, in which event Hamlet's actions will mirror those of Laertes and Hamlet's words become a dare to Laertes to leap back in. Laertes out of the grave at this point would avoid the need for Hamlet to attack him, which was Granville-Barker's main reason for rejecting the stage direction in the first place.[99] Gurr and Ichikawa note that an Elizabethan audience would see Hamlet's leap as a sign of his readiness to descend into hell in pursuit of revenge.[100] I see a further significance in Hamlet's leap. I interpret it as an expression of Hamlet's activity of delving under surfaces. Hamlet is such a delver and is so burdened by the weight of the forms he has unfolded that when he challenges Laertes with 'if thou prate of mountains let them throw / Millions of acres on us' (5.1.269–70), we believe that he would be perfectly in his element in the grave and buried deep in the ground. Laertes' own performance is less convincing. He casually consigns 'Conscience and grace to the profoundest pit' (4.5.131) as one might who has little conscience, grace or profundity.

Laertes is actually a surface-dweller. He is praised by Osric for his 'great showing' and called a 'card or calendar of gentry' (5.2.94–5). Claudius admires him for his young man's 'light and careless livery', whose sports are 'A very ribbon in the cap of youth', contrasting these attributes with the 'graveness' that clothes 'settled age' (4.7.76–80). The fact that Laertes' own will is unburdened by constraints allows him to appreciate that Hamlet's will 'is not his own'. At the start of the play, the ever-formal Polonius 'sealed' his 'hard consent' to Laertes' 'will' (1.2.60), and, adding his approval, Claudius had urged: 'Take thy fair hour, Laertes, time be thine / And thy best graces spend it at thy will' (1.2.62–3). Later, when Laertes is set on revenge for his father's death, Claudius asks 'Who shall stay you?', to which Laertes replies: 'My will, not all the world' (4.5.135–6).[101] Laertes is a superficiality, like his father; and like his father he advises that Ophelia should not 'unmask' her true feelings (1.3.36). He praises the French swordsman Lamord in suitably shallow and decorative terms as a 'brooch ... / And gem' (4.7.91–2). Not one to be concerned with the roots of things, Laertes' leap into the grave seems an uncharacteristically profound act, and yet it still has something of his showy nature in it. He pierces the surface of the earth, but remains very much on display. Likewise when he says that he would reward his friends in the way the pelican feeds its young, by piercing its own breast to yield nourishing blood (4.5.144–6), he cannot help but express the depth of his emotions in a mode that barely pierces the surface and which maintains his social front. This is how to turn a passing through form (per-form) into a performance. Laertes is quite out of his element even six feet beneath the ground. He is the *tabula rasa* who would uproot tradition and start the world afresh today. His followers are like him, for 'as the world were now but to begin, / Antiquity forgot, custom not known, / The ratifiers and props of every word, / They cry, "Choose we: Laertes shall be king!"' (4.5.103–6).

In Hamlet's case, a physical leap into the grave – the trapdoor of the stage – serves as a suitable sequel to the passing through the same trap of his father's ghost. The son follows the father by a sort of testamentary descent. The ghost was a device borrowed from Seneca, who was also in a wider sense the source of the tradition of the revenge play in early modern theatre. It is Polonius, the university actor, who summarizes the contemporary theatrical scene in the line: 'Seneca cannot be too heavy nor Plautus too light' (2.2.336–7).[102] Brian Arkins observes that the 'ghosts of Senecan drama – Atreus, Hercules, Pyrrhus, Clytemnestra, Aegisthus, Orestes, Electra ... hover in the background of *Hamlet*'.[103] Pyrrhus we have already mentioned, but Hercules also stands out for his express connection to *Hamlet* (and perhaps to the Globe theatre). In the First Folio, Rosencrantz refers to the image of Hercules in one of the play's many intensely metatheatrical passages. When Hamlet asks: 'Do the boys carry it away?', Rosencrantz replies: 'Ay, that they do, my lord, Hercules and his load too' (2.2.357–8).[104] The context for the comment is the children players at the Blackfriars theatre around the time of the first production of *Hamlet* at the Globe. Hamlet expressly contrasts himself to Hercules, ('no more like my father / Than I to Hercules' [1.2.152–3]), which indicates that Shakespeare had connected Hamlet and Hercules in his mind. One explanation for this is that Shakespeare conceived Hamlet to be like Hercules in having to labour under the burden of a task that he had to some extent willingly, and yet not fully and freely, undertaken. (Hercules had agreed to relieve Atlas of his burden temporarily, but Atlas tried to leave him with the Globe on his shoulders.)[105] A. L. Rowse takes the view that 'Hamlet has his burden imposed upon him from without, through no fault of his own'. This, he says, distinguishes Hamlet's burden from that borne by Lear, who, he argues, 'brings his tragedy on his own head'.[106] Whether Hamlet is in any way wilfully responsible for the burden he feels is a question we considered earlier. We will not agree upon any answer to that question, but we can perhaps agree that the image of Hercules and the Globe is one of a man heroically bearing the weight of the world upon his shoulders and that this is enough to connect Hercules to Hamlet. Thinking of connection leads us to the next new topic, and the challenge of a question that has been something of an unspoken burden throughout this chapter so far: What, if anything, has law got to do with all this? Having concluded our discussion of Hamlet's downwards trajectory, it is time for a sub-heading.

Law and the 'or'

I have so far deliberately downplayed the relevance of law to *Hamlet* for fear that it would skew our appreciation of the scope and complexity of the play, but it is now safe to put law in its place. It has been argued that law is not central to *Hamlet*.[107] It should be clear that I have some sympathy for that view. There is certainly some truth in it if one takes 'law' to mean the technical minutiae of rules set down in statutes and cases, but for the great idea of law to be meaningful it must mean more than that. A bigger idea of law – the sort that expresses substantial matters of justice and order in practical forms and in creative performances that are open to communal participation – is an idea that must be relevant to every great work of art. I have this bigger idea of law in mind, and not a narrow technical idea of law, when I describe theatrical performance as a 'testamentary' performance of will. Law is relevant to *Hamlet* not on technical grounds, but because performance is relevant to *Hamlet* and performance is essential to law. Thus *Hamlet* can teach us a great deal about the heart of law even if the law, narrowly conceived, can teach us a good deal less about the heart of *Hamlet*. Even when Shakespeare uses legal terminology, we have to guard against the assumption that he is making a technical point about law. It is often the case that his 'point' is to exploit the textures of legal language and to show his appreciation for lawyers as fellow practitioners in arts of wordplay and rhetoric. It also made good commercial sense to involve the law and lawyers in his plays, given that lawyers patronized the playhouses and players took their plays to the Inns of Court.[108] When Hamlet chops logic with Rosencrantz and Guildenstern and says to them, 'Shall we to the court?', they think that he is talking of the royal court, whereas Hamlet is referring to the law court.[109] Shakespeare is referring to both.

Technical legal matters may not be central to *Hamlet*, but when they do appear they frequently allude to some core matter of the play. A straightforward example is the reference to 'the law's delay' (3.1.71) in the 'To be or not to be' soliloquy, which clearly tolls with the core question of Hamlet's supposed delay in exacting 'just' revenge on Claudius. Another example is the appearance of 'Crowner's 'quest law' in the conversation between the gravedigger and his assistant (5.1.22). Their legalistic quibbling on the question of Ophelia's drowning in the 'glassy stream' (4.7.165) holds up a mirror to the central problem of Hamlet's will. When the gravedigger asks if Ophelia's downfall was 'witting' such that we can call it guilty in law, he implicitly asks if Hamlet's downfall is willing such that we can call it fault. It is therefore an allusion to a most 'necessary question of the play' (3.2.40–1). When a skull emerges from the grave, Hamlet asks: 'may not that be the skull of a lawyer?' (5.1.93–4). Why choose that profession over any other? The straightforward answer (supported by Hamlet's conjecture that the previous skull to emerge might have been that of a politician or loquacious courtier) is that Shakespeare is preparing the playgoers for the quibbling wordplay that is about to follow in conversation between Hamlet and the gravedigger. Thus Hamlet wonders what became of the (supposed) lawyer's 'quiddities', 'quillets', 'cases', 'tenures', 'tricks', 'statutes', 'recognizances', 'fines', 'vouchers', 'double vouchers', 'recoveries', 'purchases' and 'conveyances' (5.1.94–103). The ready answer to Hamlet's question is that Hamlet himself, the great player with words, is 'th'inheritor' (5.1.105) of all of them. Even as Hamlet mocks the lawyer's 'pair of indentures' (5.1.103) (which would be suitably accompanied by the action of clapping the teeth of the jaw bone to the teeth of the skull),[110] he inadvertently mocks himself as the play's great talker, quibbler, coroner-questioner and crown-quester. Even the gravedigger – the play's other 'goodman delver' (5.1.14) – can see that the question of will and performance is a central question in law, as it is in theatre. The gravedigger reveals his insight when musing on the legal question of Ophelia's death. His exposition is a bodged paraphrase of Plowden's report of *Hales* v. *Petit*:[111] 'For here lies the point: if I drown myself wittingly, it argues an act, and an act hath three branches – it is to act, to do, to perform. Argal, she drowned herself wittingly' (5.1.10–13).[112] His elaboration in the immediately subsequent lines leaves us in no doubt that the presence or absence of will – 'will he nill he' (5.1.17)[113] – is the essential question.

This brings us to the legal issue of testament and inheritance. By the time the good quarto (Q2) of *Hamlet* was published in 1604, James VI of Scotland had been crowned James I of England and Wales, and Anne of Denmark was his Queen consort. James had married Anne in 1589, and when Shakespeare's play was taking final form around 1600, the royal pair were already obvious candidates to succeed to the English throne on the death of the childless Queen Elizabeth. Anne's nationality has prompted commentators to discover in Shakespeare's tragedy of the Prince of Denmark a number of fascinating points of connection to the Danish court,[114] but if the law of Danish royal succession is one of those, the connection is slight. Hamlet's reference to Claudius having 'popped in between th'election and my hopes' (5.2.64) might allude to the fact that Denmark had an elective monarchy rather than an hereditary one (although, in practice, monarchs were usually succeeded by the eldest son),[115] but the technicalities of Danish constitutional law have no impact on the play.[116] The play's technical allusions to law are almost always allusions to English law and are usually of the domestic sort that would have most appealed to Shakespeare's playgoers. For example, Claudius's description of Gertrude as 'imperial jointress' (1.2.9) alludes to a rather homely feature of English law 'known to every Elizabethan man-on-the-street as a jointure'.[117] Jointure was typically used to describe a wife's joint ownership of a freehold with her husband and her right to succeed to possession of the freehold on her husband's death. Choosing a popular plot set in Denmark was a politic way to sidestep English constitutional politics while at the same time taking the playgoers to the heart of issues of succession, testament and will that were such significant features of the English social and legal landscape at the time. (Shakespeare's most obviously legal plays, *The Merchant of Venice* and *Measure for Measure*, also present legal issues far more relevant to England than to Venice or Vienna respectively.) It is true that Claudius nominates Hamlet to be his successor, saying to him: 'let the world take note, / you are the most immediate to our throne' (1.2.108–9), but nomination by the incumbent monarch was not a binding election in Danish law. Shakespeare is making a dramatic point, not a technical one – namely, that the death of Hamlet's father has robbed Hamlet of a voice that might have spoken for him at court in the way that Claudius speaks for him now. The play is therefore haunted by the absence of Hamlet's father's approving testimony to his son, which is the closest thing the dead king could have given to a testament on the matter of succession. Andrew Zurcher points out that in the very first words of the play, when Bernardo asks 'Who's there?', we can hear the inheritance question 'Who's th'heir'.[118]

After the visitation of the ghost, the play is doubly haunted by absent will, for the absence of the father's public 'voice' in favour of Hamlet is compounded by the absence of Hamlet's own will to make good his father's intent. John Dover Wilson was right to conclude that 'the elective throne in Shakespeare's Denmark is a mirage',[119] but he was also right to add that '[t]he usurpation is one of the main factors in the plot of *Hamlet*, and it is vital that we moderns should not lose sight of it'.[120] The significance of the inheritance issue seeps out of the script in subtle ways. For example, when Hamlet laments his father's lost 'property and most dear life' (2.2.505), it is telling that he mentions 'property' before 'life'. In similar vein, Hamlet singles out the 'estate' as the reason why Gonzago (the playlet's equivalent to his father) was poisoned. Likewise, when Rosencrantz asks Hamlet: 'what is your cause of distemper?' (3.2.328–9), Hamlet's answer (to that question we have all been asking) is: 'I lack advancement' (3.2.331). The word 'advancement' indicates improved social standing (compare 3.2.53), but as such it was closely connected to advantage conferred by inheritance and testament, hence Rosencrantz's reply: 'How can that be, when you have the voice of the king himself for your succession in Denmark?' (3.2.332–4). The word 'advancement' appears in English wills as far back as the reign of Henry V,[121] and it remains a feature of the English law of trusts and testaments to this day.[122]

Legal testamentary technicalities are not central to the play, but there is some evidence to suggest that *Hamlet* makes express reference to the leading contemporary treatise on the English law of wills. One especially resonant line is Laertes' 'Perhaps he loves you now, / And now no soil nor cautel doth besmirch / The virtue of his will' (1.3.14–16). The word 'will' hints at a testamentary double-meaning,[123] but the word 'cautel' is the more concrete clue. It is a strange word that occurs in this form nowhere else in Shakespeare's entire dramatic oeuvre.[124] In law its meaning was something like 'an exception, restriction, or reservation made for precaution's sake'.[125] Rushton conjectured that Shakespeare might have recalled it from the following passage in Swinburne's 1590 *Treatise of Testaments and Wills*:

> if a má[n] first make a testament, & then sweareth neuer to reuoke the same, yet notwithstanding he may make an other testament and thereby reuoke the former: for there is no *cautele* vnder heauen, whereby the libertie of making or reuoking his testament can be vtterly taken away.[126]

The likelihood that Shakespeare had noted this one word in Swinburne's book is no doubt very slight, but, however slight, it must be increased by the fact that 'cautele' is the only italicized word in the body text on the relevant pair of facing pages. More significant, though, is the fact that in the same passage Horatio goes on to say that Hamlet 'may not carve for himself'. This has a close counterpart in Swinburne's 'it is not lawfull for legataries to carue for themselues'.[127] Of passing interest we might also note that Swinburne quotes the authority of Fitzherbert's *Graunde Abridgement* for the statement that 'It is vnlawfull for a king to giue awaie his kingdome from his lawfull heires'.[128] Swinburne is not tempted to delve further into what he refers to as a 'deepe and dangerous question'.[129] Had he Hamlet's disposition, he surely would have. Swinburne prefers to leave such issues to the likes of Fortinbras, observing that succession to the crown is a matter for 'martial cannons' not the 'cannon lawe'.[130]

Despite possible echoes of Swinburne, the key testamentary quality of *Hamlet* is not to be found in any technical reference to the law of wills, but in the broader idea that the performance of will is 'testamentary' when it is constituted or perfected by the participation of third-party witnesses. We have seen throughout the present study that this notion of 'testamentary' applies as well to the constitution of a theatrical play through the participation of playgoers as it does to the constitution of a legal last will by the formal participation of witnesses. Hamlet is a sort of executor of his father's will and a bystander and detached commentator on the performance of his own will. In testamentary terms he is both executor and witness. He draws his fellow witnesses, the playgoers, into the action and they subject the performance to probate, which is to say that they probe the surface performance as Hamlet does in order to see what substance lies beneath. Of course I do not mean that the playgoers are a court, judge or jury in any technical sense, but that they are a group gathered together to perform a communal act of witness, scrutiny and judgment. The 'probing' of surface performance is essential to the legal notion of 'proving' evidence.[131] As the participation of witness testimony helps to prove evidence at a trial, so the participation of executors and testamentary witnesses proves a will. If the playgoers approve of what they see, we can say (to borrow testamentary language) that the play 'passes probate' (see Chapter 1). *Hamlet* contains numerous allusions to the probation of doubtful and incomplete performance, starting with the first 'Who's there?'. For Hamlet himself, it commences when he purports to look through the 'inky cloak', 'customary suits of solemn black', 'the dejected haviour of the visage' (1.2.77–8, 81) and 'forms, moods, shapes of grief' (1.2.82), all of which he dismisses as 'actions that a man might play' and mere 'trappings' and 'suits of woe' (1.2.84, 86). Of course he is himself a consummate performer, and for one who claims to 'know not "seems"' (1.2.76), he seems to have studied the forms of performance rather well.

Hamlet compares a portrait of Claudius to one of his father and mocks Claudius for lacking integrity of form and substance, calling him a 'picture' and 'counterfeit presentment' compared to Hamlet's father who was 'form and cause conjoined' (3.4.122); 'A combination and a form indeed / Where every god did seem to set his seal / To give the world assurance of a man' (3.4.58–60). Hamlet's faith in his father's integrity is undaunted by the present schism between his father's ghost and his father's corpse. He still sees his father 'in his habit as he lived' (3.4.133). Horatio is less trusting of the ghost. He acknowledges its apparent form in the legal language of evidence, admitting that it passed the test for ocular proof – 'I might not this believe / Without the sensible and true avouch / Of mine own eyes' (1.1.55–7) – and that the first eye-witnesses 'delivered, both in time, / Form of the thing, each word made true and good' (1.2.208–9), but he does not take the proof of form to be any proof of substance. Hamlet's obsession with the surface of the ghost – 'Then saw you not his face' (1.2.227) – betrays what Lorna Hutson calls a 'detective impulse', typical of contemporary modes of forensic inquisition.[132] Hutson observes that *Hamlet* is 'concerned at both a formal and an ethical level with questions of evidential probability'.[133] Whereas Hamlet probes through most formalities as far as he can, he seems far too easily satisfied by the mere face or surface form of the spectre.

Hamlet's difficulty in knowing how far to look through

forms and how far to accept them was a problem inherent in legal processes of proof, then as now. The problem is that the public expects the law to dig down to 'true' or 'absolute' justice, whereas its evidentiary processes are in practice designed to achieve the more modest aim of producing (we might say 'fabricating') formal proofs based on evident appearances.[134] The result is not to disclose absolute or naked 'truth', but to perform a fabricated and artificial 'proof' that is offered as a plausible and practically satisfactory approximation to the 'truth'. The tension between deep-probing and surface satisfaction has a parallel in Hamlet's struggle to delve down to hidden truth even as he is fixated on faces. He sees through Claudius's false forms, but he also looks to find truth in surface evidence, saying to Horatio: 'Give him heedful note, / For I mine eyes will rivet to his face / And after we will both our judgments join / In censure of his seeming' (3.2.80–3). What Hamlet is looking for here is a moment of fracture in Claudius's performance. If Hamlet finds the slightest breach or loophole in Claudius's castle wall, he will pry through it. There is method in it. Later in the play, Claudius shows that he is aware of precisely this kind of risk. Plotting with Laertes, he speaks in the language of (im)proving armour: 'Weigh what convenience … / May fit us to our shape. If this should fail / And that our drift look through our bad performance / 'Twere better not essayed. Therefore this project / Should have a back or second that might hold / If this did blast in proof.' (4.7.147–52). The technical vernacular of legal 'proof' and of proof of armour were similar and developed a concurrent concern to test external appearance by processes of probationary trial.[135] Claudius knows that 'the distracted multitude, / … like not in their judgement but their eyes' (4.3.4–5) and so he offers himself and his performance to the scrutiny and judgment of others ('It shall as level to your judgment 'pear / As day does to your eye' (4.5.150–1). The First Folio's 'pierce' instead of Q2's ''pear' usefully indicates the sense that judgment involves probing through appearances.

The creator of the questioning and questionable world of *Hamlet* knew, as the rhetoricians knew, that '[t]he whole burdein of weightie matters, and the earnest triall of all controuersies, rest onely vpon Iudgement'.[136] At the conclusion of the play, Horatio promises that when he relates Hamlet's story, the audience will 'hear' of 'accidental judgments' (5.2.366). The promise implies a plea for judgment of a better sort.[137] A similar plea is expressed in the opening prologue of *Henry V*, where the Chorus concludes by inviting the playgoers 'Gently to hear, kindly to judge our play' (*H5*, 1.prologue.34). Shakespeare seems to be saying, through Horatio and the Chorus, that fair judgment calls for a fair hearing. In the unreliable sight world of *Hamlet*, as in our own unreliable world of sights, we are cautioned never to establish judgment and proof on the basis of sight alone. We must also attune the ear to the task of judicial 'hearing'.[138] A sound judgment cannot be based solely upon the apparent or logical sense of words, but one must also lend one's ears to the actual sound sense of words.[139] Hearing does justice to the poetic. We must also engage the hands of the mind to grasp the argument of the play in order to get a feel for the performance and to weigh up that which is presented to the eye. Shakespeare's poetic use of metaphor helps us, for 'when he describes any thing, you more than see it, you feel it too'.[140]

We saw in Chapter 4 that the embodied sound sense of spoken words can touch us profoundly. The heart speaks in deep sounds and sounds can speak deeply to the heart. It is notable that when Hamlet asks for Laertes' pardon and implicitly invites the whole court and all the playgoers to judge him kindly, he speaks in the shared language of theatre and of a legal hearing. He calls the 'presence' (the king and the host of courtly attendants) his 'audience', and acknowledges that Laertes 'must needs have heard' that Hamlet is 'punished with a sore distraction' (5.2.206–7). There is something testamentary in Hamlet's words as he faces what will turn out to be a trial for his life. It sounds as if he is calling for a fair hearing not merely in the human presence of the royal court, but also in the court of the divine presence. It is the sort of plea that is frequently sounded in the Psalms, as, for example, Psalm 88.2: 'Let my prayer enter into thy presence: incline thine ear unto my cry.' The most famous, or infamous, Psalm in this regard was Psalm 130. Known as the *de profundis* on account of its opening words, in the English language Geneva Bible (1599) the first line was 'Out of the deep places have I called unto thee, O Lord'. The *de profundis* attracted the ire of protestant polemicists including James Pilkington, Bishop of Durham,[141] not merely because the speaking of the *de profundis* (usually by some boy) was a traditional feature of Roman Catholic funerals, but more specifically because of its association with Catholic belief in purgatory. The cry *de profundis* ('from the deep') is evocative of the ghost of Hamlet's father calling out from the purgatorial cellarage under the stage.[142] The example of Hamlet shows us that the most profoundly poetic human souls cry out from the deep even before they die.

Sir Walter Raleigh called the divine judge, together with the host of heaven, a 'judicious sharp spectator ... / That sits and marks still who doth act amiss'.[143] The host of playgoers can also be regarded as critical spectators and eyewitnesses in ocular mode, but they are also 'hearers' of the play. Pauline Kiernan noted in 2003 that every actor she had interviewed who had played Shakespeare's Globe had 'emphasized that the theatre is a *listening* place'.[144] (Compare the comment attributed to John Webster: 'Sit in a full Theater, and you will thinke you see so many lines drawne from the circumference of so many eares, whiles the *Actor* is the *Center*.')[145] Evidence must be presented to the eye, of course, and Kiernan concludes her observations on Shakespeare's Globe by saying that the convergence of spectators' sightlines constitutes as the '"authority" position', the point of the stage 'under the "fiery cloud" on the heavens trap, in the middle of the stage width, forward of the frons, and back from the pillars'.[146] In modern film and video productions the director controls the spectators' perspective to such an extent that bystanders and onlookers are practically powerless to create their own lines of sight even when they steal the camera used to film the thing.[147] What Shakespeare calls for in *Hamlet* is a type of judgment that respects the eye, but is not seduced by it. He calls for witnesses who will not merely watch, but who will employ sight and sound and every sense to feel what Hamlet feels. The challenge for the playgoers is to appreciate, and perhaps to imitate, Hamlet's effort to see the 'form' of the time, and see through the form of the time and all the while to feel the 'pressure of the time' (3.2.24).

What do we feel when we *really* listen to *Hamlet*? One answer is that we hear a sound that feels heavy. At the start of this chapter, I wrote that Shakespeare's 'words, words, words' (2.2.189) call for a fair hearing and that a fair hearing requires us to attend to the sound of the words as much as to their logical sense. In the original Elizabethan pronunciation, 'words, words, words' would have been filled with the sound of 'or', as in modern Received Pronunciation of 'swords, swords, swords'.[148] The sound of 'or' is a rich and heavy sound. It fills the mouth to the back of the throat, as when the 'gorge rises' (5.1.177). Furthermore, all 'or' sounds ending with the letter 'r' (as in 'orb', but not 'law') would have sounded even more full than ours do today, due to the marked rhoticity of Elizabethan pronunciation.[149] In the next few pages we will examine a number of passages and quotations in which words contain, or are conjectured to contain, the sound of 'or'. For ease of identification, I have underlined the 'or' element where it is present. I have been guided by modern pronunciation, but it should be borne in mind that Elizabethan English pronunciation will probably have lacked some of our modern 'or' sounds. It certainly had others that we have lost, including, as mentioned earlier, the 'or' sound in the word 'word' itself. It is impossible to produce an entirely definitive scheme that will show where Elizabethan pronunciation varied from ours, not least because Elizabethan pronunciation was never uniform and neither is 'ours'.[150]

The rich sound of 'or' is buried throughout *Hamlet*, like a seam of golden 'ore'. We will see that in some places

Shakespeare might actually be punning, or playing with, the metallic sense of 'ore' when he employs the sound of 'or' (puns on the golden sense of 'aur' might especially appeal to the man with the golden spear on his heraldic arms). Whether or not any pun is intended, Shakespeare is surely making use of the sense of weight that is shared by the sound and by the metallic sense of the word. The seam of the 'or' sound is nowhere richer than in the graveyard scene. Granville-Barker observes that the gravity of the graveyard scene is made more pronounced by Shakespeare's use of prose:

> We have prose for the quiet pessimism of the graveyard. What else is possible? How fatally verse would compromise the gentle gravity, the limpid clarity of ...
>
> Alas! poor Yorick. I knew him, Horatio ...[151]

The words 'poor' and 'Horatio' contain the full, rich and heavy sound of 'or'. 'Yorick' is also pronounced with the same sound, or with something very similar. This same 'or' or 'ore' is buried thick throughout the graveyard scene, so it is fitting that the scene begins with a punning reprisal of the mining theme. The gravedigger, it will be recalled, claims that the grave he is digging is 'Mine, sir' (5.1.112) ... 'it is mine' (5.1.116). 'Alas, poor Yorick. I knew him, Horatio' continues one line later with 'He hath bore me ... and now how abhorred ... My gorge rises ... Where be your gibes now – your gambols, your songs, your flashes of merriment, that were wont to set the table on a roar? Not one now to mock your own grinning' (5.1.175–82). Here, the repeated 'your' is presumably a play on the rhyme (or near rhyme) of Yorick's name; likewise when we learn from the gravedigger that 'your water is a sore decayer of your whoreson dead body' (5.1.161–2). The episode with the gravedigger ends with Hamlet's contemplation on the ultimate destination of Caesar's mortal dust, which concludes with a rhyming couplet that repeats the sound of 'or' four times: 'O, that that earth which kept the world in awe / Should patch a wall t'expel the water's flaw' (5.1.204–5). The full sound of 'or' stuffs the line with an earthiness and suits the sense of earth plugging cracks in a wall. The earlier coupling 'is this law?' and 'Ay, marry is't. Crowner's 'quest law' (5.1.21–2) produces a similarly replete effect, which is augmented further by the 'fine pate full of fine dirt' (5.1.101) that Hamlet muses may be 'the skull a lawyer'. All of which anticipates the stuffing of the crowded grave – that now has a gravedigger in it and will later have Ophelia and her brother in it, and (arguably) Hamlet too. The seam of 'or' runs thick either side of Laertes' leap into the grave, even allowing for the fact that some of the conjectured 'or' sounds might have been missing in Elizabethan pronunciation:[152]

> Hold off the earth awhile,
> Till I have caught her once more in mine arms.
> *[Leaps in the grave]*
> Now pile your dust upon the quick and dead
> Till of this flat a mountain you have made
> T'o'ertop old Pelion or the skyish head
> Of blue Olympus. (5.1.238–43)[153]

Is there a pun on the play's mining theme in Laertes' phrase 'mine arms'? Does Shakespeare intend a connection between mining and the sound of 'ore'? That may be doubtful, but the possibility is rendered at least plausible by express reference to metallic ore elsewhere in the play. The passage to which I am referring is rich with inventive instances of the 'or' sound. Gertrude reports that, after killing Polonius, Hamlet went:

> To draw apart the body he hath killed,
> O'er whom – his very madness, like some ore
> Among a mineral of metals base
> Shows itself pure –'a weeps for what is done. (4.1.24–7)

The heaviness of the 'or' sound combines again with the metallic sense when the leader of the travelling players recites the scene of Pyrrhus's revenge against King Priam.

Pyrrhus is said to have brought his sword down like the hammer of Cyclops as it forged the armour of Mars. The repetition of the 'or' sound in the passage describing the monster's metalwork is palpably and impressively intense. In the space of eleven lines we have eleven occurrences: 'storm', 'orb', 'pause', 'fall', 'forged', 'for', 'remorse', 'sword', 'falls', 'Fortune' and (arguably) 'armour' (2.2.421–31). The most intense concentration of the 'or' sound appears in the part of the passage with the most intensely metallic feel:

> And never did the Cyclops' hammers fall
> On Mars's armour forged for proof eterne
> With less remorse than Pyrrhus' bleeding sword (2.2.227–9)

At significant times throughout the play, the heavy 'or' sound is juxtaposed to the lighter sound of 'air'. This is observable even in the opening lines: 'who's there' and 'Unfold yourself'. This powerful poetic combination of contrasting vowels was presumably instinctive rather than designed. If so, the same instinct might have influenced the choice of some of the characters' names. Horatio and Laertes are a natural pair either side of Hamlet, as are Claudius and Gertrude. I am not suggesting that Shakespeare intended to alert the playgoers to any deliberate contrast between the dictionary meaning of 'ore' and 'air', but he surely sensed that the playgoers would appreciate the dramatic contrast in the weight and feel of words containing these sounds. Just occasionally we are aware of a concurrence between the sound sense of a word and its logical sense. The connection might have been unplanned, but if we appreciate the coincidence, it is likely that Shakespeare appreciated it at some level too. For example, Hamlet's line: 'I have cause and will and strength and means / To do't. Examples gross as earth exhort me' (4.4.44–5) is immediately followed by a line carrying the weighty sense of his burden: 'Witness this army of such mass and charge'. This line feels heavy, not only because of the reference to 'mass' and 'charge' (that is, 'cargo'), but also because of the 'or' sounds in the previous lines. The 'or' sounds are juxtaposed to the sound of 'air' in 'earth' and this makes the heaviness seem all the more massy and onerous. What is more, the light sound of 'air' is weighed down in 'earth', and even the earth is said to be 'gross'. A similar feeling is produced by the juxtaposition of the 'air' sound and 'or' sound when Horatio interrogates the ghost: 'Or if thou hast uphoarded in thy life / Extorted treasure in the womb of earth' (1.1.135–6). When the ghost returns to the depths we have the assonance of 'morn' and 'warning' preceding the assonance of 'earth or air' (1.1.152). It is as if the ghost, subject to the weight of tragedy, is bound to follow a downward trajectory. In this he sets a precedent for Hamlet. Hamlet muses that 'foul deeds will rise / Though all the earth o'erwhelm them' (1.2.255–6). He is thinking, of course, of the deeds of the ascending Claudius. As the foul rises, the fair sinks down. Claudius, who put the old Dane's body in the ground, betrays himself when in a single breath he talks of 'our throne' and woe thrown to earth (1.2.106–9).

The tension between lightness and weight, amplified by the sound of 'air' and 'or' and perhaps inadvertently implying the logical sense of 'air' and 'ore' (which were opposite elements in the Elizabethan world picture),[154] exaggerates the drama and especially the tragic sense that Hamlet is being inexorably pulled down to death. The same sense is palpable in the following passage:

> it goes so heavily with my disposition that this goodly frame the earth seems
> to me a sterile promontory,[155] this most excellent canopy
> the air, look you, this brave o'erhanging firmament.
> (2.2.263–6)

The 'look you' is an invitation to the playgoers to join Hamlet in observing the physical context of the play world. The word 'promontory' refers to the thrust stage; 'this most excellent canopy the air' refers to the fact that the playhouse was open to the sky; and the 'brave o'erhanging firmament' refers to the canopy protruding over the upstage (rear) part of the stage which, decorated on its underside with comets and other celestial bodies, constituted the theatrical 'heavens'. Gurr and Ichikawa propose that '[e]ach of these terms is accompanied by a gesture to the relevant features of the theatre'.[156] Compare Hamlet's 'O all you host of heaven, O earth – what else? – / And shall I couple hell?' (1.5.92–3).

Returning to the graveyard scene brings us to Ophelia, although perhaps not face-to-face with her.[157] In the narrative account of Ophelia's drowning we can see the course of her whole life in microcosm. References to her 'clothes' and 'garments' can be read as allusions to the corporal form of her flesh. The line 'Her clothes spread wide / And mermaid-like awhile they bore her up' (4.7.173–4) reminds us of the time her brother spoke to her in the image of flesh waxing in 'thews and bulk' (1.3.12). The outer 'garments' that 'Pulled the poor wretch ... / To muddy death' (4.7.179–81) were not her clothes merely, but also her mortal flesh. As Hamlet disappeared from her, sunk out of sight beneath the burden of his mortality, so she follows. Hamlet's question of will and self-slaughter, 'To be or not to be', becomes Ophelia's question of will and self-slaughter expressed by the gravedigger in the terms 'will he' or 'nill he?'. In life, Ophelia had a lightness that bore her up a while, but it could not keep her up. In the graveyard scene she becomes the sound of 'air' that is buried in 'earth'; witness Laertes' 'Lay her i'th' earth, / ... her fair and unpolluted flesh' (5.1.227–8), Hamlet's 'fair Ophelia!' and Gertrude's 'farewell!' (5.1.231–2). Even her vowel-rich name conveys something between lightness and weight. Ophelia testifies to Hamlet's burden with a triple-repeated 'or': 'a noble mind is here o'erthrown! The courtier's, soldier's, scholar's eye, tongue, sword' (3.1.149–50). She is witness to the crushing of him who should have been the rising 'rose of the fair state' (3.1.151). For her the weight of the earth is held off awhile, but when her father goes to the grave she follows him 'a-down a-down' (4.5.165) in a way that echoes Hamlet's downwards trajectory. It is no surprise that when Claudius narrates the events of Polonius's burial and Ophelia's subsequent distraction, he repeats the 'er' and 'air' sound around a core of 'or': 'we have done but greenly / In hugger-mugger to inter him; poor Ophelia / Divided from herself and her fair judgement' (4.5.83–5).

The sound sense of 'or' rises up to join the logic sense of 'or' to become the most significant word in the most significant line in the most significant speech in the entire play: 'To be or not to be?' The soliloquy purports to present a puzzle to the mind, but throughout it Shakespeare is surreptitiously employing the sound sense of words to lay the poetic weight of 'or' on the hearer's heart. We have 'outrageous fortune', 'Or to take arms', 'No more', 'mortal coil', 'Must give us pause', 'scorns of time', 'th'unworthy takes',[158] 'from whose bourn'. When we delve into the depths of this play, sounding it to its lowest note, we emerge with a buried 'or' and yet another unfathomable question. G. F. Bradby observed that 'complete agreement about *Hamlet* is unthinkable'.[159] Perhaps the possibility that Shakespeare is connecting the weighty sound of 'or' with metallic 'ore', with the buried corpse, with Hamlet's burden and with the weightiest question of the play will seem far-fetched to the very level-headed, but there are 'more things in heaven and earth, Horatio, / Than are dreamt of in your philosophy' (1.5.165–6). Herman Melville, one of the great prose writers of the nineteenth century, appreciated in the name 'Astor' precisely the same qualities of full metallic weight and richness – in short, the qualities of ore – that I have noted in the 'or' sound in *Hamlet*. The narrator of *Bartleby* describes 'John Jacob Astor' as 'a name which, I admit, I love to repeat; for it hath a rounded and orbicular sound to it, and rings like unto bullion'.[160] 'Astor' supplies the sound sense of 'or' to 'orbicular' and the metallic sense of 'ore' to the bullion.

'Horatio' is another name deserving to be heard. From the moment, early on, when he urged Hamlet to 'Season your admiration for a while / With an attent ear till I may deliver / Upon the witness of these gentlemen' (1.2.191–3), Horatio has patiently urged Hamlet to resist his deceiving eyes and to attend with a judicious ear. Horatio, the attentive witness of the whole play, is at once a playgoer who gives a fair hearing and a player who commands one. Thus it is, with substance fitting the sound of his name, that Horatio delivers something like Hamlet's funeral oration and at last delivers him weightless into angelic hands: 'Now cracks a noble heart. Goodnight, sweet Prince, / And flights of angels sing thee to thy rest' (5.2.343–4). Whatever the deep or depressive cause of Hamlet's downfall, he is, after all, a character in a poet's play, and neither poet nor play will leave Hamlet buried beneath his burdens. The oak that broke the vase rooted down only that it would rise up. Ophelia might even follow him in this, for Laertes prophesized that after death she would become in heaven a 'ministering angel' (5.1.230). Hamlet is not a passive victim, but a victim of his own success in delving so deeply. We cannot know if his will was free in life, but as he lies on the stage he is, in death, free at last. He is, in the words of Psalm 88 (again), 'counted among them that go down unto the pit … a man without strength, / Free among the dead' (Ps. 88.3–5).

With Hamlet dead, Fortinbras blusters in at last to set an epilogue on proceedings. He holds a martial truncheon and is fully armoured, as the ghost of the Dane had been.[161] He is the representation of Hamlet's father raised to life.[162] We noted earlier that Y<u>or</u>ick (his name crammed with 'or' or 'ore') was excavated from the earth under the stage. If the metal-armoured, strong-armed F<u>or</u>tinbras (whose name is equally crammed with 'or') is the successor to Hamlet's ghost, then we can say that he has risen from the same pit. Hamlet has done his work, and his work is rewarded in performative terms by the return of the figure of his father. Fortinbras has Hamlet's 'dying voice': 'I do prophesy th'election lights / On Fortinbras' (5.1.339–40), and with that cadence, as he sinks down to the heaviness of death, Hamlet foresees that his successor will rise and perhaps he also foresees the flight of his father heavenward, unburdened and at peace. Horatio directs that Hamlet, who at the last lies low on the stage, should now 'High on a stage be placed to the view' (5.2.362). In Laurence

Olivier's film version (Rank, 1948), Hamlet's body is taken up to the top of Elsinore's highest tower, to the place where the ghost had first led him. That Horatio's direction is in essence a stage direction is suggested by his 'let this same be presently performed' (5.2.377). Fortinbras confirms that the assembly should 'Bear Hamlet like a soldier to the stage' (5.2.380), and so Hamlet is 'put on' (5.2.381) and turned from one burdened by the very fact that he was born, to one who is borne up by others. The 'strong arm' Fortinbras is a sort of prop to the stage, a solidly material realization of the ghostly miner that had propped up the performance throughout. Fortinbras is thus part of the theatre and, like the theatre, is 'a symbol for making unseen realities seen, for exposing the secret places of the human heart and objectifying them in a way without which they would be unbearable to look upon'.[163] When Fortinbras commands 'Take up the bodies' (5.2.385), he not only lifts Hamlet and the others from the stage floor but also lifts the playgoers from the profundity of the drama to the height of the play. Appropriately it is he who commands the courtiers to 'call the noblest to the audience' (5.2.371). He is concerned with 'sight' and 'shows' (5.2.385–6), but also with a fair hearing.

Bradby said that Shakespeare is Hamlet's spiritual father.[164] Shakespeare might also be called the testator of the play, for, like the ghost, he charged Hamlet by his will, made Hamlet his executor to act it out and made him his witness to see it done. There is even an old legend that Shakespeare played the part of the ghost.[165] Shakespeare was certainly acting in this period, and played a part in Ben Jonson's *Every Man in His Humour* (1598), if the list of players in the 1616 Folio of Jonson's *Workes* is reliable on the point. Jonson's sequel, *Every Man Out of His Humour* (1599), makes a fascinating reference to the fact that the protestant 'abolition' of purgatory had prevented testators from returning as ghosts to see their will performed.[166] The character Carlo observes that 'heirs and executors are grown damnably careless, specially since the ghosts of testators left walking' (2.1.89–90). Burbage played the lead in *Every Man Out of His Humour*, as he did in *Hamlet*, but this time there was no part for Shakespeare. The year 1599 was a very busy one for Shakespeare,[167] so perhaps he was otherwise occupied with his own plays about succession and testament – *Hamlet*, *Julius Caesar*, *As You Like It*, *Henry V* – each of which is in some way haunted by the will of a dead father and in more than one case by an actual ghost. In 1599, Shakespeare was also occupied, to greater or lesser extent, with his father's Chancery litigation (see Chapter 3), and perhaps even then he had begun to fear that one day soon he might be called upon to act as his father's executor. As executor, there was a real risk of being burdened – we could say 'haunted' – by his father's debts.[168]

Bradby observes that 'Shakespeare has put a great deal of himself into Hamlet. Sometimes, perhaps, almost more than the character can rightly bear'.[169] We are bound to ask how Hamlet is able to delve so deep and bear so much without actually becoming mad, but Bradby consoles us with the thought that 'problems which puzzle us in the study do not trouble us on stage'.[170] Perhaps 'play's the thing' (3.1.539) that helps Hamlet to bear the burdens of life. Perhaps it is the thing that helps us all. We can do worse than to 'put an antic disposition on'. Good humour may raise the determinedly downcast eye and lift the heaviest heart. It is refreshing to think that a jig like the one that concluded *Julius Caesar* in 1599 might have closed the earliest performances of *Hamlet* too.[171] Even without a jig, it is clear that Shakespeare has been more than successful in rising to the challenge that Thomas Wilson laid down for rhetoricians, which was 'To teach. To delight. And to perswade'. To that end, Wilson recommended that 'even auncient Preachers, must now and then play the fooles in the pulpit'.[172] His special advice to them was to 'serue the tickle eares of their fleting audience ... for though their spirite bee apt, and our will prone, yet our flesh is so heauie, and humours so ouerwhelme vs'.[173] That sounds like an audience full of Hamlets. Shakespeare has someone else to play the fool. His gravedigger is the ideal comic agent. He works to put people in his graves, but expends most of his effort lifting heavy matter out of them. There is no matter more grave than a skull, but the gravedigger throws it up in the air and calls it a jester and even Hamlet can for a moment make light of it. 'The play's the thing' (3.1.539), and the thing is play. Shakespeare brings forth Hamlet to bear the burden of a 'thousand natural shocks' (3.1.61), but he also has Yorick bear him 'on his back a thousand times' (5.1.176); thus Shakespeare is 'cruel only to be kind' (3.4.176). The bottom line is that Shakespeare is playful and just, and so is *Hamlet*, and this is why we enjoy the tragedy so much.

6

From dust to dust and sealing wax: The materials of testamentary performance

In Chapter 2, we considered some of the methods employed in *Richard II*, *King John* and the prologues of *Henry V* by which Shakespeare sought to engage the hands of the playgoers' minds to touch the play and to make the play more touching. One such technique was to place characters on stage to narrate first-hand witness accounts of materials being handled. All witness narratives turn sights into sounds and therefore have the merit of appealing to playgoers as spectators and as audience. Witness accounts of materials being handled are especially potent because they excite the playgoers' senses of sight and sound and touch at the same time. Having been thus engaged to a more complete sensory imagination of the play, the playgoers are better able to get a feel for it and to weigh it up and to probe its forms and test its substance.

Richard II contains an important on-stage witness account of materials being handled. It is the scene, already considered in Chapter 2, in which the Duke of York narrates his account of the moment that the citizens of London threw dust on

Richard's head. The fact that the reported 'handlers' in that instance were the common people of London gathered to witness a great event must have enhanced the original London playgoers' ability to imagine and relate to the physical reality of the scene. Sometimes an on-stage witness account describes a more exotic scene and more luxurious materials. An example is Enobarbus's account of how 'The city cast / Her people out' to see Cleopatra and the famous 'barge she sat in' (*AC*, 2.2.223–4, 2.2.201); the words 'sat in' evoke the feel of satin and suit perfectly the description of 'silken tackle' that 'Swell with the touches of those flower-soft hands' (*AC*, 2.2.220). The poetry produces a tactile sense to the mind.

A little later in this chapter, we will consider two extended examples of Shakespeare's method of engaging the sympathy of playgoing witnesses through the evidentiary narrative of an on-stage witness. Both accounts present material evidence to be assessed by the playgoers and therefore constitute the playgoer as judge. Throughout this book, I have proposed that it is helpful to think of early modern playgoers as witnesses who are involved in a process of probing or testing the will that is performed before them on stage. The suggestion that the nature of a play can be appreciated by analogy to the process of testing (that is 'proving') a testamentary will is not so far removed from the idea that a play can be appreciated by analogy to legal processes of putting witness testimony to the proof.[1] That analogy is particularly apposite to plays in which an innocent person (almost invariably a woman) has been falsely accused, for example *Othello*, *Much Ado About Nothing*, *The Winter's Tale*.[2] One figure that connects the early modern legal world of testament and testimony is the judge known as the 'Ordinary'. These judges were clerics in the ecclesiastical courts whose task it was to decide whether or not a will passed probate. They acted under authority of the bishop (the bishop's ordained status is said to be the origin of the title 'Ordinary') and the seal of approval that they sometimes added in witness and probate of a will was the seal of the presiding bishop. Swinburne writes that:

> this office and charge of executing ... testaments and last willes hath been imposed vpon the reuerend Bishops: in the sinceritie of whose consciences all Christian laws and namely the lawe of this land, hath reposed greater confidence then in other lay people, about the performance of deade mens willes.[3]

There is a strong clerical flavour and more than a hint of probation and a red seal at the start of Shakespeare's *Henry V*. Immediately before the Archbishop of Canterbury embarks upon his lengthy formal proof of Henry's legal title to the throne of France, the king warns that if he is incited to go to war, many men 'Shall drop their blood in approbation' (1.2.19) of the legal claim. For our purposes, the title of Ordinary is convenient to remind us that the ordinary citizens of London attended the Elizabethan playhouses with the opportunity to 'prove' ('probe') and to judge the will and testament (and testimony) presented to them. With this in mind, we can now turn to our two extended examples of on-stage witness accounts: one from *Hamlet*, the other from *Macbeth*. Both narrate the same standard early modern sequence of working with materials to produce a sealed document: folding of paper, writing and sealing.

In *Hamlet*, Hamlet reports how he forged a document in the form of an order made by the king of Denmark:

HORATIO

How was this sealed?

HAMLET

Why even in that was heaven ordinant:
I had my father's signet in my purse –
Which was the model of that Danish seal –
Folded the writ up in the form of th'other,
Subscribed it, gave't th'impression, placed it safely.
(*Ham*, 5.2.47–52)

The word 'ordinant' will now put the reader in mind of the

seal affixed by the clerical Ordinary, and it may be that the word had similar resonance for the first playgoers.

In *Macbeth*, we have the Gentlewoman's report of Lady Macbeth's nocturnal compositions:

GENTLEWOMAN
Since his majesty went into the field, I have seen
her rise from her bed, throw her nightgown upon
her, unlock her closet, take forth paper, fold it,
write upon't, read it, afterwards seal it, and again
return to bed, yet all this while in a most fast sleep.
DOCTOR
... besides her
walking and other actual performances, what, at any
time, have you heard her say?
GENTLEWOMAN
That, sir, which I will not report after her.
DOCTOR
You may to me: and 'tis most meet you should.
GENTLEWOMAN
Neither to you, nor any one, having no witness to
confirm my speech. (*Mac,* 5.1.4–18)

These accounts of the act of producing a documentary form are accounts of 'actual performances', as the *Macbeth* passage expressly confirms. Both narratives also describe performances in the theatrical sense of gestured and propertied action. In each instance, the sequence by which the form is created ends in the impression of wax, presumably blood-red, and can therefore be said to plot in microcosm the tragic trajectory of the entire play in which the sequence appears. The fact that the sequence of folding–writing–sealing in both *Hamlet* and *Macbeth* appears early in the final act creates a tangible sense of events unfolding that are written in the fates and bound for a bloody end. The reader will recall from Chapter 5 that *Hamlet* began with the documentary and performative connotations of an invitation to 'unfold', and that Hamlet's own idea of the acting aspect of theatrical performance was one which called for the players to show 'the time his form and pressure' (*Ham*, 3.2.24). Perhaps there is a pun here on the pressing of a seal on a documentary form.

In the two documentary episodes under consideration, the witness narratives of Hamlet and the Gentlewoman are of a special sort. They resemble the legal process of 'attestation', whereby a witness affirms the veracity of writing, signature and seal. In Shakespeare's day, the law reflected the fact that the national population was largely illiterate. Testators did not have to write their wills in person, or sign them, or seal them. Following the 1540 Statute of Wills, a devise of land by will was required to be in writing, but that was as far as the formalities went during Shakespeare's lifetime.[4] Neither did witnesses have to subscribe the will or seal it or otherwise attest to it in writing. In cases of doubt, their oral testimony was sufficient.[5] Writing, signing and sealing by the testator and witnesses were, of course, encouraged, and it was expedient for the avoidance of doubt. Shakespeare's own will was subscribed by witnesses and signed by Shakespeare in his own hand. A subscribing testator is always, in a sense, acting as witness to their own will. The example of Shakespeare's will makes this clear. It recites a standard form of words: 'In witnes Whereof I have hereunto put my ~~Seale~~ *hand*'. As a gentleman, Shakespeare must have owned a signet or seal matrix bearing his arms, but for some reason it was not used and the word 'Seale' is deleted. The idea of performers acting as witnesses to their own wills is a very potent one. It speaks of actors being in a sense alienated from their acts. Where this decays into deep alienation from oneself, it can produce a destructive schism between act and will. This is the case with Lady Macbeth in the episode set out above, and something like it (but for very different reasons) is true of Hamlet throughout most of *Hamlet* (as we saw in Chapter 5). Hamlet is not, however, alienated from his actions in the episode quoted above. In that episode the sequential process of documentary performance (pressed on by the urgency of a deadline) engages his will to act in a way that we seldom witness elsewhere in the play. Whatever block it is that Hamlet suffers from, it is not writer's block. Hamlet shows us in this scene that a character on stage (and, where appropriate, an actor on stage) can engender a sense that he or she is a witness to their own performance. Where a person does this, it invites the playgoers to witness the performance with them. Playgoers cannot help but join with Hamlet and the Gentlewoman and the Doctor in witness to the performances described in the two episodes. The playgoers might also relate to the on-stage depiction of quotidian rituals of manual work, in this case writing. The presence of similar writing sequences in both plays is, in addition to its other significations, a sign of a professional writer attesting to the work of his own hands by representing his everyday practices on stage.

Early modern writing called for a fairly standard set of materials. These included: paper (rarely parchment); scissors to cut the paper; a ruler to fold the paper and to rule lines; an inkstand ('standish'); an inkwell; ink; feathers (*pennae*) for quills; a penknife (to cut the *penna* into quill pens); a whetstone to sharpen the knife; a dustbox or sandbox or pouncebox from which to sprinkle dust, sand or 'pounce';[6] a candle to see by and to melt the sealing wax; string or ribbon for the seal; a signet ring or other seal matrix; and, finally, a chair to sit at, and a desk to stage the whole performance.[7] When items such as these become properties on stage, they have the 'power to puncture dramatic illusion by pointing to alternate social dramas of economic production, exchange, and ownership'.[8] One of the best examples of this is the gage or glove that we considered in Chapter 2. As the son of a glover, the glove was an obvious thing for Shakespeare to focus on, but playgoers did not have to be glovers to be able to imagine a personal connection to the thing. It was common enough as an item of fashionable dress or labouring garb.

As words move us through their effect on the mind, especially through the material connotations that metaphors create, so physical material can have the same effect unmediated by words. In earlier chapters, we considered John Austin's notion of 'performative utterances' (or 'speech acts' as he later termed them), but we can also speak of 'performative materials' or 'performative properties'. The art of rhetoric is most effective when it appreciates the material reality of words and marries this to the moving potential of silent action and material stuff.[9] This is real rhetoric. Some wordless sights and objects have the quality that Shakespeare calls 'a prone and speechless dialect / Such as move men' (*MM*, 1.2.173–4). The word 'object' denotes something that is conceptually 'thrown against' the senses, and we have seen through the course of this book that some of the most striking and significant stage objects are not only thrown conceptually, but are also thrown physically (e.g. dust, gloves, warder, skulls). When an object is thrown against another thing, it will move it, all other things being equal. As Newton's laws explain material encounters in the physical world, so we can talk of dramatic laws through which stage properties have a metaphysical power to move people. There is something proto-Newtonian in the hope expressed by Claudius that a visit to England will move Hamlet to change: 'Haply the seas and countries different / With variable objects shall expel / This something-settled matter in his heart' (*Ham*, 3.1.170–2). Newton's language of 'force' and 'gravity' and 'motion' would not have existed without a rhetorical tradition that understood the matter of the mind to be moved by emotional force. Consider, for example, the proto-Newtonian quality of Thomas Wilson's observation that 'Affections therefore (called Passions) are none other thing, but a stirring or forsing of the minde'.[10]

Legal documentary performance combines word, act and thing. The word 'deed' is a clue to the speech act by which the legal word is performed and the deed is also a documentary thing. It operates not only as a performative utterance, but also as a performative property. The seal is the most significant material aspect of a legal deed, and a clue to this is the fact that the word itself derives from the Latin for 'little sign' (*sigillum*). The seal is evidence of the wilful participation of the one who impresses it.[11] When, in *King John*, Salisbury says 'we swear / A voluntary zeal' (*KJ*, 5.2.9–10), Shakespeare is implying a fluid poetic connection between will and seal: 'voluntary' corresponds to 'will'; 'zeal' corresponds to 'seal'. 'Seal' and 'zeal' are expressly identified with each other where the Duke of Austria says: 'Upon thy cheek lay I this zealous kiss, / As seal to this indenture of my love' (*KJ*, 2.1.19–20) (the association is also intimated at 2.1.244, 250). More demanding on the imagination – and in that respect more engaging – are the moments where Shakespeare connects 'seal' and 'zeal' indirectly through reference to their shared qualities. If one had to choose a word to describe the property of blood (or a blood-red substance) which becomes hot, congeals when cool and is used to confirm the performance of deeds, 'seal' and 'zeal' would both be apt. Shakespeare plays with this poetic connection – between 'zeal' and 'heat' and 'blood' and 'voluntary' and 'deeds' and 'seal' – throughout *King John*. On 'will' and 'heat', we have the 'fiery voluntaries' of the English camp (*KJ*, 2.1.67). On 'zeal' and 'blood', we have Hubert's 'If zealous love should go in search of virtue … Whose veins bound richer blood than Lady Blanche?' (*KJ*, 2.1.428–31). On 'blood' and 'heat', we have the Bastard's line 'the rich blood of kings is set on fire!' (*KJ*, 2.1.351) and King John's 'France, I am burn'd up with inflaming wrath; / A rage whose heat hath this condition, / That nothing can allay, nothing but blood, / The blood, and dearest-valued blood, of France' (*KJ*, 3.1.340–3). On 'zeal' and 'heat' and 'blood' together, we have Cardinal Pandulph's 'This act so evilly borne shall cool the hearts / Of all his people, and freeze up their zeal' (*KJ*, 3.3.149–50) (compare *R2*, 1.1.47, 51). On 'zeal' and 'heat' and 'wax', we have Queen Elinor's 'Lest zeal, now melted by the windy breath / Of soft petitions, pity and remorse, / Cool and congeal again to what it was' *(KJ*, 2.1.477–9). Malone argued that Elinor is referring to zeal as the congealed ice of resolution, and Honigmann's suggestion that Shakespeare might be contrasting the heat of English zeal to the iciness of French zeal is not implausible,[12] but I agree with John Dover Wilson that Shakespeare is here quibbling on 'zeal' as a hot humour associated with a wax 'seal'.[13] On 'blood' and 'heat' and 'wax' together, we have Melun's 'Have I not hideous death within my view, / Retaining but a quantity of life, / Which bleeds away, even as a form of wax / Resolveth from his figure 'gainst the fire?' (*KJ*, 5.4.22–5).

Melun's words are 'testamentary' in the most obvious sense of having 'death within ... view', but they are also testamentary in their connection to the play's central concern with inheritance. The connection to the play's inheritance theme can be inferred into Melun's phrase ''gainst the fire?' (5.4.22–5). The phrase is echoed in King John's 'all my bowels crumble up to dust: / I am a scribbled form, drawn with a pen / Upon a parchment, and against this fire / Do I shrink up' (*KJ*, 5.7.31–4). This intensely material reiteration of the material processes of writing, takes us directly to what Pettet calls the play's 'dominant image, in both the words and the stage spectacle', which is Arthur – the play's symbol of the true royal succession – sitting bound against the fire (the brazier of hot coals) in Scene 4.1. Pettet concludes that 'the fire imagery of *King John* does something, superficially, towards unifying the play' but that 'it contributes nothing at all to the meaning'.[14] I disagree. It seems to me that the heat image is essential to the sealing of the testamentary performance and is therefore a most meaningful signifier of the play's intense concern to engage the sensory participation of the playgoing witnesses. Their participation becomes politically charged when the play invites them to join in passing judgment on the willful acts of a king. Hubert, a citizen comrade to the original London playgoers, presents the documentary evidence of John's order to kill Arthur:

HUBERT
Here is your hand and seal for what I did.
KING JOHN
O, when the last account 'twixt heaven and earth
Is to be made, then shall this hand and seal
Witness against us to damnation!

> How oft the sight of means to do ill deeds
> Make deeds ill done! Hadst not thou been by,
> A fellow by the hand of nature mark'd,
> Quoted and sign'd to do a deed of shame,
> This murder had not come into my mind.
> (*KJ*, 4.2.215–24).

John does not deny that the document is his, but he tries to deny responsibility for the deed by shifting the blame on to Hubert and to 'nature'. This is a dramatically interesting variation on the legal plea '*non est factum*' ('this is not my deed').[15] This legal plea asserts that the pleader did not appreciate the import of what it was that he or she had signed. A successful plea of *non est factum* renders the instrument void from its inception.[16] The plea normally applies to *inter vivos* instruments (documents created during the creator's lifetime), but even in Shakespeare's day the plea had a counterpart in the law of wills. According to Swinburne, '[i]t is the minde and not the words which giveth life to the testament', so a will was void and 'no testament' if it lacked *animum testandi*.[17] This covered the case of a testator who was found to have made his will 'rashly, unadvisedly' or otherwise 'not seriously, nor with a firme purpose to make his will',[18] and it covered cases of fraud.[19] Shakespeare's King John, likewise Bolingbroke in *Richard II*, perform acts of trade with the crown (see Chapter 2), and it is notable that they both attempt similar pleas of *non est factum* in order to deny responsibility for deeds. In *Richard II*, there is an episode in which Bolingbroke purports to deny responsibility for the deed of killing the rightful king in almost exactly the same way that King John does, although in Bolingbroke's case the deed is not written down. When Exton presents Richard's body, Bolingbroke decries Exton's 'deed of slander', to which Exton replies: 'From your own mouth, my lord, did I this deed' (*R2*, 5.6.37). In the same play, Aumerle attempts a plea of *non est factum* in more orthodox form when he repents the deed by which he sealed his treason against Bolingbroke, saying: 'Read not my name there; / My heart is not confederate with my hand' (*R2*, 5.3.51–2). The denial of deeds is fundamentally alienating behaviour. A legal documentary deed is a deed of action (of the hand and mind) represented as a physical thing. When the actor playing King John denies his own act and the actor Hubert (in the role of executor and executioner) refuses his role, the performance as a whole becomes a detached or alien object thrown against the playgoers as something to be handled and assessed. With apologies to the melancholy Jaques, one person can at any time 'play many parts', and here, as John turns from testator to witness of his own will, and as Hubert turns from executor to judge, so the playgoing witnesses are engaged to all perspectives at once. They witness the wills of others in performance and, through a process of trial or probation, they pass judgment on others with a will of their own.

In *Julius Caesar*, Brutus did not in express terms seek to deny his deed, but Harry Keyishian notes that in the assassination scene in Stuart Burge's film version (Commonwealth United Entertainment, 1970), when the conspirators held their 'hands palms-outward, so as not to stain their clothes', they 'in some *gestural* sense repudiate their deed even as they praise it'.[20] The motif of the 'bloody deed' is ubiquitous in Shakespeare's tragedies. In *Hamlet*, Gertrude says 'bloody deed is this!' *(Ham*, 3.4.25) in reference to the accidental execution of Polonius. (That's execution of a 'formality' if ever there was one.) Hamlet immediately echoes her: 'A bloody deed' (*Ham*, 3.4.26). The 'bloody deed' is frequently employed as a pun or trope on a legal deed. As blood marks the violent performance of will, so the red mark of wax seals the legal performance of will in testamentary and lifetime documents. Hamlet says that he will 'speak daggers' to his mother in the form of 'words', but will not give his words 'seals' by wounding her physically (*Ham*, 3.2.386–9). Early modern drama frequently employs physical properties of red on white – typically a stain of blood on white flesh or white cloth – to associate murderous deeds and executions with the legal execution of documentary deeds. The signal contrast between red and white is primal.

It may be as close as we get to a universal sign of the performance of human life. With regard to the Ndembu people, the anthropologist Victor Turner observed that:

> when the colors are considered in abstraction from social and ritual contexts, Ndembu think of white and black as the supreme antitheses in their scheme of reality. Yet ... in rite after rite white and red appear in conjunction and black is seldom directly expressed ... in action contexts red is regularly paired with white.[21]

In Shakespeare's usage, the mark of red on white has ritual and liminal significance. It denotes loss of innocence; witness Hubert's 'this hand of mine / Is yet a maiden and an innocent hand, / Not painted with the crimson spots of blood' (*KJ*, 4.2.251–3). Desdemona's 'handkerchief / Spotted with strawberries' (*Oth*, 3.3.437–8), which was adduced by Iago in evidence of her infidelity, seems to be a similar sign – always assuming that the handkerchief was white (in Iqbal Khan's 2015 RSC production it was black, and so was Iago). Violence, death, mourning and remembrance of the dead are frequently signalled by the sign of red and white and by the prop of a bloodied handkerchief (*JC*, 3.2.134; *R3*, 4.4.274–7). Shakespeare and other early modern playwrights followed the medieval theatrical tradition of using blood symbolically to evoke the performative power of the blood of Christ and His saints.[22] They were also reviving a tradition, dating back to ancient Greek drama, in which the stain of blood was used to represent the violence inherent in the performance of will, including will expressed through the imposition of rigid rules and inflexible forms of law. An important early example appears in Sophocles' *Antigone*.[23] Creon, King of Thebes, had decreed that Polyneices (eldest son of Oedipus's incestuous union with his mother Jocasta), who had died in an assault upon his native Thebes, must be left unburied in the public street as punishment for his treachery. Antigone, a sister of Polyneices, was imprisoned at Creon's command when it emerged that she had secretly performed burial rites for her brother by sprinkling earth on his corpse. Antigone's dungeon cell became her tomb when she killed herself by hanging and it was in that state that Haemon, Creon's son and Antigone's lover, discovered her pale corpse. Impassioned with rage, he assailed Creon and accidentally killed himself upon his own sword. The line that sets the seal on the tragic scene is delivered by a messenger to Haemon's mother, Eurydice. Through the messenger's report (an ancient precedent for the theatrical technique of using on-stage witness narrative), we learn that when Haemon (the 'man of blood') took Antigone in a final embrace, 'he spurted a quick stream of bloody drops onto her white cheek' (1238–9). This sealed the violent performance of Creon's will and law. Red blood on a white cheek was an established sign of ritual mourning. (Euripides' *The Suppliant Women* records that the Argive mothers were directed to mourn their dead sons with the words: 'Bloody the white fingernail along the cheek, and stain the skin!')[24] The blood on Antigone's white cheek was also a sign of her lost innocence, and as such it set a tragic seal on her will to marry Haemon.[25]

The climactic crypt scene in Shakespeare's *Romeo and Juliet* is in some salient respects similar to the climactic dungeon scene in Sophocles' *Antigone*. When Romeo finds Juliet in the crypt, he associates her facial appearance with the sign of red and white, observing that 'Beauty's ensign yet / Is crimson in thy lips and in thy cheeks, / And death's pale flag is not advanced there' (*RJ*, 5.3.94–6). Believing Juliet to be dead, Romeo kills himself, as Haemon did, by an act that is at once deliberate and unintended. Shakespeare has Romeo express his performance in the legal terminology of a deed that has been sealed and thereby finalized or 'engrossed', but he does so with typically poetic disregard for legal technical distinctions between doctrinal categories. He blends the sense of contractual act and testamentary consequence:

Eyes, look your last;
Arms, take your last embrace, and lips, O you

> The doors of breath, seal with a righteous kiss
> A dateless bargain to engrossing death. (5.3.112–15)

Shakespeare returned to a similar set of thoughts in *Henry V*, where the Duke of Exeter narrates the report of a touching encounter between the dying Duke of York and the body of his comrade, the Duke of Suffolk. He tells how York kissed 'the gashes / That bloodily did yawn upon his face' (4.6.13–14), and:

> So did he turn, and over Suffolk's neck
> He threw his wounded arm and kissed his lips,
> And so, espoused to death, with blood he sealed
> A testament of noble-ending love. (4.6.24–7)

In *Henry V*, Shakespeare describes written evidence of the treachery of the Earl of Cambridge, Lord Scroop and Sir Thomas Grey in terms that seem to allude to the legal idea of the deed 'engrossed'. Henry considers the written evidence to be truth 'as gross / As black on white' (2.2.103–4). In the next act of the same play, allusion to legal documentation acquires something of a testamentary sense through the use of the word 'attest'. Henry challenges his troops to 'attest / That those whom you called fathers did beget you. / Be copy now to men of grosser blood' (3.1.22–4). 'Copy' and 'gross' both refer to deeds in their final, and thus finest, form.

In *Julius Caesar*, when Antony speaks of 'a parchment, with the seal of Caesar' (3.2.129) and later produces 'the will, and under Caesar's seal' (3.2.233), there can be little doubt that he is holding a white parchment sealed with red wax. If the parallel sign of blood on Caesar's white toga and corpse does not confirm it, then it is confirmed by Antony's prophesy that if the plebeians were to read the will, they would 'go and kiss dead Caesar's wounds, / and dip their napkins in his sacred blood' (3.2.133–4). The motif of the napkin dipped in blood was not exclusive to tragedy. In Shakespeare's intensely testamentary comedy *As You Like It* (see Chapter 3), we have the curious incident of Orlando being delayed by a violent encounter with a lioness. He sends a bloodied handkerchief as proof of his valour and as an evidentiary explanation for his tardiness. *A Warning for Fair Women*, an anonymous domestic tragedy contemporary with both *Julius Caesar* and *As You Like It*, seems to have inspired elements of Shakespeare's plays or to have been inspired by them. In *A Warning*, the murderer Browne kills his lover's husband and dips his 'hankerchief in his bloud' in order to 'send it as a token' to her (1385–6).[26] Browne makes express what is only implied in Shakespeare's plays – that the stained handkerchief represents bloody performance: 'Upon this bloody Handkercher the thing, / As I did promise and have now performed' (1412–13). Subha Mukherji observes that 'in its statement of promise and performance, this gesture enacts a perverse marriage sequence'.[27] (As such, it reminds us of the inverted nuptials witnessed in the death tryst of Haemon and Antigone.) The resonance between *A Warning* and *Julius Caesar* is loudest where both plays refer to the speaking tongues of bloody wounds. In *Julius Caesar*, 'sweet Caesar's wounds' are 'poor poor dumb mouths' (3.2.218) and Antony wishes that his oratory could 'put a tongue / In every wound of Caesar' (3.2.221–2). In *A Warning*, Browne reports that 'In ev'ry wound there is a bloudy tongue, / Which will speake … / By a whole Jury I shall be accusde' (1995–9). There is something more here than the mere evident sight of blood on white flesh. There is also the testimonial sound of speech. The playgoers are presented with a signal object as a thing to be seen, but also as a thing to be heard. A true case of hearing the evident.[28]

As the mark of red on white is a stage property that signals tragedy, so the 'ring' is a stage property that signals comedy. The distinction is not strict, of course (we have already noted the bloody handkerchief in *As You Like It*, and the sealed bond in *The Merchant of Venice* is a tragic element in the context of a play that is formally comedic), but as a general rule the bloody mark is a tragic sign and the ring is a comedic symbol. In Chapter 3, we considered how the ring operates in comedy to symbolize the folly of willing submission to bonds (bands) and the folly of repeating errors in a never-ending circle of 'here we are all over again'. I will only add here that the placement of the ring conceit within the plot of the comedic action is strikingly consistent across Shakespeare's plays. Where a comedy contains confusion and tricks with rings, the relevant scenes nearly always come towards the end of the play. As such they speak of comedy's cyclical errors – its errors without end. They also put a seal on the 'testamentary performance' (including the 'deed' or 'action' of the play) as a signet ring does. Examples of concluding or late scenes involving ring games and ring conceits include the following: *The Comedy of Errors* (4.2–4.4, 5.1); *The Two Gentlemen of Verona* (4.4, 5.4); *The Merchant of Venice* (5.1: in this play, 'ring' is the very last word); *The Merry Wives of Windsor* (5.5); *All's Well That Ends Well* (5.3). *Twelfth Night, or What You Will* is the exception in which the ring game comes early in the play (1.5, 2.2, 3.1), but that comedy is sealed in the most poignant re-joining of twin brother and sister as if re-joining a signet ring to the counterpart of the wax seal. It is, I think, the most touching ending to any of Shakespeare's comedies, even before one conjectures that it might imagine the reunion of Shakespeare's own daughter Judith to the twin brother she had lost. With such an ending, it is little wonder that Shakespeare broke with his pattern and pushed the folly of the ring game to the beginning of the play.

In *As You Like It* we have no actual ring game, but the repeated reference to spring as a 'pretty ring time' in the stanzas of a song comes in Scene 5.3, which is exactly where we would expect it. Coming at the end of the play, the ring sets a seal on the comedy by focusing not upon the mark made by the ring (as the fatal finality of a tragedy must), but upon the never-ending nature of the circle itself. In comedy, errors go on, but so does life. The ring in *All's Well That Ends Well* has a distinctively testamentary quality, but not in any morbid sense. The ring is testamentary in the sense that it had been 'Conferr'd by testament to th' sequent issue' (*AW*, 5.3.196) down six generations. It is also testamentary in the fact that it performs an evidentiary function in the trial of Diana's virtue. Presented with the evidence of the ring, her accuser blushes red on his white cheeks (the comedic equivalent of Juliet's or Antigone's tragic 'blush'). The ring becomes the chief witness in this scene because Parolles, who was summoned as a witness to give oral evidence in the matter, cannot be relied upon on; he is 'So bad an instrument' (*AW*, 5.3.201). There is a joke for the lawyers in this, for parol (oral) evidence is the exact opposite of the documentary evidence that an 'instrument' supplies.

Like the classical pairing of the mask of tragedy with the mask of comedy, the blood-red wax of tragedy and the ring of comedy are two sides of the same dramatic performance. We noted earlier that when Shakespeare was writing, the seal was usually created by pressing a signet ring or other matrix into the hot wax (*Ham*, 5.2.47–52). Taking this as our metaphor, we can say that the signet ring of comedy leaves its impression on the bloody wax of tragedy and that it succeeds as comedy because it has touched the tragic but come away untainted. Aristotle used the image of wax and signet to explain the unity of body and soul. He argued that the body is not of the same substance as the soul, but that body and soul are imprinted with the same identity: 'Hence we need not ask whether the soul and body are one, any more than we need to ask this about the wax and the seal or, in general, about the matter and the thing of which it is the matter'.[29] The signet made of gold imparts its form to the wax, but does not impart its golden substance. Extending the allegory in the direction of Christian theology, we might say that during the life of a person the golden signet of the soul is pressed into constant contact with the wax of the earthly body, so that the waxen flesh bears the seal or identity of the soul. At death, the wax is melted and the same golden signet makes a new and more perfect impression on the new and more perfect wax of the eternal body.[30]

As we perform our lives in flesh, so we perform ourselves in dress, including the material form of clothes. Parolles is considered to be an unreliable instrument because his soul 'is his clothes' (2.5.43–4), but even such stuff as clothes can bear the sincere imprint of our identity. The actor who played the courtly Parolles would very likely have been wearing the clothes that a dead gentleman or nobleman had left to the company or which had been sold to the company by a beneficiary of a gentleman's testament.[31] When Richard Burbage, playing Hamlet, pondered the material remains that the human soul leaves behind at death, did he pause to contemplate that his costume was (we can conjecture) a material remnant of another man's life?

Talking of material remnants brings us back to the glove or gage. We have noted that it is a sign of the hand's action in executing documents and performing all sorts of acts of will in the worlds of theatre and law. The glove also has a prior material connection to legal performance in the fact that gloves were made of the same stuff (animal skin) as the most important legal deeds. Skin is simultaneously the very definition of a superficiality and the very definition of a materially significant remnant of life. Shakespeare, whose father was among many other things a glove-maker and seller of skins, grew up in Stratford-upon-Avon surrounded by material connections between hand and deed. Hamlet has just been discussing legal formalities at the graveside when he asks 'Is not parchment made of sheepskins?'. We should not be surprised that Horatio's response is very precise: 'Ay, my lord, and of calves' skins too' (*Ham*, 5.1.107–8).

We will stay in Stratford-upon-Avon. It seems the proper place to conclude this study of testamentary will as we mark the four-hundredth anniversary of Shakespeare's last will and testament. When most people think of Shakespeare's will, one thing comes immediately to mind. It is a thing that I have preferred to leave until last, as he seemingly did. I am referring, of course, to the solitary provision by which Shakespeare made a bequest in favour of his wife (without actually mentioning Anne's name). The provision, added between the lines towards the end of his will, simply reads:

'Itm, I gyve vnto my wief my second best bed wth the furniture.' That bed has generated much entertaining speculation on the nature of Shakespeare's relationship to Anne.[32] I will let them lie in it. My only suggestion is that Shakespeare was probably content to think that Anne would be looked after by their daughter Susanna and her husband Dr John Hall. If we have learned anything from our study of performance and will, it is that formal appearances are never the end of the matter. With legal forms, we must be especially careful to read between the lines, and beyond the lines. As Hamlet points out, 'They are sheep and calves which seek out assurance' in legal documents (*Ham*, 5.1.109–10). What he is saying is that to put one's hope in legal forms is to follow the flock. The legal suitor is, on this view, someone who pursues the sight of the form without questioning what lies behind it or where it might lead. I like to think that Shakespeare is mocking legalistic habits of unthinking formalism and all routine forms of behaviour that are devoid of imaginative acts of will.

Another interlineal addition to Shakespeare's will was an item describing gifts of money to Shakespeare's 'fellows' in the London theatre: John Heminges, Richard Burbage and Henry Condell. The money was given for the express purpose of purchasing rings (to remember Shakespeare by). We now know that Heminges and Condell went a good deal further, for it is in large part down to their efforts that we have the First Folio edition of *Mr. William Shakespeares Comedies, Histories, & Tragedies*.[33]

Shakespeare's son Hamnet, who had predeceased his father by almost twenty years, was nowhere expressly referred to in his father's will. It would have been most strange if he had been. There is nevertheless a sense in which the absent Hamnet is present in the will. Park Honan observes that the weak point of Shakespeare's own estate was 'its terrible lack of a male heir',[34] and the wording of the will, even allowing that it was a variation on a standard form, seems to strain to make up for that lack. It provides no less than seven times that the estate should pass by entail to 'heires Males of the bodie' of Shakespeare's daughters and their issue (on 'entail', see Chapter 3). Hamnet is an absent presence in the will. Shakespeare explores something like this sense of absent presence in a passage in *King John*, written around the time of Hamnet's death. Constance speaks movingly of a parent's grief at the loss of a son:

> Grief fills the room up of my absent child,
> Lies in his bed, walks up and down with me,
> Puts on his pretty looks, repeats his words,
> Remembers me of all his gracious parts,
> Stuffs out his vacant garments with his form. (*KJ*, 3.3.93–7)

Perhaps these words reflect some of Shakespeare's thoughts on the loss of his son. That is what I hear, and I make no apology for taking the romantic view. John Dover Wilson was of a very different opinion. For him this description of grief seemed 'conventional and frigid'.[35] There can be no argument on matters of taste, but there may be some middle ground to be found in the fact that Shakespeare would surely not have intended the grief in this passage to be appreciated by the playgoers as a representation of his own grief. It is poetry intended to be performed on stage (and by the time of the First Folio, if not before, intended to be read on the page). As such, the passage demonstrates Shakespeare's poetic capacity to animate material stuff (even the mundane 'room', 'bed' and 'garments') so as to make them humanly touching. This is poetry with testamentary power, for as it gives life to inanimate things it connects the world of the living to the world after death. It is with this power that Shakespeare still fills up the house.

NOTES

'Performance is a kind of will or testament'

1 Etymologies are from *Chambers Dictionary of Etymology*, R. K. Barnhart (ed.) (London: H. Wilson and Company, 1988) unless otherwise stated.

2 An internet search will quickly reveal that the pun is a common one in the titles of books about Shakespeare.

3 I discuss the 'science fiction' of law in *Equity Stirring: The Story of Justice Beyond Law* (Oxford: Hart, 2009), 10–14.

4 Almost one-third of academic articles on the legal database *Westlaw UK* that contain 'rhetoric' in their title also contain the word 'reality' (31 of the 100 most recent articles as at 26 April 2015). Disjunction between the words is always implied, and is usually expressed – as in the phrases 'rhetoric or reality?' and 'from rhetoric to reality'.

5 'There is something wrong with a state of the law which makes it necessary to create fairy tales' (*AIB Group (UK) plc v. Mark Redler and Co Solicitors* [2014] UKSC 58, [2014] 3 WLR 1367, per Lord Toulson at para [69]).

6 Ibid., para [1].

7 For further insight into the rhetorical nature of legal language the reader is directed to Marianne Constable, *Our Word is Our Bond: How Legal Speech Acts* (Stanford, CA: Stanford University Press, 2014) and to the writings of James Boyd White (see J. Etxabe and G. Watt [eds], *Living in a Law Transformed: Encounters with the Works of James Boyd White* [Michigan: Michigan University Press, 2014]) and to the work of Peter Goodrich.

8 Quotations from Shakespeare's works are from the most recent edition published by Bloomsbury Arden Shakespeare unless otherwise stated.

9 This was in large part a matter of superstition (see E. A. J. Honigmann and Susan Brock, *Playhouse Wills, 1558–1642* [Manchester: Manchester University Press, 1993], 17. The authors note that in their sample, the average time between the making of the will and burial is just two weeks). A short gap between will and death was also practically advantageous because early modern wills were not effective to dispose of lands acquired by the testator after the date of the will (Joseph Chitty [ed.], *William Blackstone's Commentaries on the Laws of England*, (1765–69), [London: William Walker, 1826], II.23, 378).

10 Jane Cox, 'Shakespeare's Will and Signatures', in *Shakespeare in the Public Records* (London: Public Records Office, 1985), 25.

11 Compare *Per*, 4.2.90–1.

12 Robert Cover, 'Violence and the Word', 95 *Yale Law Journal* 1603 (1985–6) 1602 fn.2. I am grateful to Angela Luk Fan, a student on the joint degree in law and literary studies at the University of Hong Kong, for bringing this quotation to my attention.

13 These are the general rules. In the case of emergencies, as also in the case of soldiers on active duty, exceptions have been made since ancient times.

14 Harley Granville-Barker, 'Shakespeare's Dramatic Art', in *A Companion to Shakespeare Studies*, H. Granville-Barker and G. B. Harrison (eds) (Cambridge: Cambridge University Press, 1934), 45–87, 86. On the participation of playgoer as judge see Julen Etxabe, *The Experience of Tragic Judgment* (Abingdon: Routledge, 2012).

15 Lorna Hutson, '"Lively Evidence": Legal Inquiry and the *Evidentia* of Shakespearean Drama', in *Shakespeare and the Law*, B. Cormack, M. Nussbaum and R. Strier (eds) (Chicago: University of Chicago Press, 2013), 72–97, 73.

16 On the significance of the painter's lines to the equitable

doctrine of 'specific performance' of a contract, see Luke Wilson, *Theaters of Intention: Drama and the Law in Early Modern England* (Palo Alto, CA: Stanford University Press, 2000), 178–82; Gary Watt, *Equity Stirring: The Story of Justice Beyond Law* (Oxford: Hart, 2009), 114–16.

17 *Throckmerton* v. *Tracy* (1555) 1 Plow 145, 159, 162–3, per Sir Robert Broke, Chief Justice of the Common Pleas.

18 On the rhetorical cultures that connected early modern theatre and law, see for example Quentin Skinner, *Forensic Shakespeare* (Oxford: Oxford University Press, 2014); Lorna Hutson and Victoria Kahn (eds), *Rhetoric and Law in Early Modern Europe* (New Haven, CT: Yale University Press, 2001).

19 Harley Granville-Barker, *Prefaces to Shakespeare* (London: Batsford, 1930), 5.

20 Compare *KJ*, 4.2.231–7. On signs and deeds in *King John*, see Chapters 2 and 6.

21 The earliest theatrical usage cited in the *Oxford English Dictionary* is Robert Green's *Green's Neuer too Late* (1590): 'Men greedie of gaines did fall to practise the acting of such Playes' (ii. sig. B4v). On the terminology of 'acting', see Andrew Gurr, *The Shakespearean Stage, 1574–1642*, 4th edn (Cambridge: Cambridge University Press, 2009), 118.

22 'Stone tools, language and the brain in human evolution', *Phil. Trans. R. Soc. B* (2012), 367, 75–87, 81.

23 Elias Canetti, *Crowds and Power*, Carol Stewart (trans.) (New York: Continuum, 1973), 217.

24 Cicely Berry, *From Word to Play: A Handbook For Directors* (London: Oberon Books, 2008), 127.

25 Henry Swinburne, *A Briefe Treatise of Testaments and Last Willes* (London: John Windet, 1590).

26 William West, *Symbolæography* (London: Totthill, 1590).

27 Edmund Plowden, *Les Commentaries, ou les Reportes* (London: Tottyl, 1571).

28 Thomas Wilson, *Arte of Rhetorique* (1560), G. H. Mair (ed.) (Oxford: Clarendon Press, 1909).

29 Peter Mack, *Elizabethan Rhetoric: Theory and Practice* (Cambridge: Cambridge University Press, 2002), 80–95. Classical originals that Shakespeare would probably have encountered include Cicero's *De officiis* and *De inventione*, Quintilian's *Institutio oratoria* and the anonymous *Rhetorica ad Herennium*. The latter was frequently and erroneously attributed to Cicero.

30 Holger Schott Syme, *Theatre and Testimony in Shakespeare's England: A Culture of Mediation* (Cambridge: Cambridge University Press, 2012), 19.

31 John 1.14 (Geneva Bible, 1599).

32 Erika T. Lin, *Shakespeare and the Materiality of Performance* (New York: Palgrave Macmillan, 2012), 9.

33 'The brother's possession of the fee simple makes the sister the heir.'

34 Sir Edward *Coke*, *Institutes of the Laws of England* (London: Society of Stationers, 1628), I.15b (note).

35 William Lowes Rushton, *Shakespeare's Testamentary Language* (London: Longmans, Green and Co., 1869).

36 J. L. Austin, 'Performative Utterances', in *J. L. Austin: Philosophical Papers*, J. O. Urmson and G. J. Warnock (eds), 3rd edn (Oxford: Clarendon Press, 1979), 233, 236. Austin developed this idea of 'performative utterance' into his theory of the 'speech act': J. L. Austin, *How To Do Things With Words: The William James Lectures delivered at Harvard University in 1955*, J. O. Urmson (ed.) (Oxford: Clarendon Press, 1962).

37 See Michael Weiss, 'Indo-European Languages', in M. Gagarin and E. Fantham (eds), *The Oxford Encyclopedia of Ancient Greece & Rome* (Oxford: Oxford University Press, 2010), 61–3, 63.

38 Benjamin W. Fortson, *Indo-European Language and Culture: An Introduction*, 2nd edn (Oxford: Wiley-Blackwell, 2010), 303.

39 *The Institutes of Gaius*, II.101–4. See George Willis Botsford, *The Roman Assemblies: From Their Origin to the End of the Republic* (New York: Macmillan, 1909), 159.

40 Buckland, *Manual of Roman Law* (Cambridge: Cambridge University Press, 1928), 174, §65.

41 Ibid., 174, §64.

42 *Gaius*, II.103.

43 *Gaius*, II.104. Francis de Zulueta (trans.), *The Institutes of Gaius* (Oxford: Clarendon Press, 1946).

44 *Gaius*, II.104.

45 Ibid. (R. W. Lee, *The Elements of Roman Law*, 4th edn [London: Sweet and Maxwell, 1956], 188).

46 Lee, ibid., 187.

47 *Vox Graculi, or Iacke Dawes Prognostication for the Elevation of All Vanity, etc.* (1623), cited in Glynne Wickham et al., *English Professional Theatre, 1530–1660* (Cambridge: Cambridge University Press, 2000), 416.

48 Which are conjectured to have been situated in the elevated galleries immediately adjacent to, or at the rear of, the stage. See Gabriel Egan, 'The Situation of the "Lords Room": A Revaluation', *Review of English Studies* 48 (1997), 297–309; Derek Peat, 'Looking Back to Front: The View from the Lords' Room', in *Shakespeare and the Sense of Performance: Essays in the Tradition of Performance Criticism in Honor of Bernard Beckerman*, Marvin Thompson and Ruth Thompson (eds) (Newark: University of Delaware Press, 1989), 182, 185; E. K. Chambers, *The Elizabethan Stage* (Oxford: Clarendon Press, 1923), III.118.

49 Egan, ibid.

50 Thomas Platter's report of his visit to the Globe on the afternoon of 21 September 1599. Quoted in Jean Wilson, *The Shakespeare Legacy: The Material Legacy of Shakespeare's Theatre* (Godalming: Bramley Books, 1995), 62.

51 C. W. R. D. Moseley, 'Judicious, Sharp Spectators? Form, Pattern and Audience in Early Modern Theatre', *Cahiers Élisabéthains* 85 (2014), 16.

52 Mark Rylance, 'Playing the Globe: Artistic Policy and Practice', in *Shakespeare's Globe Rebuilt*, J. R. Mulryne and M. Shewring (eds) (Cambridge: Cambridge University Press, 1997), 169–76, 171.

53 Honigmann and Brock, *Playhouse Wills*, 12 (citing West, *Symbolæography*, s.639); Cox, 'Shakespeare's Will', 24.

54 See Clarkson and Warren, *Law of Property*, 269.

55 Ibid., 270.

56 Swinburne, *Testaments*, 18.

57 Swinburne, *Testaments*, 3. West takes a similar view: *Symbolæography*, s.680. Technically speaking, the term 'testament' should also have been reserved for a will not including land, but this was a rule more honoured in the breach than the observance. A devise of land by will was commonly referred to as, and for most purposes treated as if it were, a testament.

58 West, ibid.

59 Ibid.

60 *Alvared Graysbrook, Executor of the Testament of Thomas Kene* v. *Robert Fox* (1564) 1 Plowden 275, 280; 75 E.R. 419, 428.

61 See the discussion near the end of Chapter 5.

62 Johannes Rothmann, *Cheiromantia ... etc.*, George Wharton (trans.) (1595) (London: Nathaniel Brooke, 1652), 175–6, 183.

63 John Bulwer, *Chironomia* (London: Thomas Harper, 1644). On the hand as legal instrument, see Peter Goodrich, 'The Missing Hand of the Law', in *Legal Emblems and the Art of Law: Obiter Depicta as the Vision of Governance* (Cambridge: Cambridge University Press, 2013), Ch. 6.

64 Aristotle, *Peri psyches* ('on the soul'), III.432a.

65 Section 1.

66 34 Hen. 8 c.5, s.14.

67 Sir Edward *Coke*, *Institutes of the Laws of England* Volume I: 'Coke's *Littleton*' (London: Society of Stationers, 1628), 59 b. The surrender of copyholds to uses specified in testaments was part of the custom by Shakespeare's day. See, for example, the 1559 will of Robert Brown (*Ward* v. *Downing* (1592) Pop. 10; 79 E.R. 1132, Court of King's Bench).

68 In 'Pelham's Case' the impanelled jurors testified as follows:

'the City of London is an ancient city, and ... all lands and tenements within the said city are, and from the time whereof the memory of man is not to the contrary, were devisable and bequeathable by testament in writing' (*Page deceased, Bowes* v. *Griffin* (1588) 1 Co.Rep.3a, 4a). That might have been overstating the point, but land held by the custom of 'tenure in burgage', which was rare outside London, could certainly be devised by will instead of passing by feudal inheritance (Sir Edward *Coke*, *Institutes of the Laws of England* Volume I: 'Coke's *Littleton*' [London: Society of Stationers, 1628], 109).

69 Stephen Greenblatt, *Renaissance Self-Fashioning: From More to Shakespeare* (Chicago: The University of Chicago Press, 1980), 1.

70 L. C. Knights, *Drama and Society in the Age of Jonson* (1937) (Harmondsworth: Penguin Books, 1962), 27.

71 S. B. Liljegren, *The Fall of the Monasteries and the Social Changes in England Leading Up to the Great Revolution* (Lund/Leipzig: Gleerup/Harrassowitz, 1924), 130–1. Cited in Knights, ibid., 90.

72 Andrew Zurcher, *Shakespeare and the Law*, Arden Shakespeare (London: Bloomsbury, 2010), 185.

73 E. M. W. Tillyard, *The Elizabethan World Picture* (1943) (Harmondsworth: Penguin, 1966).

74 Richard Wilson, *Will Power: Essays on Shakespearean Authority* (Hemel Hempstead: Harvester Wheatsheaf, 1993), 203.

75 Swinburne, *Testaments*, 9.

76 35 Hen. 8 c.1 (1544).

77 Marie Axton, 'The Influence of Edmund Plowden's Succession Treatise', *Huntington Library Quarterly* 37(3) (1974), 209–26, 220.

78 28 Hen. 8 c.7 (1536), s.18.

79 27 Hen. 8 c.10.

80 See A. W. B. Simpson, *An Introduction to the History of the Land Law*, 2nd edn (Oxford: Clarendon Press, 1986), Ch. 8; Neil Jones, 'Uses, Trusts and a Path to Privity', *Cambridge Law Journal* 56 (1) (1997), 175–200; Neil Jones, 'Trusts

in England after the Statute of Uses', in *Itinera Fiduciae: Trust and Treuhand in Historical Perspective*, Richard Helmholz and Reinhald Zimmermann (eds) (Berlin: Duncker and Humblot, 1998), 173–205, 173. (The church had a long-standing interest in assisting landholders to give lands to the church by deathbed gifts; see *H5*, 1.1.9–10.)

81 Eileen Spring, *Law, Land, and Family: Aristocratic Inheritance in England, 1300 to 1800* (Chapel Hill: The University of North Carolina Press, 1993), 72, 33.

82 11 February 1531.

83 30 January 1649 (1648 Old Style).

84 Renamed *The Tragedy of Ferrex and Porrex* when it was revised in 1570, it is best known as a possible inspiration for elements of Shakespeare's *King Lear*.

85 E. M. W. Tillyard, *Shakespeare's History Plays* (1944) (London: Chatto & Windus, 1956), 95.

86 West, *Symbolæography*, s.680.

87 Nowadays, we are keenly aware of the potential downsides of excessively liberal trade. See, generally, Ian Ward, *Shakespeare and the Legal Imagination* (London: Butterworths, 1999), Ch. 5.

88 Cited in *Throckmerton* v. *Tracy* (1555) 1 Plow. 145, 161; 75 Eng. Rep. 222, 250 (Brook, C.J.).

89 A statistic of 1604 records that '[t]he masse of the whole trade of the realme is in the hands of some 200 persons' (*Orig. Jrnls. House of Commons* [21 May 3 f. 251v]).

90 William Kempe, *Kempe's Nine Daies Wonder* (1600), G. B. Harrison (ed.) (London: The Bodley Head, 1923), 9. Cited in M. C. Bradbrook, *The Rise of the Common Player* (London: Chatto & Windus, 1962), 105.

91 Robert Weimann, *Shakespeare and the Popular Tradition in the Theater: Studies in the Social Dimension of Dramatic Form and Function* (Baltimore and London: Johns Hopkins University Press, 1978), 222.

92 The Latin 'platea' derives from Ancient Greek πλατεῖα (plateîa), meaning 'street'.

Handling tradition: Testament as trade in *Richard II* and *King John*

1 In all five quarto editions of the play published before the First Folio of 1623, the play is called *The Tragedie of King Richard the Second*, but in the first folio it appears with the Histories as *The Life and Death of King Richard the Second*. The compositors might have borrowed the type-set already prepared for the preceding play in the collection, *The Life and Death of King John* (Charles R. Forker, *Richard II*, The Arden Shakespeare, 3rd series [London: Bloomsbury, 2002], 179 n). In this chapter, all references to *Richard II* are to Forker's edition unless otherwise stated. References to *King John* are to E. A. J. Honigmann, *King John*, The Arden Shakespeare, 2nd series (London: Methuen, 1954).

2 West describes probate as 'probation of the testament' (William West, *Symbolæography* [London: Totthill, 1590], s.684).

3 James Boyd White, 'Shakespeare's *Richard II*: Imagining the Modern World', in *Acts of Hope: Creating Authority in Literature, Law and Politics* (Chicago: University of Chicago Press, 1994), Ch. 2, 51.

4 Ibid., 57.

5 On the play's capacity to constitute the playgoers as self-aware witnesses of the spectacle, see Bridget Escolme, *Talking to the Audience: Shakespeare, Performance, Self* (Abingdon: Routledge, 2005). Phyllis Rackin argues that *Richard II* casts the playgoers in 'a carefully calculated role' ('The Role of the Audience in Shakespeare's *Richard II*', *Shakespeare Quarterly* 36(3) [1985], 262–81, 263). See also Jeffrey S. Doty, 'Shakespeare's *Richard II*, "Popularity", and the Early Modern Public Sphere', *Shakespeare Quarterly* 61 (2) (2010), 183–205, 185.

6 Andrew Gurr (ed.), *King Richard II* (Cambridge: Cambridge University Press, 2003), 20. On Henry VIII's will, see Chapter 1.

7 On Hooker's influence, see Paul Raffield, *Shakespeare's*

Imaginary Constitution: Late-Elizabethan Politics and the Theatre of Law (Oxford: Hart, 2010), 23–33; White, *Acts of Hope*, Ch. 3.

8 He is 'old Adam's likeness, / Set to dress this garden' of England's 'other Eden' (3.4.72–3; 2.1.42), echoing Genesis 2.15. (Compare 'Adam was a gardener', *2H6*, 4.2.124.)

9 Gurr, *Richard II*, 20.

10 See, generally, P. A. Jorgensen, 'Vertical Patterns in *Richard II*', *The Shakespeare Association Bulletin* 23 (3) (1948), 119–34.

11 Ibid., 119.

12 'Chairs of state on the Elizabethan stage ... were not just centrally positioned on the horizontal axis ... they were also raised on a 'halpace' or low dias', thus '[t]he monarch physically climbed up the steps to take his or her seat on the state' (Janette Dillon, *Shakespeare and the Staging of English History*, Oxford Shakespeare Topics [Oxford: Oxford University Press, 2012], 40).

13 The word 'gage' continues to have commercial connotations to this day, notably in the form of real security that goes by the name of 'mortgage'.

14 Psalm 62.9 contains the words 'weights' and 'vanitie' and might therefore be an even stronger analogy. See, generally, Naseeb Shaheen, *Biblical References in Shakespeare's Plays* (1989) (Newark: University of Delaware, 2011), 377. Biblical quotes are from the Geneva Bible unless otherwise stated.

15 L. C. Knights, *Drama and Society in the Age of Jonson* (London: Chatto & Windus, 1968), 144.

16 Jorgensen, 'Vertical Patterns', 129.

17 Forker, *Richard II*, 88.

18 Katherine Duncan-Jones and H. R. Woudhuysen, *Shakespeare's Poems*, The Arden Shakespeare (London: Bloomsbury, 2007), 333.

19 E. A. J. Honigmann and Susan Brock, *Playhouse Wills, 1558–1642* (Manchester, Manchester University Press, 1993), 19. For a template see West's 'verie perfect forme of a Will' (*Symbolæography*, s.689).

20 David Cressy notes that '[t]he word 'handfasting', which called attention to the ritual action, was more commonly used in the north'. It involved 'holding and releasing of hands, the plighting of troths, kissing, drinking, and the ritual exchange of betrothal rings' (*Birth, Marriage, and Death: Ritual, Religion, and the Life Cycle in Tudor and Stuart England* [Oxford: Oxford University Press, 1997], 269, 273). The word 'gage' (with its associations to the hand) survives in the modern betrothal language of 'engagement'.

21 Germaine Greer, *Shakespeare's Wife* (London: Bloomsbury, 2007), 87.

22 Daniel Nicholas, deposition of 19 June 1612 (*Bellott–Mountjoy*, Court of Requests). The italicized words are scored through in the original, which perhaps raises a doubt as to the veracity of that part. See, generally, Charles Nicholl, *The Lodger: Shakespeare on Silver Street* (London: Allen Lane, 2007), Ch. 27.

23 See Cressy, *Birth, Marriage, and Death,* Ch. 18.

24 Honigmann and Brock, *Playhouse Wills*, 19.

25 Transcription based on Honigmann and Brock, *Playhouse Wills*, 105. Italic additions in square parentheses indicate characters not appearing in the original will.

26 Compare Ecclesiastes 3.20.

27 See Chapter 1.

28 For a Derridean appreciation of the dust in *Richard II* as a sign of the 'crumbling of the principle of sovereignty', see Geoffrey Bennington,'Dust', *Oxford Literary Review* 34 (1) (2012), 25–49, 42.

29 John Preston, 'Ben Whishaw on his new role as Richard II', *Telegraph* (online), 30 June 2012.

30 Cited in Forker, *Richard II*, 106.

31 Frederick S. Boas, *Shakspere and his Predecessors* (1896) (London: John Murray, 1940), 250.

32 John Dover Wilson (ed.), *Richard II* (Cambridge: Cambridge University Press, 1939), xx.

33 A. B. Steel, *Richard II* (Cambridge: Cambridge University Press, 1941), 1.

34 E. M. W. Tillyard, *Shakespeare's History Plays* (1944) (London: Penguin Books, 1991), 259, citing Steel ibid.

35 Ibid., 268.

36 Ibid., 265.

37 Jack Tinker, *Daily Mail*, 28 January 1989.

38 Shaheen, *Biblical References*, 386.

39 Matthew 10.4–5.

40 Gary Watt, 'The Law of Dramatic Properties in *The Merchant of Venice*', in *Shakespeare and the Law*, P. Raffield and G. Watt (eds) (Oxford: Hart, 2008), 237–51.

41 The production of *Richard II* for the series *The Hollow Crown* (BBC, 2012) presents this scene in flashback and shows dung landing on Ben Whishaw's King Richard. The act of throwing this 'dust' is not shown.

42 Hands clap in the parallel episode in one of Shakespeare's 'sources': Samuel Daniel, *The First Fowre Bookes of the Civile Wars* (registered 1594, printed 1595), stanzas 67–9.

43 On 'trade' and 'tread' see the discussion later, and in Chapter 1.

44 See, further, William O. Scott, 'Landholding, Leasing, and Inheritance in *Richard II*', *Studies in English Literature* 42 (2002), 275–92; Dennis R. Klinck, 'Shakespeare's *Richard II* as Landlord and Wasting Tenant', 25 (1) *College Literature Law, Literature, and Interdisciplinarity* (1998), 21–34. The Wilton Diptych represents Richard's connection to the land in the form of his insignia, the White Hart, tethered to the land by a chain (see Raffield, *Imaginary Constitution*, Ch. 3). At the end of Gregory Doran's production of *Richard II* (RSC, 2013) the stage floor was raised to reveal David Tennant's Richard chained to the dungeon floor. Thus Richard, who began at the top of the social 'chain of being' under God, is shown sunk to its lowest level.

45 These lines have close counterparts in the anonymously authored play *Thomas of Woodstock* (c. 1591–5). See P. Corbin and D. Sedge (eds), *Thomas of Woodstock* (Manchester: Manchester University Press, 2002), 4.1.147–8; 5.3.106–7.

46 Joshua Williams, *Principles of the Law of Real Property* (London: S. Sweet, 1845), 9–10. F. H. Lawson agrees that the landlord–tenant relationship was not feudal, but an 'alien commercial element' (*Introduction to the Law of Property* [Oxford: Clarendon Press, 1958]).

47 Bradin Cormack, 'Shakespeare Possessed: Legal Affect and the Time of Holding', in *Shakespeare and the Law*, P. Raffield and G. Watt (eds) (Oxford: Hart, 2008), 83–100.

48 On 'stasis', see Chapter 4.

49 J. H. Baker, *An Introduction to English Legal History* (London: Butterworths, 1990), 298.

50 Coke, *Littleton*, 191a.

51 Ivor B. John (ed.), *The Tragedy of King Richard II*, The Arden Shakespeare (1912) 3rd rev. edn (London: Methuen and Co, 1934), xxv.

52 It is said that shortly before her death Queen Elizabeth was told by Robert Cecil that she 'must' go to bed, to which her indignant response was: '*Must*! Is *must* a *word* to be addressed to princes?'

53 Forker, *Richard II*, 354 n.158. This would accord with the shared English etymology of 'trade' and 'tread'.

54 In Elizabethan pronunciation, 'tread' rhymed with 'head' (*LLL*, 4.3.274–7) and 'red' (*MND*, 3.2.390–1) as it does today, but it is likely the Elizabethan 'trade' did too. See Fausto Cercignani, *Shakespeare's Works and Elizabethan Pronunciation* (Oxford: Clarendon, 1981), 78.

55 See, generally, Steven Marx, *Shakespeare and the Bible* (Oxford: Oxford University Press, 2000); John W. Velz, 'Shakespeare and the Geneva Bible: The Circumstances', in *Shakespeare, Marlowe, Jonson: New Directions in Biography*, T. Kozuka and J. R. Mulryne (eds) (Aldershot: Ashgate, 2006), 113–18; Shaheen, *Biblical References*.

56 *Eikon basilike, The pourtraicture of His Sacred Majestie in his solitudes and sufferings* (9 February 1649) s.3, 15–16.

57 Lukas Erne, *Shakespeare and the Book Trade* (Cambridge: Cambridge University Press, 2013), 206.

58 National Archives, SP 12/278, no. 78, fol. 130r.

59 See Paul E. J. Hammer, 'Shakespeare's *Richard II*, the Play of 7 February 1601, and the Essex Rising', *Shakespeare Quarterly* 59(1) (2008), 1–35; Jonathan Bate, *Soul of the Age: the Life, Mind and World of William Shakespeare* (London: Penguin, 2008), 249–86; but see Blair Worden, 'Which play was performed at the Globe Theatre on 7 February 1601?', *London Review of Books*, 10 July 2003.

60 *Eikonoklestes in answer to a book intitl'd Eikon basilike etc* (London: Matthew Simmons, 1649), 28.

61 The story is historically doubtful; see Bate, *Soul*, Ch. 14.

62 Gurr, *Richard II*, 16.

63 Mark Rose, *Shakespearean Design* (Cambridge, MA: The Belknap Press, 1972), 142. Doty favours the garden scene (3.4) where 'the commoners finally appear onstage to discuss the shifting fortunes of Richard and Bolingbroke' ('Popularity', 200).

64 The deposition scene did not appear in print until Q4 (1608). See, generally, Cyndia Susan Clegg, '"By the choise and inuitation of al the realme": *Richard II* and Elizabethan press censorship', *Shakespeare Quarterly* 48 (1997), 432–48.

65 'Grab' and 'grave' share the same etymology.

66 The land is Richard's *demesne*, which indicates his possession 'in hand' (Cormack, 'Shakespeare Possessed', 86).

67 If the 'let us sit' is played as an invitation, the king's attendants are bound to join him on the ground, but see Forker, *Richard II*, 329, for performative alternatives.

68 John Palmer, *Political Characters of Shakespeare* (Basingstoke: Palgrave Macmillan, 1945), 159. Cited in Forker, *Richard II*, 32 n.

69 E. K. Chambers, *Shakespeare: A Survey* (Oxford: Oxford University Press, 1926), 91. Cited in Forker, ibid.

70 Harry Berger, '*Richard II* 3.2: An Exercise in Imaginary Audition', *ELH* 55(4) (1988), 755–96, 756.

71 On the use of 'dust' in Elizabethan writing, see Chapter 6.

72 F. W. Maitland, 'The Crown as Corporation', in *Collected*

Papers, H. A. L. Fisher (ed.) (Cambridge: Cambridge University Press, 1911), III.251.

73 Ernst Kantorowicz based his famous reading of Richard II's deposition (*The King's Two Bodies: A Study in Mediaeval Political Theology* [Princeton: Princeton University Press, 1957]) on *The Case of the Duchy of Lancaster*: 'the King has in him two bodies, viz. a body natural, and a body politic. His body natural (if it be considered in itself) is a body mortal ... his body politic is a body that cannot be seen or handled' (Mich. Term. 4 Eliz (1561) 1 Plow. 212, 213; 75 English Reports 325, 326). This case confirmed that Henry IV had successfully separated his Lancastrian inheritance from the Crown estate. It remains part of the monarch's privy purse to this day; inheritable, but not alienable by sale. Shakespeare's Bolingbroke alludes to the legal theory of the two bodies when he claims that he was banished as Hereford, but returns as Lancaster (*R2*, 2.3.113–14).

74 As David Tennant did (Gregory Doran, RSC, 2013).

75 Philip C. McGuire, 'Choreography and language in *Richard II*', in *Shakespeare the Theatrical Dimension*, P. C. McGuire and D. A. Samuelson (eds) (New York: AMS Press, 1979), 61–84, 75–6.

76 Charles Moseley identifies impressive similarities between Richard's fate and Ovid's account of the Phaëthon myth (*Shakespeare's History Plays* [London: Penguin, 1988)] 122).

77 David Tennant employed this technique (Gregory Doran, RSC, 2013).

78 *The Plays of William Shakespeare* (8 vols) vol. IV (London: Longman et al., 1797), 190n.

79 On seal and blood, see Chapter 6.

80 Hebrews 10.16; quoting Jeremiah 31.33. In Hebrews 8.10, the same verse from Jeremiah is paraphrased with the word 'testament' substituted for 'covenant'.

81 Contrast Thomas Cromwell's fatal submission to parliament under Henry VIII: 'I am a subject and born to obey laws' (J. D. Mackie, *The Earlier Tudors, 1485-1558*, Oxford History of England [Oxford: Clarendon Press, 1952], 415).

82 Alice Hunt, *The Drama of Coronation: Medieval Ceremony in Early Modern England* (Cambridge: Cambridge University Press, 2008), 36.

83 W. S. Holdsworth, *An Historical Introduction to the Land Law* (London: Oxford University Press, 1927), 288.

84 Coke, *Littleton*, 60–6. P. S. Clarkson and C. T. Warren, *The Law of Property in Shakespeare and the Elizabethan Drama* (1942) (New York: Gordian Press, 1968), 113.

85 Holdsworth, *Historical Introduction,* 112–13.

86 Henry de Bracton, *De Legibus et Consuetudinibus Angliae*, 2.18.12; Coke, *Littleton*, 48a.

87 Frederick Pollock and Frederic William Maitland, *The History of English Law Before the Time of Edward I*, 2nd edn (Cambridge: Cambridge University Press, 1898), II.86.

88 Pollock and Maitland, *History,* II.85.

89 Holinshed, *Chronicles* (London: J. Harison, 1587), VI.493 (An. Reg. 21. Richard II).

90 William S. Holdsworth, *A History of English Law* (10 vols) (London: Methuen, 1922–32), III.69 n.3.

91 Jorgensen, 'Vertical Patterns', 123.

92 John, *Richard II*, xxiii.

93 J. G. Frazer, *The Golden Bough* (New York: Macmillan, 1922), Ch. 3.

94 Compare Polonius's line 'Take this from this' (*Ham*, 2.2.153). The context suggests that he means 'take my head off my body' and would gesture accordingly, but Edward Dowden opined that Polonius might be saying something like 'take this staff of office from my hand' (*Hamlet*, The Arden Shakespeare [London: Methuen, 1899]).

95 Darlene Farabee notes the contrast between the movement in the metaphor of the bucket 'dancing in the air' and the 'stage image' of the 'static crown'. ('Grounded Action and Making Space in *Richard II*', in *Shakespeare's Staged Spaces and Playgoers' Perceptions* [London: Palgrave Macmillan, 2014], Ch. 2, 49.)

96 Jack Benoit Gohn, '*Richard II*: Shakespeare's Legal Brief on

the Royal Prerogative and the Succession to the Throne', *Georgetown Law Journal* 70 (1981–82), 943, 973.

97 Tillyard, *History Plays*, 240.

98 A broad, but by no means total, consensus dates them *Richard II* (1595) and *King John* (1596).

99 Robert Lane, '"The Sequence of Posterity": Shakespeare's "King John" and the Succession Controversy', *Studies in Philology* 92 (4) (1995), 460–81, 467.

100 Henry Swinburne, *A Briefe Treatise of Testaments and Last Willes* (London: John Windet, 1590), 68.

101 William Camden, *Annales Rerum Anglicanarum et Hibernicarum regnante Elizabetha* (London: William Stansby for Simon Waterson, 1615), I.14.

102 Robert Parsons, *Conference About the Next Succession to the Crowne of England* (Antwerp: A. Conincx, 1594 [1595]), 194.

103 Holinshed, *Chronicles*, VI.156 (An. Reg. 10. Richard I).

104 Lane, 'Succession Controversy', 466.

105 Ibid.

106 Swinburne, *Testaments*, 162.

107 Lane, 'Succession Controversy', 467.

108 Dillon, *Staging*, 49.

109 Lane, 'Succession Controversy', 464.

110 See Julen Etxabe, *The Experience of Tragic Judgment* (Abingdon: Routledge, 2013).

111 Emma Smith, *The Cambridge Shakespeare Guide* (Cambridge: Cambridge University Press, 2012), 78.

112 Here 'owe' means 'own' and is intended to contrasts Arthur's 'true' title with John's presumptive title based on possession.

113 Compare Stephen Hawes's poem 'Example of Virtue' (c.1503–4). Dedicated to the Prince of Wales (the future King Henry VIII), it contains the line 'Prince Henry is sprung, our King to be, / After his father, by right good equity' (J. M. Berdan, *Early Tudor Poetry* [New York: Macmillan, 1931], 43).

114 11 May 1612.

115 Nicholl, *Lodger,* 252.

116 Christian A. Smith, '"That smooth-faced gentleman … Commodity": Shakespeare's critique of exchange-value in *King John*', *Shakespeare* 4 (2013), 1–14.

117 Ibid., 5.

118 Ibid., 4.

119 Sigurd Burckhardt, '*King John*: The Ordering of this Present Time', *ELH* 33(2) (1966), 133-153, 141.

120 Michael Neill, *Putting History to the Question: Power, Politics, and Society in English Renaissance* (New York: Columbia University Press, 2002), 456 n.43.

121 Frederick S. Boas, *Shakspere and his Predecessors* (1896) (London: John Murray, 1940), 243.

122 Henry S. Maine, *Ancient Law* (London, John Murray, 1861).

123 Ben Ross Schneider Jr., '*King Lear* in Its Own Time: The Difference that Death Makes', *Early Modern Literary Studies* 1 (1) (1995), 3.1–49, 31.

124 Smith, *Cambridge Shakespeare Guide*, 79.

125 Lane, 'Succession Controversy', 478.

126 *Chambers Dictionary of Etymology*, R. K. Barnhart (ed.) (London: H. Wilson and Company, 1988).

127 Douglas Bruster, 'The Dramatic Life of Objects in the Early Modern Theatre', in *Staged Properties in Early Modern English Drama*, J. G. Harris and N. Korda (eds) (Cambridge: Cambridge University Press, 2002), 67–96, 70–1.

128 Following Zeno's metaphor.

129 S. Duncan, 'Some Signals and Rules for *Taking Speaking Turns in Conversations*', *Journal of Personality and Social Psychology* 23 (1972), 283–92, 287.

130 Coke, *Institutes*, IV.60. See Bradin Cormack, *A Power to Do Justice: Jurisdiction, English Literature, and the Rise of Common Law, 1509–1625* (Chicago: University of Chicago Press, 2008), 93–4.

131 William Blackstone, *Commentaries on the Laws of*

England (4 vols) 1st edn (Oxford: Clarendon Press, 1765–69), II.4.

132 I am grateful to RSC Voice coach Emma Woodvine for letting me participate in a demonstration of the technique.

133 Cicely Berry, *The Actor and the Text* (1987) (London: Virgin Books, 2000), 82.

134 Ibid., 83.

Worlds of will in *As You Like It* and *The Merchant of Venice*

1 *As You Like It,* The Arden Shakespeare, 3rd series, Juliet Dusinberre (ed.) (London: Bloomsbury, 2006), 65. Quotations are from this edition unless otherwise stated. Quotations from *The Merchant of Venice* are from The Arden Shakespeare, 3rd series, John Drakakis (ed.) (London: Bloomsbury, 2011).

2 An entail or 'fee tail' is an 'estate of inheritance' that passes from generation to generation for so long as the original grantee or any of his lineal descendants are still alive. The typical form 'in tail male' was designed to pass the fee to the eldest male descendant.

3 William West, *Symbolæography*, vol. I (London: Totthill, 1590).

4 On the 'gage', see Chapter 2.

5 West, *Symbolæography*, s.17.

6 This second Jaques was probably the part left behind when the melancholy one sprang out of the play's proto-Jaques. See Helen Gardner, '*As You Like It*', in *More Talking of Shakespeare,* John Garrett (ed.) (London: Longmans, Green, 1959), 17–32, 19.

7 Gary Watt, 'The Law of Dramatic Properties in *The Merchant of Venice*', in *Shakespeare and the Law*, Paul Raffield and Gary Watt (eds) (Oxford: Hart, 2008), 237–52, 244.

8 Stemming especially from C. L. Barber, *Shakespeare's Festive*

Comedy: A Study of Dramatic Form and its Relation to Social Custom (Princeton: Princeton University Press, 1959) (paperback 1972), and Northrop Frye, *A Natural Perspective: The Development of Shakespearean Comedy and Romance* (New York: Columbia University Press, 1965).

9 Struan Leslie's choreography employed circles in the forest and lines at court (Michael Boyd, RSC, 2009).

10 Emma Smith, *The Cambridge Shakespeare Guide* (Cambridge: Cambridge University Press, 2012), 13. Smith cites the Stratford production (Adrian Noble, RSC, 1985) in which Duke Senior and Duke Frederick were doubled.

11 See Howard Jacobson, 'Shylock's Troubled Heart' (RSC, 2015, programme).

12 *Guardian*, 22 May 2015.

13 Billington (ibid.) acknowledges that Tritschler's choral music gave a sense of location to Findlay's production.

14 On 'sound' judgment, see Chapter 5.

15 Thomas Wilson, *Arte of Rhetorique* (1560), G. H. Mair (ed.) (Oxford: Clarendon Press, 1909), 217.

16 Jean Wilson, *The Shakespeare Legacy: Material Legacy of Shakespeare's Theatre* (Godalming: Bramley Books, 1995), 127.

17 On these themes see, further, Gary Watt, *Dress, Law and Naked Truth: A Cultural Study of Fashion and Form* (London: Bloomsbury Academic, 2013).

18 Georg Gottfried Gervinus, *Shakespeare Commentaries* (London: Smith, Elder, & Co., 1875), 235.

19 Nancy E. Wright and A. R. Buck, 'Cast out of Eden: Property and Inheritance in Shakespearean Drama', in *The Law in Shakespeare*, Constance Jordan and Karen Cunningham (eds) (Basingstoke: Palgrave Macmillan, 2007), 73–90, 73.

20 Michael Hattaway, 'Dating *As You Like It*, Epilogues and Prayers, and the Problems of "As the Dial Hand Tells O'er"', *Shakespeare Quarterly* 60 (2) (2009), 154–67.

21 The National Archives, C2/Eliz/5/24/21; C33/95 f.140v.; C33/98 f.57v.

22 James Shapiro, *1599: A Year in The Life of William Shakespeare* (London: Faber & Faber, 2005), 278–9.

23 Nowadays the terms of wills can be varied post-mortem by various means (see Gary Watt, *Trusts and Equity*, 7th edn [Oxford: Oxford University Press, 2016], Ch. 9).

24 An excellent starting point for further reading is Richard Wilson, *Will Power: Essays on Shakespearean Authority* (Hemel Hempstead: Harvester Wheatsheaf, 1993), Ch. 7.

25 See, generally, Jane Freeman, '"Fair Terms and a Villain's Mind": Rhetorical Patterns in *The Merchant of Venice*', *Rhetorica* 20(2) (2002), 149–72.

26 On the rhetorical relation between stasis and persuasive sweetness, see Chapter 4.

27 John Dover Wilson, *Shakespeare's Happy Comedies* (London: Faber & Faber, 1962), 73.

28 On '*traditio*', 'trade' and 'tradition', see the discussion in Chapters 1 and 2.

29 The transformation theme in Shakespearean comedy owes a great deal to Ovid's *Metamorphoses*. See, generally, Jonathan Bate, *Shakespeare and Ovid* (Oxford: Clarendon Press, 1994).

30 The actress Athene Seyler once observed that *comedy is 'a comment on life from outside' (*Athene Seyler and S. Haggard, *The Craft of Comedy* (1943) [Abingdon: Routledge, 2013], 24–5).

31 Dympna Callaghan argues that Orlando is speaking here in 'the language of political radicalism' on behalf of the socially downtrodden. The point is that 'courtesy of nations' is not an unchanging divine or natural law, but something that can vary over time (Dympna Callaghan, *Who Was William Shakespeare?: An Introduction to the Life and Works* [Oxford: Wiley-Blackwell, 2012]).

32 Wilson, *Will Power*, 203.

33 Ibid., 186–7.

34 Thomas Lodge, *Rosalynde. Euphues golden legacie: found after his death in his Cell at Silexedra. Bequeathed to Philautus sonnes noursed up with their father in England.*

Fetcht from the Canaries (London: Thomas Orwin for T. G. and John Busbie, 1590). See Alex Davis, 'Thomas Lodge's *Rosalynde* as Testamentary Fiction', *Journal of the Northern Renaissance* 5 (2013), 15.

35 Davis, ibid.

36 Russell was a second son twice over. He was second-born son to his father Sir Thomas Russell and, after his father's death and his mother's remarriage, he ranked behind the natural son of his new stepfather Sir Henry Berkeley. (Leslie Hotson, *I, William Shakespeare* [London: Jonathan Cape, 1937], 23–4.)

37 The role of the overseer is to 'oversee ... will' (*Luc*, 1205) by ensuring that the executors fulfil the terms of the testament.

38 Dusinberre, *As You Like It*, 56.

39 *Chambers Dictionary of Etymology*, R. K. Barnhart (ed.) (London: The H. Wilson Company, 1988).

40 Notably the conflict between Cain and Abel (Genesis 4), and also, without the physical violence, the conflict between Esau and Jacob (Genesis 25).

41 The name of the old servant in *The Tale of Gamelyn* and the inspiration for the name of the retainer in *As You Like It*.

42 Gardner, '*As You Like It*', 18.

43 Andrew Zurcher, *Shakespeare and Law* (London: Arden Shakespeare, 2010), 114.

44 A wonderful inventory of playgoers for the period 1567–1642 appears as the first Appendix to Andrew Gurr, *Playgoing in Shakespeare's London*, 3rd edn (Cambridge: Cambridge University Press, 2004).

45 Gardner, '*As You Like It*', 21. The reference is to Suzanne Langer, *Feeling and Form* (London: Routledge, 1953), 348.

46 Joseph S. Jenkins, *Inheritance Law and Political Theology in Shakespeare and Milton: Election and Grace as Constitutional in Early Modern Literature and Beyond* (Farnham: Ashgate, 2012), 95–6.

47 Dusinberre, *As You Like It*, 33.

48 Gardner, '*As You Like It*', 22.

49 Sherman Hawkins, 'The Two Worlds of Shakespearean Comedy', *Shakespeare Studies*, 3 (1967), 62–75, 64.

50 Ibid., 64.

51 Barber, *Festive Comedy*, 223.

52 R. Chris Hassel Jr, *Faith and Folly in Shakespeare's Romantic Comedies* (Athens: University of Georgia Press, 1980) (paperback 2011), 118.

53 Amiens uses the phrase 'What you will' when addressing Jaques in *As You Like It* (2.5.16). The phrase 'as you like it' might have been inspired by 'If you like it, so' in the preface to Lodge's *Rosalynde*.

54 Hawkins, 'Two Worlds', 63. Note the song in *As You Like It* that describes the wedding contract as a 'blessed bond of board and bed' (5.4.140) and Touchstone's pithy observation that 'marriage binds' (5.4.57).

55 Hawkins, 'Two Worlds', 63.

56 Henry Swinburne, *A Treatise of Spousals or Matrimonial Contracts etc* (London: Robert Clavell, 1686); David Cressy, *Birth, Marriage, and Death: Ritual, Religion, and the Life Cycle in Tudor and Stuart England* (Oxford: Oxford University Press, 1997), 267.

57 Erika T. Lin, *Shakespeare and the Materiality of Performance* (New York: Palgrave Macmillan, 2012), 7.

58 Northrop Frye, *A Natural Perspective*, 133.

59 Smith, *Cambridge Guide*, 15.

60 See Adam Nicolson, *Earls of Paradise* (London: HarperCollins, 2008), 141.

61 Smith, *Cambridge Guide*, 15.

62 Susan Baker, 'Personating Persons: Rethinking Shakespearean Disguises', *Shakespeare Quarterly* 43(3) (1992), 303–16, 313.

63 Henry Swinburne, *A Briefe Treatise of Testaments and Last Willes* (London: John Windet, 1590), 47–8. On the significance of the freedom of an unmarried woman ('feme sole') to write a will, see Michelle M. Dowd, *The Dynamics of Inheritance on the Shakespearean Stage* (Cambridge: Cambridge University Press, 2015), 44–6.

64 Andrew Gurr, *The Shakespearean Stage 1574–1642*, 4th edn (Cambridge: Cambridge University Press, 2009), 60.

65 On apprenticeship in the playing companies, see E. A. J. Honigmann and Susan Brock, *Playhouse Wills, 1558–1642* (Manchester: Manchester University Press, 1993), 3.

66 Gurr, *Shakespearean Stage*, 90.

67 In one of the earliest English wills in the Court of Probate, the testator directs his executors to pay for the costs of the 'qwytaunce' of another party's 'enditement' ('debt') (the 1426 will of William Hanyngfeld esq of Chelmsford, Essex in F. J. Furnivall, *Fifty Earliest English Wills* [London: Early English Text Society, 1882], 71).

68 Swinburne, *Testaments*, 236.

69 Gardner, '*As You Like It*', 21.

70 Ibid.

71 As I have noted elsewhere: Watt, 'Dramatic Properties', 238.

72 The Puritan authors of the 1572 Admonition to the Parliament alleged that 'the use of the ring in marriage is Foolish' (Cressy, *Birth, Marriage, and Death*, 344). On rings, see Chapter 6.

73 Richard insists on the 'unstooping firmness of my upright soul' (1.1.121), and his biggest mistake was wilfully to ignore York's warning that he should not seize Bolingbroke's inheritance; see Chapter 2.

74 Caesar boasts, 'I am constant as the northern star' (3.1.60), just before he falls to earth; see Chapter 4.

75 Gardner, '*As You Like It*', 21.

76 Zurcher, *Shakespeare and Law*, 118.

77 Wright and Buck, 'Eden', 87.

78 Ibid.

79 The melancholy Jaques is apparently unaware of this when he bequeaths to Oliver his 'land and love and great allies' (5.4.187).

80 Seyler and Haggard, *Craft of Comedy*, 24–5.

81 In the form '*Totus mundus agit histrionem*', see Shapiro, '*1599*', 257; Dusinberre, *As You Like It*, 42 n.3.

82 'The play creates a special relation with its audience, who become not just watchers but participants' (Dusinberre, *As You Like It*, 61).

83 Dusinberre, *As You Like It*, 7.

84 Barber, *Festive Comedy*, 228.

85 Ibid.

86 Sir Thomas Egerton, letter written to Robert Devereux, 2nd Earl of Essex (1598), cited in Dusinberre, *As You Like It*, 104.

87 Edward I. Berry, 'Rosalynde and Rosalind', *Shakespeare Quarterly* 31 (1) (1980), 42–52, 44.

88 Dusinberre, *As You Like It*, 142.

89 Ibid.

90 The play's two worlds of will are also the two worlds of William Shakespeare. In the Elizabethan period the river Avon divided Warwickshire into two parts, each with a distinct topography (see G. M. Trevelyan, *English Social History*, 3rd edn [London: Longmans, Green and Co., 1946], 144). Shakespeare's hometown of Stratford, straddling the river, had one foot touching forest and one foot touching field. To the north of the river was the region of the ancient Forest of Arden, more sparsely wooded in Shakespeare's lifetime than it had been in previous centuries; and to the south of the river was the rural Feldon, a gently rolling landscape of pasture and arable land. (The distinction is clearly discernable even as late as 1695, as can be seen from Robert Morden's map of Warwickshire.)

91 Shapiro, *1599*, 247. The dubious anecdote was attributed by Edward Capell to a very old Stratford man 'of weak intellects, but yet related to Shakespeare' (*Commentary*, 1774).

'Shall I descend?': Rhetorical stasis and moving will in *Julius Caesar*

1 In this chapter, all references to *Julius Caesar* are to David Daniell (ed.), *Julius Caesar*, The Arden Shakespeare, 3rd series (London: Bloomsbury, 1998) unless otherwise stated.

2 Thomas Wilson, *Arte of Rhetorique* (1560), G. H. Mair (ed.) (Oxford: Clarendon Press, 1909), 99. On Shakespeare's familiarity with Wilson's *Rhetoric*, see Chapter 1.

3 F. J. Furnivall and A. W. Pollard (eds), *The Macro Plays* (London: Oxford University Press, 1904), 75–188, lines 153–4.

4 On the connection between the groundlings and the Roman citizen in the context of the 1999 production at the Shakespeare's Globe, see *Andrew Gurr, Around the Globe* 11 (Autumn 1999), 33; Michael E. Mooney, '"Passion, I See, Is Catching": The Rhetoric of "Julius Caesar"', *The Journal of English and Germanic Philology* 90 (1) (1991), 31–50, 32.

5 Shakespeare possibly played a part in the grant of arms to his father in 1596 (see Raymond Carter Sutherland, 'The Grants of Arms to Shakespeare's Father', *Shakespeare Quarterly* 14 (4) [1963], 379–85). Heraldic arms were a standard indicator of gentlemanly status.

6 See generally Martin Luther, *The Bondage of the Will*, J. I. Packer and O. R. Johnson (eds) (Grand Rapids: Fleming H. Revell Company, 1957) (translating Luther's *De Servo Arbitrio* [1525]).

7 Mark Rose, 'Conjuring Caesar: Ceremony, History, and Authority in 1599', *English Literary Renaissance* 19 (3) (1989), 291–304, 292.

8 Casca is spelled Caska in the First Folio. Daniell follows this in his Arden edition. I have adopted the original Roman spelling.

9 This Brutus features in Shakespeare's *The Rape of Lucrece* (1594). In a scene anticipating *Julius Caesar*, the people revolt following the display of Lucrece's body in the Roman forum. (Lines 1734–5 are among many that bear comparison

with the play [see *JC*, 3.2.175–6].) The poem contains one of the few Shakespearean uses of the word 'testament': 'My stained blood to TARQUIN I'll bequeath, / ... / ... as his due writ in my testament' (1181–3). (Katherine Duncan-Jones and H. R. Woudhuysen (eds), *Shakespeare's Poems*, The Arden Shakespeare, 3rd series [London: Bloomsbury, 2007].)

10 *The Description of England* (London: 1577), III.4.

11 John Calvin, *The Institutes of the Christian Religion* (1536), Thomas Norton (trans.) (London: Wolfe & Harrison, 1561), II.3.4. See R. M. Frye, *Shakespeare and Christian Doctrine* (Princeton: Princeton University Press, 1963), 183.

12 *Moral Philosophie of the Stoicks* (c. 1585), Thomas James (trans.) (London: Thomas Man, 1598), 47.

13 Norman Council, *When Honour's at the Stake: Ideas of Honour in Shakespeare's Plays* (London: George Allen & Unwin, 1973), 12.

14 Wilson, *Rhetorique*, 100.

15 R. W. Zandvoort, 'Brutus's Forum Speech in *Julius Cæsar*', *Review of English Studies* 61 (1940), 62–6. A compact example of *chiasmus* is 'Censure ... your senses' (3.2.16–17).

16 Brian Vickers, 'Shakespeare's Use of Rhetoric', in *A Reader in the Language of Shakespearean Drama*, Vivian Salmon and Edwina Burness (eds) (Amsterdam: John Benjamin, 1987), 398.

17 On rebellion of the nobility, see the discussion of the 'Essex Rebellion' in Chapter 2.

18 On the significance of bloody napkins and Caesar's bloody toga, see Chapter 6.

19 Shakespeare's main 'source' for Roman history was *Plutarch's Lives of the Noble Grecians and Romans*, Thomas North (trans.) (1579); references are to Walter W. Skeat (ed.) (London: Macmillan and Co., 1875).

20 On Caesar's 'transmutation of private land into public spaces', see Michael Mangan, '"I Am No Orator": The Language of Public Spaces', in *Longman Critical Essays: Julius Caesar*, Linda Cookson and Bryan Loughrey (eds) (Harlow: Longman, 1992), 66–77, 77.

21 '"A Savage Spectacle": Reproducing Caesar', in Cookson and Loughrey, *Essays*, 17–26, 24.

22 North, *Plutarch: Brutus*, §15.

23 Don J. Kraemer Jr, '"Alas, Thou Hast Misconstrued Every Thing": Amplifying Words and Things in *Julius Caesar*', *Rhetorica: A Journal of the History of Rhetoric* 9 (2) (1991), 165–78, 166.

24 See further, Peter Goodrich, 'The Missing Hand of the Law', in *Legal Emblems and the Art of Law: Obiter Depicta as the Vision of Governance* (Cambridge: Cambridge University Press, 2013), Ch. 6.

25 Peter Ure, *Julius Caesar: A Casebook* (London: Macmillan, 1969), Introduction, 14–15.

26 Harry Keyishian, *The Shapes of Revenge: Victimization, Vengeance, and Vindictiveness in Shakespeare* (Atlantic Highlands, NJ: Humanities Press, 1995), 87.

27 Robert Hapgood, 'Speak Hands for Me: Gesture as Language in *Julius Caesar*', *Drama Survey* 5 (1966), 162–70, 164.

28 See J. R. Mulryne, 'Speak Hands For Me: Image and Action in *Julius Caesar*', in *Shakespeare et le corps à la Renaissance* (Société Française Shakespeare, Actes du Congrès 1990) (Paris: Les Belles Lettres, 1991), 101–12.

29 On the toga, see Jonathan Edmondson and Alison Keith (eds), *Roman Dress and the Fabrics of Roman Culture* (Toronto: University of Toronto Press, 2008).

30 Harley Granville-Barker, *Prefaces to Shakespeare* (London: Batsford, 1930), 12.

31 *A Theory of Meter* (London: Mouton & Co, 1964), 39; quoted in George T. Wright, *Shakespeare's Metrical Art* (Berkeley: University of California Press, 1988), 150.

32 Jean Fuzier, '*Rhetoric versus Rhetoric: A Study of Shakespeare's Julius Caesar*, Act lll, Scene 2', *Cahiers Élisabéthains* 5 (1974), 25–65, 48.

33 Daniell, *Julius Caesar*, 257 n.74.

34 Sam Leith, *You Talkin' to Me?: Rhetoric from Aristotle to Obama* (London: Profile Books, 2011), 49.

35 Ibid., 50.

36 Fausto Cercignani's *Shakespeare Works and Elizabethan Pronunciation* (Oxford: Oxford University Press, 1981), 184–5. Shakespeare rhymes 'Rome' with 'doom' (*Luc*, 715–17, 1849–51) and he puns 'Rome' and 'Roam' (*1H6*, 3.1.51), so it is possible that 'room', Rome' and 'roam' were homonyms or that pronunciation of Rome was in flux and beginning to acquire its modern sound (see Helge Kökeritz, *Shakespeare's Pronunciation* [New Haven: Yale University Press, 1953], 141–2).

37 And possibly also 3.1.289; 3.2.164–5; 4.3.39.

38 Wilson, *Rhetorique*, 100–1.

39 Even without referring to physical gesture or to the final four syllables, Lynette Hunter sees in the first six syllables something 'like a widening arc embracing the audience' ('Persuasion', in *Reading Shakespeare's Dramatic Language: A Guide* [London: Arden Shakespeare, 2001], 113–29, 125).

40 Wright, *Metrical Art*, 109. Carol Marks Sicherman argues that in this play 'Shakespeare wrote short lines with deliberate thought' ('Short Lines and Interpretation: The Case of *Julius Caesar*', *Shakespeare Quarterly* 35 (2) [1984], 180–95, 181.)

41 For this observation I am indebted to my sometime workshop colleague, the RSC actor Keith Osborn.

42 E.g. Cedric Watts, *Julius Caesar* (Ware: Wordsworth Editions, 1992), 118 n.85; Daniell, *Julius Caesar*, 257 n.79.

43 To cite just three examples of 'ambitious' appearing in strongly metrical passages: *Cor*, 4.5.113; *3H6*, 2.2.19, 3.3.27.

44 Shakespeare may be alluding to future theatrical performances of Caesar's fall or alluding more generally to political assassinations. See Cedric Watts, '*Julius Caesar*, III.1.111-113', in Cookson and Loughrey, '*Essays*', 48–55, 54. On the continuing political relevance of the play, see John Drakakis, '"Fashion it thus": *Julius Caesar* and the Politics of Theatrical Representation', *Shakespeare Survey: Shakespeare and Politics* 44 (1991), 65–74.

45 John Russell Brown, *Shakespeare's Dramatic Style* (London: Heinemann, 1970), 119.

46 Wilson, *Rhetorique*, 102 ('hault' means 'haughty'; compare 'haught': *R2*, 4.1.254).

47 Hodges portrays the pulpit (rostra) as 'a firmly-built structure of commanding height'. It is a platform erected against the centre of the *frons* and accessed by a flight of stairs leading up from the stage. The usual 'state' structure (of dais and throne) is used to represent Caesar's chair of State in the Senate (C. Walter Hodges, *Enter The Whole Army: A Pictorial Study of Shakespearean Staging 1576–1616* [Cambridge: Cambridge University Press, 1999], 42–8).

48 Ernest Schanzer, *The Problem Plays of Shakespeare* (London: Routledge and Kegan Paul, 1963), 48.

49 Garry Wills, *Rome and Rhetoric: Shakespeare's Julius Caesar* (New Haven: Yale University Press, 2011), 54–7.

50 Schanzer, *Problem Plays*, 48.

51 Wilson, *Rhetorique*, Preface.

52 Ibid.

53 L. C. Knights, *Further Explorations: Essays in Criticism* (Stanford: Stanford University Press, 1965), 42.

54 Herbert R. Coursen, Jr, 'The Fall and Decline of *Julius Caesar*', *Texas Studies in Literature and Language* 4(2) (1962), 241–51, 242.

55 Andrew Gurr, 'Staging at The Globe', in *Shakespeare's Globe Rebuilt*, R. Mulryne and Margaret Shewring (eds) (Cambridge: Cambridge University Press, 1997), 159–68, 164.

56 Marvin Spevack (ed.), *Julius Caesar*, The New Cambridge Shakespeare (Cambridge: Cambridge University Press, 1988), 21. They have been likened to the formality of 'speeches in a courtroom drama' (Mangan, 'Public Spaces', 67).

57 T. S. Dorsch (ed.), *Julius Caesar*, The Arden Shakespeare (London: Methuen, 1955), lii.

58 Wilson, *Rhetorique*, 5.

59 Aristotle, *The Art of Rhetoric*, I.2.3.

60 Wilson, *Rhetorique*, 6.

61 Hapgood, 'Gesture', 169.

62 Wilson, *Rhetorique*, 134.

63 Desiderius Erasmus, *The Praise of Folly*, John Wilson (trans.) (1668) (New York: Black, 1942), 140.

64 Zandvoort, 'Brutus's Speech', 65.

65 Compare Hapgood, 'Gesture', 167.

66 Quintilian, *Institutio Oratoria*, 11.3.147. On Roman rhetorical gesture, see Fritz Graf, 'Gestures and Conventions: The Gestures of Roman Actors and Orators', in *A Cultural History of Gesture*, J. Bremmer and H. Roodenburg (eds) (Cambridge: Polity Press, 1991), 36–58; Gregory S. Aldrete, *Gestures and Acclamations in Ancient Rome* (Baltimore: The Johns Hopkins University Press, 2003).

67 On the use of pauses, see J. L. Styan, *Shakespeare's Stagecraft* (Cambridge: Cambridge University Press, 1967), 189–92.

68 *Omne trium perfectum* ('all perfection is threefold').

69 Almost the entirety of Wilson's wisdom on rhetoric is traceable to classic sources, chiefly Cicero and Quintilian. Here his immediate source appears to be Cicero's *De optimo genere oratorum*: 'The supreme orator … is the one whose speech instructs, delights and moves the minds of his audience' ('The Best Kind of Orator', H. M. Hubbell (trans.) Loeb Classical Library [Cambridge, MA: Harvard University Press, 1949], I.3–4).

70 Wilson, *Rhetorique*, 4.

71 *Palladis Tamia: Wit's Treasure* (London: P. Short for Cuthbert Burbie, 1598).

72 Wilson, *Rhetorique*, 4.

73 I am grateful to Keith Osborn for pointing this out.

74 On rhetoric's 'Newtonian' capacity to move, see Chapter 6.

75 Mangan, 'Public Spaces', 67.

76 Ibid.

77 Luke 19.40.

78 Hor. Ars 394 (C. Smart trans.).

79 Charles Hoole, *A New Discovery of the Old Art of Teaching Schoole* (London: J. T. for Andrew Crook, 1660) (Syracuse, NY: C. W. Bardeen, 1912), 219 (based on treatises written by Hoole in the 1630s).

80 Jonathan Bate, *The Genius of Shakespeare* (London: Picador, 1997), 63.

81 Spevack, *Julius Caesar*, 11.

82 Ibid., 12.

83 See, generally, John Anson, '*Julius Caesar*: The Politics of the Hardened Heart', *Shakespeare Studies* 2 (1966), 11–33.

84 'The Dynamics of Stasis: Classical Rhetorical Theory and Modern Legal Argumentation', *The American Journal of Jurisprudence* 34(1) (1989), 171–97, 171.

85 Wilson, *Rhetorique*, 86.

86 *The Art of Rhetoric*, III.17.1.

87 See Quentin Skinner, *Forensic Shakespeare* (Oxford: Oxford University Press, 2014), 198.

88 Gary Watt, 'Rule of the Root: Proto-Indo-European Domination of Legal Language', in *Law and Language*, Current Legal Issues, Fiona Smith and Andrew Lewis (eds) (Oxford: Oxford University Press, 2013), 571–89. On sound symbolism generally see, for example, David Reid, *Sound Symbolism* (Edinburgh, T&A Constable Ltd, 1967); Roman Jakobson and Linda R Waugh, *The Sound Shape of Language* (Bloomington, Indiana University Press, 1979); Leanne Hinton, Johanna Nichols and John J. Ohala (eds), *Sound Symbolism* (Cambridge, Cambridge University Press, 1994).

89 For another example, see *H8*, 1.2.84–7.

90 Spevack, *Julius Caesar*, 58.

91 Spevack, *Julius Caesar*, 59.

92 Ure, *Casebook*, 22.

93 Historically, Decimus Brutus.

94 In David Farr's production at the Swan Theatre (RSC, 2004), Gary Oliver's Antony tore up the will and dropped it into a bucket of blood (Patricia Elizabeth Tatspaugh, 'Shakespeare

Onstage in England, 2004–2005', *Shakespeare Quarterly* 56(4) [2005], 448–78, 466).

95 Mark Van Doren, *Shakespeare* (New York: H. Holt, 1939), 185.

96 See, generally, Gayle Greene, '"The Power of Speech to Stir Men's Blood": The Language of Tragedy in Shakespeare's *Julius Caesar*', *Renaissance Drama* 2 (1980), 67–93.

97 Wills, *Rhetoric*, 97–8.

98 Mark Rose, 'Conjuring Caesar: Ceremony, History, and Authority in 1599', *English Literary Renaissance* 19 (3) (1989), 291–304, 298.

99 The remaining line in the group calls for judgment of the gods. If Brutus is Caesar's 'angel' up there, perhaps Antony is implying that the commoners are 'gods' down there. After all, Antony is certainly addressing the plebeians with his apostrophe 'O Masters!' and also, I would suggest, in his 'O judgment' (3.2.105). The remainder of that line 'Thou art fled to brutish beasts' is clearly an allusion to Brutus. A revolutionary, but perfectly suitable, gesture for this line would be to gesture down to the people on 'O judgment!' (contrary to the instinct to appeal upwards for justice from the gods; compare *TA*, 4.3.11–13) and to gesture upwards to Brutus on 'fled to Brutish beasts'.

100 Wright, *Metrical Art*, 107. Wright adds that the same is true of hypometrical lines.

101 Ibid., 164.

102 Daniell (*Julius Caesar*, 261 n.162) associates the citizen's call to make 'Room for Antony' (3.2.164) with the medieval practice of making playing room in the popular throng. Daniell cites Chambers, who quotes lines from the start of a Leicestershire Mummers Play: 'Room, a room! brave gallants, give us room to sport; / For in this house we do resort' (*The Medieval Stage*, 2 vols [Oxford: Clarendon, 1903], 2.276).

103 D. J. Hopkins, *City/Stage/Globe: Performance and Space in Shakespeare's London* (London: Routledge, 2008), 170. Hopkins conjectures that in early performances Antony might have moved as far down as the groundlings in the yard, but the association between the stage level and the common street (both share the space of the 'platea'; see Chapter 1) would make such an extreme descent dramatically unnecessary. On the other hand, some modern productions have placed the citizens in the orchestra pit. (John Ripley, *Julius Caesar on Stage in England and America, 1599–1973* [Cambridge: Cambridge University Press, 1980], 240.)

104 Hopkins, ibid., 164.

105 'The stage is hung with black; and I perceive / The auditors prepared for a tragedy' (Anon, *A Warning for Fair Women* [c.1590], induction). The stage skirt seems to be represented in Johannes De Witt's famous 1596 drawing of the Swan theatre.

106 Gary Watt, *Equity Stirring: The Story of Justice Beyond Law* (Oxford: Hart, 2009).

107 John I. M. Stewart, *Character and Motive in Shakespeare* (London: Longmans, Green, 1949), 53.

108 Wilson, *Rhetorique*, 133.

109 North, *Plutarch: Brutus*, §10. Cited in Spevack, '*Julius Caesar*', 11.

110 North, *Plutarch: Brutus*, §32.

111 Jennifer Richards, *Rhetoric*, The New Critical Idiom (Abingdon: Routledge, 2008), 91.

112 Ibid., 93.

'His will is not his own': Hamlet downcast and the problem of performance

1 In this chapter, quotes are from *Hamlet*, The Arden Shakespeare, 3rd series, Ann Thomson and Neil Taylor (eds) (London: Bloomsbury, 2006) unless otherwise stated. Thomson and Taylor is based on the Second Quarto of 1604–5 (hereafter, 'Q2').

2 Andrew Gurr and Mariko Ichikawa, *Staging in Shakespeare's Theatres* (Oxford: Oxford University Press, 2000), 131.

3 Charles Forker, 'Shakespeare's Theatrical Symbolism and Its Function in Hamlet', *Shakespeare Quarterly* 14(3) (1963), 215–29, 221.

4 Hamlet holding the globe of his head fits with the play's many references to Hercules holding the burden of the world on his shoulders – an image which is supposed to have been the emblem of the Globe theatre. That supposition goes back to Steevens and Malone, and, although it is not universally credited, it has the approval of some more recent critics, including, for example, Harold Jenkins, editor of *Hamlet*, The Arden Shakespeare, 2nd series (London: Methuen, 1982).

5 J. K. Harmer, 'Hamlet's Introspection', *Essays in Criticism* 61(1) (2011), 31–53, 35.

6 R. A. Foakes, '"Armed at Point Exactly": The Ghost in *Hamlet*', *Shakespeare Survey* 58 (2005), 34–47, 44.

7 Harmer, 'Introspection', 31.

8 Harmer, 'Introspection', 34–5.

9 There was a theatrical tradition in which a point of Hamlet's performance was to crawl along the stage from Ophelia towards Claudius so as to see the king's face more closely during the performance of 'The Mousetrap' (Thomson and Taylor, *Hamlet*, 304 n.106).

10 See, generally, Stanley Wells, 'Staging Shakespeare's Ghosts', in *The Arts of Performance in Elizabethan and Early Stuart Drama: Essays for G. K. Hunter*, Murray Biggs, Philip Edwards, Inga-Stina Ewbank and Eugene M. Waith (eds) (Edinburgh: Edinburgh University Press, 1991), 50–69.

11 James L. Calderwood, *To Be and Not to Be: Negation and Metadrama in Hamlet* (New York: Columbia University Press, 1983), 196.

12 R. W. Emerson, *Essays*, 2nd series (Boston: James Munroe & Co., 1844), 21–4.

13 Hamlet has, for instance, proven fertile ground for psychoanalytic critique. See, for example, Jacques Lacan, 'Desire and the Interpretation of Desire in *Hamlet*', *Yale French Studies* 56 (1977), 11–52.

14 On the material base of Hamlet's emotion, see Gail Kern Paster, *Humoring the Body: Emotions and the Shakespearean Stage* (Chicago: University of Chicago Press, 2004).

15 E. M. W. Tillyard, *The Elizabethan World Picture* (1943) (Harmondsworth: Penguin, 1966), 79.

16 Jenkins (*Hamlet*, 245 n.159) confirms that the reference is to the 'centre' of the earth.

17 In the event, Claudius is caught in a 'Mousetrap'.

18 See the discussion and image in Andrew Gurr, *The Shakespearean Stage, 1574–1642*, 4th edn (Cambridge: Cambridge University Press, 2009), 1–3.

19 Robert Green (attributed), *Groats-Worth of Wit* (London: William Wright, 1592). Stephen Greenblatt sees a reposte in Polonius's 'That's an ill phrase, a vile phrase; "beautified" is / a vile phrase' (Greenblatt, *Will in the World – How Shakespeare Became Shakespeare* [London: Random House, 2004], 215).

20 A modern indoor theatre can exaggerate the radiance of Claudius's court to create a dazzling shift from the midnight of 1.1 to the too much sun (or 'son') of 1.2 (Michael Pennington, *Hamlet: A User's Guide* [New York: Limelight Editions, 1996], 35, 38).

21 Gurr and Ichikawa, *Staging*, 131; but see Jenkins, *Hamlet*, 425.

22 Jenkins, *Hamlet*, 458.

23 Here I prefer the First Folio to Q2's 'We'll teach you for to drink ere you depart'.

24 I'm grateful to Kimberley Brownlee for directing me to the case of the philosopher John Stuart Mill, whose own mental breakdown featured his father (see Bruce Mazlish, *James and John Stuart Mill* (1975) [New Brunswick, NJ: Transaction, 1988], 209). On some accounts, a ghost also makes a fleeting appearance.

25 Compare Othello's 'tyrant custom' (*Oth*, 1.3.230).

26 Aristotle, *The Nicomachean Ethics*, II.1. See Dean Frye, 'Custom and Utterance in Hamlet', in *Literature and Ethics: Essays Presented to A. E. Malloch*, Gary Wihl and David

Williams (eds) (Montreal: McGill-Queen's University Press, 1988), 18–31, 20.

27 '*Usus est altura natura*' (Desiderius Erasmus, *Adagia*, 4.9.25).

28 It was a common theme in plays traditionally dated to 1599, for example: *JC*, 3.1.269; *AYL*, 3.5.3.4.

29 Robert I. Lublin, '"Apparel oft proclaims the man": Visualizing *Hamlet* on the Early Modern Stage', *Shakespeare Bulletin* 32 (4) (2014), 629–47, 639.

30 *Adagia* 3.1.60. We cannot assume that Shakespeare agreed with the maxim (witness his use of the saying *cucullus non facit monachum*, 'a hood does not a monk make' [*TN*, 1.5.51–2; *MM*, 5.1.261]).

31 Spenser considers the example of Lydian warriors who were turned effeminate by soft clothing (Edmund Spenser, *A View of the State of Ireland: Written Dialogue-Wise between Eudoxus and Ireneus* [1598, published 1633], reprinted in *The Works of Edmund Spenser* [London: Henry Washbourne, 1850], 500).

32 Peter Stallybrass and Ann Rosalind Jones, 'Fetishizing the Glove in Renaissance Europe', *Critical Inquiry* 28(1) (2001), 114–32, 116.

33 This passage appears in the First Folio, but not in Q2. The citation refers to line numbers in Jenkins, *Hamlet.*

34 Richard Lovelace (1618–58), *To Althea, from Prison* c.1642 (*The Oxford Book of English Verse: 1250–1900*, Arthur Quiller-Couch (ed.) [Oxford: Clarendon, 1919], 348).

35 Paul A. Cefalu, '"Damnéd Custom … Habits Devil": Shakespeare's *Hamlet*, Anti-Dualism, and the Early Modern Philosophy of Mind', *ELH* 67(2) (2000), 399–431, 400. Cefalu adds (at 400, 410) that 'In the *Confessions*, Augustine … describes his divided will as a "disease of the mind … weighed down by habit … which develops almost naturally because of the unruliness of our mortal inheritance"'.

36 Harley Granville-Barker, *Prefaces to Shakespeare* (London: Batsford, 1930), 60.

37 Cefalu, 'Damnéd Custom', 401.

38 *Ethics*, II.1.

39 Ibid.

40 As a variation on the traditional pose of skull held up to the eye, Mel Gibson's persuasively depressed Hamlet placed the skull on a mound of turf and lay down to contemplate it face to face (Zeffirelli, Warner Bros, 1990).

41 See J. A. Reynolds, 'Variations on a Theme in the Western Tradition', in *Sweet Smoke of Rhetoric*, N. G. Lawrence and J. A. Reynolds (eds) (Coral Gables, FL: University of Miami Press, 1964), 83–92, 90–2.

42 See Jenkins, *Hamlet*, 436.

43 Section XXVI.

44 Compare Proverbs 16.9.

45 Although if 'compatibilists' are correct in their belief that free will and determinism are not logically inconsistent, we can be held morally responsible even if we lack free will to act other than we do. I am grateful to Kimberley Brownlee for this insight.

46 On this passage, see Richard Mallette, 'Gyves to Graces: *Hamlet* and Free Will', *The Journal of English and Germanic Philology* 93 (3) (1994), 336–55, 346.

47 The line reference is to Jenkins, *Hamlet*.

48 Jenkins, *Hamlet*, 484–92.

49 John Barton, *Playing Shakespeare* (London: Methuen, 1984), 6.

50 Classical authors were cautious when comparing the art of rhetoric and the art of acting, but did acknowledge their shared appreciation of the relationship between word and action. See Cicero, *De Oratore*, III.17; Quintilian, *Institutio Oratoria*, XI.3.

51 Paul Prescott, 'The Play in Performance', in *Hamlet*, Penguin Shakespeare, T. J. B. Spencer (ed.) (London: Penguin, 2005), lix–lxxi, lxv.

52 Jenkins concludes that 'the essential *Hamlet* ... was being acted on the stage just possibly even before the end of 1599 and certainly in the course of 1600' (*Hamlet*, 13).

53 If the same actor did play both parts, the identity of that

actor is unknown. John Heminges is one candidate (Andrew Gurr, *The Shakespeare Company 1594–1642* [Cambridge: Cambridge University Press, 2010], 15).

54 J. Willett (trans.), *Brecht on Theatre* (London: Methuen, 1964), 144.

55 Ibid., 136.

56 This is a variation on the old idea that Hamlet's flaw was one of (in his own words) 'thinking too precisely' (4.4.40). This is the so-called Schlegel-Coleridge reading approved by A. C. Bradley, *Shakespearean Tragedy* (1904) (London: Penguin, 1991), 106ff. Compare Sir Sidney Lee, *A Life of William Shakespeare* (London: Spottiswode & Co., 1898), 225: Hamlet is 'foiled by introspective workings of the brain that paralyse the will'. Also, Charles Forker: 'Hamlet may ... be viewed as a symbolic focus for the idea of tragic conflict – man divided against himself ... torn between the compulsion to act (*to do*) and the need to pretend and hence *not* to do' ('Theatrical Symbolism', 219). In my view, Hamlet is not occupied with the activity (or as Forker puts it, the inactivity) of pretending, but with activities of inquiry and probation.

57 Bernard R. Conrad, 'Hamlet's Delay – A Restatement of the Problem', *PMLA* 41 (3) (1926), 680–7.

58 On the skull in *Hamlet*, see Andrew Sofer, *The Stage Life of Props* (Ann Arbor: The University of Michigan Press, 2003), 95–100.

59 The stage direction appears in the First Quarto (registered 1602, published 1603, hereafter 'Q1') and not in Q2 or the First Folio. Q1 is thought to be an unauthorized text largely based on memories of actual performances, so its stage directions may be one of its more reliable aspects. On Q1 stage directions, see Gurr and Ichikawa, *Staging*, 125.

60 In Chapter 1, I cited the example of 34 Hen. 8 c.5, s.14.

61 Calderwood, *Negation*, 9.

62 Granville-Barker, *Prefaces*, 127n; also, Jenkins, *Hamlet*, 348.

63 Juliet Dusinberre, '*King John* and Embarrassing Women', *Shakespeare Survey* 42 (1990), 37–52, 38 n.7.

64 Gurr and Ichikawa, *Staging*, 134.

65 B. L. Joseph, *Shakespeare's Eden: The Commonwealth of England 1558–1629* (London: Blandford Press, 1971), 95.

66 David Garrick exploited the absence of a hat to employ a mechanical hair-raising wig for his encounter with the ghost (see Aoife Monks, *The Actor in Costume* [London: Palgrave Macmillan, 2010], 125–7).

67 'The stage is hung with black; and I perceive / The auditors prepared for a tragedy' (Anon, *A Warning for Fair Women* [c. 1590], induction).

68 As is the rhetorical notion of 'timesis' (see Calderwood, *Negation*, Ch. 6). Timesis is a species of rhetorical digression that Wilson calls a 'swarve sometimes from the matter ... as well as if we had kept the matter still'; for example, when giving evidence against a murderer, one might digress to mention the merits of the victim (Thomas Wilson, *Arte of Rhetorique* [1560] G. H. Mair (ed.) [Oxford: Clarendon Press, 1909], 181).

69 Gurr and Ichikawa, *Staging*, 135.

70 Granville-Barker, *Prefaces*, 39.

71 On mining imagery in Shakespeare's works, see Ann Thompson and John O. Thompson, *Shakespeare: Meaning & Metaphor* (Iowa City: University of Iowa Press, 1987), 104–9.

72 Wilson, *Rhetorique*, Preface.

73 Carolyn Sale, '"The King is a Thing": The King's Prerogative and the Treasure of the Realm in Plowden's Report of the "Case of Mines" and Shakespeare's *Hamlet*', in *Shakespeare and the Law*, Paul Raffield and Gary Watt (eds) (Oxford: Hart Publishing, 2008), 137–57, 149.

74 Cicero, *Tusculan Disputations*, Loeb Classical Library, J. B. King (ed.) (Cambridge, MA: Harvard, 1927). The grammatical variation from Cicero is probably attributable to Shakespeare's poetic licence.

75 E. A. J. Honigmann, 'To be or not to be', in *In Arden: Editing Shakespeare – Essays In Honour of Richard Proudfoot*, Ann Thompson and Gordon McMullan (eds) (London: Bloomsbury Arden, 2015), 209–10.

76 Cicero: 'who would be such a madman as to pass his life continually in toil and peril?' (King, '*Tusculan*', I.14).

77 Cicero: 'All men are anxious ... about what will happen after death' (King, '*Tusculan*', I.14).

78 Jenkins, *Hamlet*, 489.

79 King, '*Tusculan*', I.41.

80 I am grateful to Keith Osborn for this thought.

81 M. Tullii Ciceronis, *Tusculanarum quæstionum seu disputationum libri quinque* (London: Richard Field, printed John Harrison, 1591).

82 David Crystal, 'Sounding Out Shakespeare: Sonnet Rhymes in Original Pronunciation', in *Jezik u Upotrebi: primenjena lingvistikja u cast Ranku Bugarskom*, Vera Vasic (ed.) [Language in Use: Applied Linguistics in Honour of Ranko Bugarski] (Novi Sad and Belgrade: Philosophy faculties, 2011), 295–306, 300.

83 John Dover Wilson, *What Happens in Hamlet* (1935), 3rd edn (Cambridge: Cambridge University Press, 1951), Ch. 2. The tradition goes at least as far back as J. W. von Goethe, *Wilhelm Meisters Lehrjahre* ('*Wilhelm Meister's Apprenticeship*') (Berlin: Johann Friedrich Unger, 1795–6).

84 Wilson, ibid., 39.

85 Ibid., 45.

86 Ibid., 50.

87 Ibid., translating Goethe, *Lehrjahre*, IV.13.

88 Ibid.

89 Rebecca West, 'Was Hamlet without Will?', *The Court and the Castle* (London: Macmillan & Co. Ltd, 1958), 6.

90 Andrew Zurcher argues that such lines as 4.5.123–5 heighten playgoers' critical awareness by raising reasonable doubt against the accusation that Claudius murdered Hamlet's father (*Shakespeare and Law*, Arden Critical Companion [London: Bloomsbury, 2010], 264–7).

91 Myron Taylor, 'Tragic Justice and the House of Polonius', *Elizabethan and Jacobean Drama* 8(2) (1968), 273–81, 273. James Boyd White writes that 'Polonius represents real evil',

and that '[t]here is in a real sense no one there in the words, and the person behind them is a monster' (*Living Speech: Resisting the Empire of Force* [Princeton, NJ; Princeton University Press, 2006], 59–60).

92 This exact phrase (only once used by Shakespeare) appears in North's account of Antony's speech at Caesar's funeral (*Plutarch's Lives of the Noble Grecians and Romans*, Thomas North (trans.) [1579], Walter W. Skeat (ed.) [London: Macmillan and Co., 1875], §15).

93 Jenkins, *Hamlet*, 74.

94 Glynne Wickham and Herbert Berry (eds), *English Professional Theatre, 1530–1660* (Cambridge: Cambridge University Press, 2001), 181–3.

95 John C. Meagher takes this view ('The Stage Directions, Overt and Covert, of Hamlet 5.1', in *Stage Directions in 'Hamlet': New Essays and New Directions*, Hardin L. Aasand (ed.) [Madison, NJ: Fairleigh Dickinson University Press, 2003], 140–60, 147).

96 Anthony Scoloker referred to '*Friendly Shakespeare's Tragedies*, where the *Commedian* rides, when the *Tragedian* stands on Tip-toe: Faith it should please all, like Prince *Hamlet*. But in sadnesse, then it were to be feared he would runne mad' (*Daiphantus, or the Passions of Love, Epistle to the Reader*, 1604).

97 Ibid.

98 Granville-Barker, *Prefaces*, 139n.

99 Sheldon P. Zitner also assumes that only a wild Hamlet would leap, and rejects the leap for that reason ('Four feet in the grave', *TEXT* 2 [1985], 139–48, 145–6).

100 See, further, Gurr and Ichikawa, *Staging*, 153.

101 Here Q2 has 'world's'.

102 Hamlet was from the beginning a 'university play', as is clear from the title page of the First Quarto.

103 Brian Arkins, 'Heavy Seneca: His Influence on Shakespeare's Tragedies', *Classics Ireland* 2 (1995), 5.

104 Jenkins, *Hamlet*, 257.

105 Wilson, *What Happens*, 473.

106 A. L. Rowse, *Prefaces to Shakespeare's Plays* (London: Orbis, 1984), 208.

107 Derek Dunne, 'Decentring the law in *Hamlet*', *Law and Humanities* 9(1) (2015), 55–77.

108 On the relationship between Shakespeare, rhetoric and the Inns of Court, see P. Raffield, *Images and Cultures of Law in Early Modern England: Justice and Political Power 1558–1660* (Cambridge, Cambridge University Press, 2004).

109 Gurr and Ichikawa, *Staging*, 134.

110 The indenture was a deed so-called because its terms were duplicated on a single sheet cut with a toothed serration into two precisely interlocking parts, so that each party would take their part with some security against fraud. Sometimes the indenture was in triplicate or more. (Coke, *Littleton*, 229; William S. Holdsworth, *A History of English Law* [London: Methuen, 1922–32] (10 vols), III.227.)

111 *Hales* v. *Petit* (3 Eliz.) 1 Plow. 253. Lady Margaret Hales sought to defend her interest in land that had been jointly owned with her husband, the judge Sir James Hales. The land had been forfeited as a result of a coroner's decision that Sir James had committed felonious self-slaughter. The episode of Ophelia's drowning might also owe something to Shakespeare's childhood memory of an inquest that took place in Stratford in 1580 concerning a lady who drowned in the Avon in December 1579. Her name: Katherine Hamlet. (Rowse, *Prefaces*, 191.)

112 Defending counsel in *Hales* v. *Petit* argued that the performance of the act of self-destruction has three stages: 'imagination', 'resolution' and 'perfection' (an extract from the case is reproduced in Jenkins, *Hamlet*, 547). See, further, Carolyn Sale, 'The "Amending Hand": *Hales* v. *Petit*, *Eyston* v. *Studd*, and Equitable Action in *Hamlet*', in *The Law in Shakespeare*, Constance Jordan and Karen Cunningham (eds) (Palgrave Macmillan, 2007), 189–207; Luke Wilson, '*Hamlet*, *Hales* v. *Petit*, and the Hysteresis of Action', *English Literary History* 60 (1993), 17–55 (also Luke Wilson, *Theaters of*

Intention: Drama and the Law in Early Modern England [Stanford, CA: Stanford University Press, 2000], Ch. 1).

113 This is the phrase in the First Folio (Jenkins, *Hamlet*, 377). Q2 has 'willy-nilly'.

114 See Gunnar Sjögren, '*Hamlet* and the Coronation of Christian IV', *Shakespeare Quarterly* 16 (1965), 155–60; Richard Wilson, *Free Will: Art and Power on Shakespeare's Stage* (Manchester: Manchester University Press, 2013), Ch. 4.

115 Every sixteenth-century King of Denmark was an eldest (or only) son succeeding to the throne vacated by his father.

116 A. P. Stabler, 'Monarchy in the Sources of *Hamlet*', *Studies in Philology* 62 (5) (1965), 654–61.

117 Paul S. Clarkson and Clyde T. Warren, *The Law of Property in Shakespeare and the Elizabethan Drama* (New York: Gordian Press, 1968), 84. See, for example, *Johnson* v. *Smythe* (1586) C33/71 ff 472, 563, which concerned a 'trust to take a bond of £1000 for the assurance of a jointure'.

118 Zurcher, *Shakespeare and Law*, 229.

119 *What Happens in Hamlet* (1935) 3rd edn (Cambridge: Cambridge University Press, 1951), 38.

120 Ibid., 34. On the importance of issues of land and inheritance, see Margreta De Grazia, '*Hamlet*' *without Hamlet* (Cambridge: Cambridge University Press, 2007).

121 See, for example, the 1411 will of Sir William Langeford of Bradfield, which directed that all his lands be sold and the proceeds spent to the advancement of his daughters. (Reproduced in F. J. Furnivall, *Fifty Earliest English Wills* [London: Early English Text Society, 1882], 18–21, 20.)

122 Gary Watt, *Trusts and Equity*, 7th edn (Oxford: Oxford University Press, 2016), 298.

123 And perhaps to a sexual pun (Thomson and Taylor, *Hamlet*, 190 n.16).

124 The word 'cautelous' appears on one occasion each in *Coriolanus* (4.1.33) and *Julius Caesar* (2.1.128).

125 *Oxford English Dictionary*, '(n.) 4'.

126 Henry Swinburne, *A Briefe Treatise of Testaments and Last*

Willes (London: John Windet, 1590), 61. Similar references to '*cautele*' occur at 263 and 266. See William Lowes Rushton, *Shakespeare's Testamentary Language* (London: Longmans, Green and Co., 1869), 42–3.

127 Swinburne, *Testaments*, 50 (see also 289).

128 Sir Anthony Fitzherbert, *La Graunde Abridgement* (1514) (published in numerous editions, including London: Tottell, 1565) tit deuise, n.5.tit. executors. n.108 (Swinburne, '*Testaments*', 67).

129 Swinburne, '*Testaments*', 68.

130 Ibid.

131 See Gary Watt, 'Shakespeare on Proof and Fabricated Truth', in *Dress, Law and Naked Truth: A Cultural Study of Fashion and Form* (London: Bloomsbury, 2013), Ch. 3.

132 Lorna Hutson, *The Invention of Suspicion: Law and Mimesis in Shakespeare and Renaissance Drama* (Oxford: Oxford University Press, 2007), 67.

133 *Ibid.*, 139.

134 Watt, *Dress*, 51, 80.

135 Ibid., 56–8, discussing the language of proof in *Othello*. See, further, the essays in Jean-Pierre Schandeler and Nathalie Vienne-Guerrin (eds), *Les Usages de la preuve d'Henri Estienne à Jeremy* (Québec: Les Presses de l'Université Laval; Paris: Hermann, 2014).

136 Wilson, *Rhetorique*, 86, writing 'Of an Oration iudiciall'.

137 Focusing on Sophocles' *Antigone*, Julen Etxabe encourages a heightened awareness of the difficulty of judgment in his book *The Experience of Tragic Judgment* (London: Routledge, 2013). Etxabe proposes a model of judgment akin to the transformative experience that an audience undergoes when engaging with a play.

138 Richard Dawson, *Justice as Attunement: Transforming Constitutions in Law, Literature, Economics and the Rest of Life* (Abingdon, Routledge, 2013).

139 John Russell Brown recommends as an exercise for approaching Shakespeare's language that we should first listen to 'words themselves, as sound ... without being conscious of meaning' (*Shakespeare's Dramatic Style* [London: Heinemann, 1970], 17).

140 John Dryden, *Essay of Dramatick Poesie* (London: Henry Herringman, 1668), para. 87.

141 See David Cressy, *Birth, Marriage, and Death: Ritual, Religion, and the Life Cycle in Tudor and Stuart England* (Oxford: Oxford University Press, 1997), 399.

142 See Stephen Greenblatt, *Hamlet in Purgatory* (Princeton: Princeton University Press, 2001).

143 Sir Walter Raleigh, 'On the Life of Man', in *Silver Poets of the Sixteenth Century*, Gerald Bullet (ed.) (London: Dent, 1960), 296.

144 Pauline Kiernan, 'The New Globe', in Frank Occhiogrosso, *Shakespeare in Performance* (Newark: University of Delaware Press, 2003), 113–22, 115.

145 Anon [Webster?], 'An Excellent Actor' (1615) (reproduced in Andrew Gurr, *Playgoing in Shakespeare's London*, 3rd edn [Cambridge: Cambridge University Press, 2004], 274).

146 Kiernan, 'The New Globe', 121.

147 See the actor Keith Osborn's account of the filming of Gregory Doran's *Hamlet* (RSC; BBC2/Illuminations, 2009) with David Tennant in the title role (*Something Written in the State of Denmark: An Actor's Year With the Royal Shakespeare Company* [London: Oberon Books, 2010], 231–2).

148 'Word' sounded like modern 'ward' (Helge Kökeritz, *Shakespeare's Pronunciation* [New Haven: Yale University Press, 1953], 153, 172, 254) and 'lord' (ibid., 459).

149 The 'or' sound ɔ: would have generally sounded ɚ: In his *English Grammar*, Ben Jonson likens it to the growl of a dog: 'R is the dog's letter, and hurreth in the sound.' Compare *RJ*, 2.4.190.

150 For an entertaining and scholarly introduction to the subject that is focused on original pronunciation in performance, see David Crystal, *Pronouncing Shakespeare* (Cambridge: Cambridge University Press, 2005).

151 Granville-Barker, *Prefaces*, 176.

152 For example, although we presume that Shakespeare pronounced 'o'er' monosyllabically (ɔ:) to rhyme with 'before' (*Son*, 30.10–12), 'sore' (*Luc*, 1567–8) and 'swore' (*MND*, 3.2.134) (Kökeritz, *Shakespeare's Pronunciation*, 467), he might sometimes have intended it to be pronounced bisyllabically (ibid., 366) with the first syllable pronounced '0:'.

153 The 'or' in 'Olympus' is included at the reader's discretion.

154 Tillyard, '*World Picture*', 79.

155 Syncope (phonemic loss) is always possible with promontory (promont'ry) but the full 'or' sound will be effective here to emphasize how 'heavily' it goes with Hamlet.

156 Gurr and Ichikawa, *Staging*, 135.

157 Carol Chillington Rutter, 'Snatched Bodies: Ophelia in the Grave', *Shakespeare Quarterly* 49(3) (1998), 299–319.

158 The sound change that 'word' has undergone since Elizabethan pronunciation also occurred to 'worth', which originally rhymed with 'forth' (*AW*, 3.4.13–15). See, further, Kökeritz, 168, 183.

159 *Short Studies in Shakespeare* (London: John Murray, 1929), 186.

160 Herman Melville, *Bartleby* (1853), in *Billy Budd, Sailor and Other Stories*, Penguin Classics, Harold Beaver (ed.) (London: Penguin, 1985), 59–99, 60.

161 Gurr and Ichikawa, *Staging*, 161.

162 Ibid.

163 Forker, 'Theatrical Symbolism', 217.

164 Bradby, *Short Studies*, 178.

165 It first appeared in print in Nicholas Rowe, *Some Account of the Life &c. of Mr. William Shakespear* (London: 1709).

166 Helen Ostovich (ed.), *Every Man Out of His Humour* (Manchester: Manchester University Press, 2001). See, further, Tom MacFaul, *Problem Fathers in Shakespeare and Renaissance Drama* (Cambridge: Cambridge University Press, 2012), 7.

167 See Shapiro, *1599*.

168 The fact that executors were liable to discharge the testator's debts 'was a common reason for renouncing the duty if the estate was known to be encumbered with debts which might exceed assets' (Honigmann and Brock, *Playhouse Wills,* 250). The fact that a statute ('An Act concerning Executors of last Wills and Testaments', 21 Hen. 8 c. 4) was passed to deal with executors' refusal to act indicates how widespread the problem must have been. Executors' fear might be the reason Shakespeare refers to 'executors pale' (*H5*, 1.2.203), although most editors think that he had 'executioners' in mind at this point.

169 Bradby, *Short Studies*, 178.

170 Ibid., 194.

171 C. W. R. D. Moseley, *Shakespeare's History Plays* (London: Penguin, 1988), 50; Gurr and Ichikawa, *Staging*, 162.

172 Ibid., 3.

173 Wilson, *Rhetorique*, 4.

From dust to dust and sealing wax: The materials of testamentary performance

1 A great deal of fine scholarship has engaged with the trope of trial in law. The following list is by no means conclusive, but represents a good basis for further reading: Lorna Hutson, *The Invention of Suspicion: Law and Mimesis in Shakespeare and Renaissance Drama* (Oxford: Oxford University Press, 2007); Subha Mukherji, *Law and Representation in Early Modern Drama* (Cambridge: Cambridge University Press, 2006); Barbara Shapiro, *A Culture of Fact; England, 1550–1730* (Ithaca, NY: Cornell University Press, 2000); Luke Wilson, *Theaters of Intention: Drama and the Law in Early Modern* (Stanford, CA: Stanford University Press, 2000).

2 See Daniela Carpi, 'A Just and Open Trial': The Trial Based

on Circumstantial Evidence in *The Winter's Tale*', in P. Kennan and M. Tempera *(eds) International Shakespeare. The Comedies* (Bologna: Clueb, 2004), 75–84.

3 Henry Swinburne, *A Briefe Treatise of Testaments and Last Willes* (London: John Windet, 1590), 206, citing Perkins, *De Testamentis*, fol. 94.

4 E. A. J. Honigmann and S. Brock, *Playhouse Wills, 1558–1642* (Manchester, Manchester University Press, 1993), 12–13.

5 All the words of the testator's will must be expressed in writing or not at all (*Thomas Brett* v. *John Rigden* (1567) 1 Plow. 340, 345; 75 E.R. 516, 525). Even if the testator does not witness the will by signature or seal, and even if the witnesses do not, the Ordinary in the ecclesiastical court may do so if satisfied that the writing presented is proved to be the testator's will. The Ordinary therefore acts as a sort of witness of last resort (see *Alvared Graysbrook, Executor of the Testament of Thomas Kene* v. *Robert Fox* (1564) 1 Plow. 275, 280; 75 E.R. 419, 428 [1 January 1564]).

6 Also known as 'pin-dust' (typically comprising ground pumice or cuttlefish). It was used to prepare the paper by rubbing, and for blotting ink after writing.

7 See the detailed account in James Daybell, *The Material Letter in Early Modern England: Manuscript Letters and the Culture and Practices of Letter-Writing, 1512–1635* (Basingstoke, Palgrave Macmillan, 2012), 30–41.

8 Jonathan Gil Harris and Natasha Korda (eds), *Staged Properties in Early Modern English Drama* (Cambridge: Cambridge University Press, 2002), 15.

9 The connection between thing (*res*) and word (*verba*) is a long-standing concern in rhetorical studies.

10 Thomas Wilson, *Arte of Rhetorique* (1560), G. H. Mair (ed.) (Oxford: Clarendon Press, 1909), 130.

11 *Eyre of Kent* (S.S.) II.10 (Spigurnel, J.), cited William S. Holdsworth, *A History of English Law* (London: Methuen, 1922–32), III, 417 n.4; *Sharington and Pledall* v. *Strotton* Court of King's Bench (1564) 1 Plow. 298, 309; 75 E.R. 454, 470–1.

12 E. A. J. Honigmann, *King John*, The Arden Shakespeare, 2nd series (London: Methuen, 1954), 47.

13 John D. Wilson, *King John* (Cambridge: Cambridge University Press, 1936), 127.

14 *E. C. Pettet, 'Hot Irons and Fever: A Note on Some of the Imagery of King John', Essays in Criticism* 4(2) (1954), 128–44, 136.

15 For a more literal rendering of the plea on stage, see Ben Jonson's *Volpone*, where the Advocate Voltore ('Vulture') says: 'it is my hand; / But all that it contains is false' (5.8).

16 *Stone and Withypolls Case* (1587) 1 Leonard 113, 114; 74 E.R. 106.

17 Swinburne, *Testaments*, 261.

18 Ibid.

19 Ibid., 240.

20 Harry Keyishian, 'Storm, Fire, and Blood: Patterns of Imagery in Stuart Burge's *Julius Caesar*', in *Shakespeare in Performance*, Frank Occhiogrosso (ed.) (Newark: University of Delaware Press, 2003), 101.

21 Victor W. Turner, *The Forest of Symbols: Aspects of Ndembu Ritual* (Ithaca: Cornell University Press, 1967), 74.

22 See, generally, John Spalding Gatton, '"There Must Be Blood": Mutilation and Martyrdom on the Medieval Stage', in *Violence in Drama*, J. Redmond (ed.) (Cambridge: Cambridge University Press, 1991), 79–91.

23 Mark Griffith (ed.), *Sophocles: Antigone* (Cambridge: Cambridge University Press, 1999).

24 F. W. Jones (trans.), *Euripides: The Suppliant Women*, in *The Complete Greek Tragedies,* vol. 4, D. Grene and R. A. Lattimore (eds) (Chicago: University of Chicago Press, 1974), 139.

25 L. J. Bennett and W. B. Tyrrell, 'What is Antigone Wearing?', *The Classical World* 85(2) (1991), 107–9.

26 Charles Dale Cannon, *A Warning for Fair Women: A Critical Edition* (The Hague and Paris: Mouton, 1975).

27 *Law and Representation in Early Modern England* (Cambridge: Cambridge University Press, 2006), 120.

28 On judgment by sight and sound, see the discussion in Chapter 5. See, also, James Parker, *Acoustic Jurisprudence* (Oxford: Oxford University Press, 2015).

29 Aristotle, *Peri psyches* ('on the soul'), III.432b.

30 1 Corinthians 15.52: 'the dead shall be raised up incorruptible, and we shall be changed' (Geneva Bible, 1599).

31 Peter Stallybrass, 'Worn Worlds: Clothes and Identity on the Renaissance Stage', in *Subject and Object in Renaissance Culture*, Margreta de Grazia, Maureen Quilligan and Peter Stallybrass (eds) (Cambridge: Cambridge University Press, 1996), 289–320.

32 For a measured view, see E. A. J. Honigmann, 'Shakespeare's Will and Testamentary Traditions', in *Shakespeare and Cultural Traditions*, Tetsuo Kishi, Roger Pringle and Stanley Wells (eds) (Newark: University of Delaware, 1994), 127–37.

33 London: Printed by Isaac Jaggard and Edward Blount, 1623.

34 Park Honan, *Shakespeare: A Life* (Oxford: Oxford University Press, 1999), 233. Hamnet Sadler, after whom Shakespeare's son was almost certainly named, acted as a witness to Shakespeare's will. See Susan Brock, 'Last things: Shakespeare's neighbours and beneficiaries' in *The Shakespeare Circle: An Alternative Biography*, Paul Edmondson and Stanley Wells (eds) (Cambridge: Cambridge University Press, 2015), 213–30.

35 John Dover Wilson (ed.), *King John* (Cambridge: Cambridge University Press, 1936), vii.

INDEX

Lightning Source UK Ltd.
Milton Keynes UK
UKHW02f1943050118
315581UK00005B/366/P